I GOT A NAME

THE JIM CROCE STORY

I GOT A NAME
THE JIM CROCE STORY

INGRID CROCE & JIMMY ROCK

DA CAPO PRESS
A Member of the Perseus Books Group

Set in 10 point Antique Olive Light by the Perseus Books Group
A list of permissions appears at the end of this book.

Cataloging-in-Publication data for this book is available
from the Library of Congress.

First Da Capo Press edition 2012
ISBN 978-0-306-82121-9 (hardcover)
ISBN 978-0-306-82123-3 (e-book)

Published by Da Capo Press
A Member of the Perseus Books Group
www.dacapopress.com
www.jimcroce.com

Da Capo Press books are available at special discounts for bulk purchases in the U.S. by corporations, institutions, and other organizations. For more informa- tion, please contact the Special Markets Department at the Perseus Books Group, 2300 Chestnut Street, Suite 200, Philadelphia, PA 19103, or call (800) 810-4145, ext. 5000, or e-mail special.markets@perseusbooks.com.

10 9 8 7 6 5 4 3 2 1

To Rich Croce
and to Jim Croce's fans

But in looking back at the faces I've been,

I would sure be the first one to say when I look at myself today,

I wouldn't have done it any other way.

—JIM CROCE

CONTENTS

FOREWORD

AS MUCH AS THIS STORY is said to be about Jim Croce, the story I read in-between the lines is, in many ways, my story too. I remember a night in 1969 at a club called The Main Point just outside of Philadelphia. Jim and Ingrid were opening a show for me. I recall talking with them downstairs under the stage, in the dressing rooms with my girlfriend at the time, Jackie Hyde. Jackie was nervous about something.

While Jim and Ingrid were singing onstage Jackie finally said, "I'm pregnant." I looked at Jackie and said, "Great! We'll have to move to the country and give him an Indian name." Since that night I have had to look at my life through her eyes and her heart, as well as my own. Surely neither Jim or I knew at that time that our lives would be opened to others through the voices of the women we loved. Some of it is pretty good, some of it, as you can imagine, not so pretty. And although Jim is long gone, and I'm still here, the telling of those tales continues without us, whether or not we are walking around.

There is no one I'd trust more to tell my story than my long-time love, wife, and partner. Ingrid has not—and never will—give death an ounce of sympathy or retreat one little bit from the full acknowledgment of what love truly is: a part of herself in the form of Jim Croce. The details of this book are about Jim and Ingrid, but the story is about anyone who has had the good fortune and unbelievable luck to find someone who will tell it with love.

So I say to my old friend, Jim, "Buddy, you got more than a name. You've got yourself one hell of a gal."

—Arlo Guthrie

PREFACE

FROM THE OUTSIDE, it's impossible to fathom what two people who love each other feel: why the attraction starts and how a relationship grows. But I can tell you that in the case of Jim Croce and me, it felt right. The music, chemistry, and youthfulness that brought us together formed an intense and unbreakable bond. And though Jim has been gone from this Earth for almost forty years, there isn't a day in my life that goes by without him.

When Jim and I fell crazy in love, we were just kids. He wasn't famous then, but he was a star to me. He made me happier than I'd ever been. And because he showed me in so many wonderful ways that I made him feel that way too, I knew we'd be together forever.

When we met in the early '60s, I was a teenager, and Jim was a sophomore at Villanova University. Music brought us together, and it was the music business that not only tested our relationship but plagued it, constantly challenging our survival.

We were both intense individuals. When it was good, it was magnificent, passionate, and soulful. But when we hurt each other, when our friendship and trust were challenged, it was horrific, painful, and empty.

Although Jim Croce was a private man, people feel they know him through his songs. His voice, stories, humor, and sincerity touch them in a way that makes them believe Jim understood what they felt, that his experiences were theirs too. And yet the stories I tell here, about the life behind the songs, reveal something closer to who Jim really was and how he came to create such timeless music.

For many years, I felt compelled to write about my life with Jim, but I was reluctant. Now I feel the time is finally right.

SPEEDBALL TUCKER

September 20, 1973

"H EY, MAURY," JIM CALLED over his left shoulder to his best friend and lead guitarist. "Watch this—Bob's gonna let me land the plane."

"Do you think you're ready?"

"Is the pope Catholic?"

Robert Elliott, the pilot, instructed Jim to increase the flaps 10 degrees and watch his air speed. From the copilot's seat of the privately chartered plane, Jim looked down on the old plantation city of Natchitoches, Louisiana, perched on the grassy banks of the shallow Cane River. The chestnut, pecan, and chinquapin trees that crowded the city made it humid, nearly tropical. It was late September, but shimmering heat waves rose from the runway. With the pilot's help, Jim angled down over a sparse stand of pecan trees and set the twin-engine Beechcraft onto the tarmac.

The flying lessons were helping make the routine of traveling bearable. But Jim was beyond exhausted, and as he looked out through the plane's window at the tiny airport, he wondered how much longer he could keep this going.

The concert at Northwestern University in Natchitoches would be his fourth in four days, tenth in two weeks, over three hundredth in the past year. And although each night he managed to call me, the brutal road schedule and forced separation had been painful for us.

Thank God he'd finally put his foot down and demanded this concert tour be his last for a while. He'd told me before he left, "Ing, if I don't stop this craziness myself, something else will."

Although he was only five foot ten, his rugged looks and the unruly characters he wrote and sang about made Jim seem much larger to his fans. But now he appeared pale and drawn as he stepped off the wing of the plane. The stifling, sultry air weighed him down and added to his depression. The constant touring leached every drop of energy from his body and soul. He just hoped he had the guts to stick to his word and demand enough time off to get his life back together.

Jim's traveling companions climbed out after him, stretching and yawning. The last to deplane was Maury. At twenty-four years old, Maury Muehleisen looked pasty, thin, and delicate under his long, light brown hair. He had toured with Jim for the past two years, and the wear of the road had taken its toll on him, too.

Since Jim had no band, his concerts typically featured just Maury and him onstage with their acoustic guitars.

As Maury ducked through the door of the plane, he immediately began to sneeze. The wind was whipping up ribbons of pollen from a nearby field of golden-rod, and he doubled over in a sneezing fit. Jim scarcely heard Maury's loud honks. His companion's constant allergic reactions had become background noise.

Jim's attention focused on a black Pontiac convertible that had wheeled around the corner of the hangar. The GTO squealed to a stop just a few feet from him, and a robust bear of a man struggled to step out. He had a broad, friendly face. Grinning, he extended a huge paw.

"Welcome to Louisiana, Mr. Croce," the big man drawled, pumping Jim's hand vigorously. "I'm Doug Nichols, vice chairman of the Big Name Entertainment Committee at NU. It's my job to make you happy."

Jim returned his grin and glanced at Doug's convertible. He was dreading the cramped drive to town with all six passengers in the tiny rented sedan they'd hired: Maury; Jim; Jim's agent, Ken Cortese; road manager Dennis Rast, a disc jockey whose on-air name was Morgan Tell; opening-act comedian George Stevens; and the pilot, Bob Elliott.

"Can you give us a lift?"

"Sure, you bet. That's what I'm here for."

Jim gestured to Maury, who was leaning against the plane, trying to recover. "Let's take a ride," he told him.

Maury's red bandanna, dangling between thumb and forefinger, waved damply in the breeze. He nodded, picked up his guitar case, and walked to the Pontiac, his route interrupted midway by another bout of sneezing. While Jim and Maury got in the convertible, the rest of the troupe unloaded backpacks and guitars from the plane and squeezed into the rental car.

At Jim's urging, Doug soon had the Pontiac flying along the back roads. A canopy of trees stretched overhead, and the wind felt fresh and cool as it hit Jim's mustachioed face. He felt his spirits rise as they drove. This, he thought, was the type of freedom he missed.

He looked at Doug and laughed. Although the man appeared strong enough to wrestle a grizzly bear and outweighed Jim by more than 150 pounds, he was ob-viously nervous.

The effect his celebrity status had on some people amused and embarrassed Jim. Drumming his fingers on the steering wheel, Doug tried to start a conversation.

"How's the tour going?"

Jim didn't answer right away. He was starting to feel relaxed and didn't want to think about it. Besides, he thought, if he was honest, he'd probably just disappoint Doug.

The truth was that even though his hit songs, "You Don't Mess Around with Jim," and "Bad, Bad Leroy Brown," had recently topped the charts around the country, Jim was broke, fatigued, and homesick.

"It's okay," he finally answered, without conviction.

Doug gave him a quizzical look and then had to brake quickly as a logging truck pulled in front of them from a side road. A huge load of freshly cut tree trunks was lashed to the top of the truck. "Jeez, look at that boy," Doug drawled. "He must be three times full."

Jim raised his thick eyebrows at the turn of phrase, pulled out a tattered notebook from his shirt pocket, and made a note.

"Do you mind if I borrow that?"

Doug grinned. "Don't mind at all. You think you could put that in a song like 'Speedball Tucker'? That's my favorite." He broke into the refrain but was off-key, and stopped.

Jim laughed.

"Maury, did you hear that?" he yelled over his shoulder. "I don't need you anymore. I got me a new partner."

Maury grimaced. "What, Jim? I can't hear a damn thing you're saying back here!"

"I said, 'You're fired'!" Jim hollered through cupped hands.

"Oh," said Maury, "is that all?" He lay back down to get out of the wind.

When the oncoming lane was clear, a well-muscled arm emerged from the cab of the lumber truck and waved the convertible around. Doug punched the accelerator. The pavement gave way to the antebellum bricks of Front Street in Natchitoches, and they hummed under the wheels. The convertible pulled level with the cab of the truck, and Jim waved in thanks.

The driver grabbed the lanyard and responded with a blast of his air horn. Doug jumped. Jim grinned and shouted, "Hey, Maury, excuse yourself."

Doug laughed and relaxed, surprised by Jim's unpretentiousness. He had developed a low opinion of the entertainers he had escorted to the university concerts for the past two years. "Snooty prima donnas" was how he described most of them. Once he had driven eighty miles to Shreveport to pick up Sly Stone, who emerged from the airplane wearing a brilliantly sequined suit, which he wore around town all day before the concert. Doug had not been impressed.

"You sure are down-to-earth," he said to Jim. "I was wondering if maybe your work shirt and worn-out blue jeans was just an act. But that's how you dress all the time, isn't it?"

"Yeah," Jim said, amused. What Doug didn't know was that the clothes he was wearing represented the best of what was left of his wardrobe.

Doug was glad that Jim had been selected to play at Northwestern University. The Big Name Entertainment Committee had favored a more glitzy, high-powered entertainer like Tom Jones, but Will Mitchell, chairman of the committee, pulled seniority and insisted on booking Jim, certain he would be a star.

Jim had originally been scheduled to appear in the spring, but severe throat problems forced him off the concert tour and delayed the NU gig until September. In the interim, Jim's first album, *You Don't Mess Around with Jim*, shot to the top of the charts, and now his second album, *Life and Times*, was charting too, with "Operator" and "Bad, Bad Leroy Brown." Jim's concert price had risen to $10,000 a night. Doug had let everyone on the concert committee know what a great deal they were getting, as Jim had been secured at the earlier price of $750.

Since Jim seemed to be enjoying himself on the ride through the countryside, Doug felt at ease enough to ask him a few questions.

"How many concerts do you do a year?"

"About three hundred," Jim answered disinterestedly. It wasn't his favorite subject.

"Wow!" Doug said. He did some quick arithmetic in his head. Three hundred concerts a year times $10,000 per concert, plus royalties. "You're on your way to being a millionaire. Good for you!"

Jim wished Doug was right. In spite of his success, he was living on expense money on the road while management sent his family $200 a week.

As they reached the center of town, Doug asked, "Do you wanna check out the motel now?"

"Not yet." Jim was enjoying the sun and the company. "I don't need to be any-place until sound check this afternoon. So if you don't mind, can we just drive around for a while? Oh, and would you mind stopping by a post office? I need to send a letter to my wife."

By 7 PM the sun had slipped far down toward the horizon, but the heat had barely diminished. Jim and Maury felt relieved to be inside in the university's air-conditioned Prather Coliseum. They warmed up for the concert in the basketball locker room, which doubled as their dressing room, the faint odors of the last basketball season still lingering in the air. They both sat on metal folding chairs, tuning their guitars.

5

Maury, a perfectionist, toiled and kept an ear cocked. A lit Marlboro was stuck under a string at the end of his guitar. Jim was restless. He finished tuning quickly and walked over to inspect the sandwiches donated by the Southern Hospitality Committee. The committee consisted of two dozen or so anxious, lush-lashed sorority sisters who catered the entire NU concert series. It was their opportunity to meet and flirt with the stars.

Jim picked up one of the triangular-shaped sandwiches and laughed. "Hey, Maury," he called out. "Take a look at this!" He held up the white-bread sandwich with the crust removed and wiggled it in Maury's direction. A toothpick attempted to secure a sliced, stuffed olive to the top. The olive dropped off. "This may be the South, but it ain't South Philly. And this sure isn't Italian bread. Don't they know it's a capital offense to cut off the crust?"

He carefully replaced the delicate morsel as if it were a small, wounded bird. Maury paid little attention, still fiddling with his guitar. He barely noticed that a small entourage had collected in the dressing room. It included Doug and several of his friends, mostly students.

Jim wandered over, picked up his guitar, and sat down. Maury finally finished tuning. Jim strummed a few chords and began to play the old Sam Cooke tune "Chain Gang." Without looking over, Maury picked up the lead on his guitar. They entertained the private party for over a half-hour, with a mixture of material from slow Delta blues to English bawdy ballads. With a cigarette dangling out of the corner of his mouth, smoke rising to the ceiling, Jim treated them to the song "Careful Man" from his upcoming album.

> *I don't gamble, I don't fight,*
> *I don't be hangin' in the bars at night;*
> *Yeah, I used to be a fighter, but now I am a wiser man.*
> *I don't drink much, I don't smoke,*
> *I don't be hardly messin' round with no dope;*
> *Yeah, I used to be a problem, but now I am a careful man.*
> *But, if you want to see a co-mo-tion,*
> *You should a seen the man that I used to be;*
> *I was trouble in per-pet-u-al motion,*
> *Trouble with a cap-i-tal "T."*
> *Stayin' out late, havin' fun,*
> *Done shot off ev'ry single shot in my gun;*

Yeah, I used to be a lover,
But now I am an older man.

The small crowd applauded.

"Thanks," he told them. "This is a lot of fun. In fact, it's my favorite part of playing." Maury looked up and brushed back his shoulder-length hair.

"Maybe we should pass the hat," he said, smiling. "We could use the extra change."

They were interrupted by Jim's Midwest agent, Ken Cortese, who reminded them of a scheduled newspaper interview. Jim knew about the interview but was uneasy asking the students to leave while they were enjoying the private performance. He excused himself:

"Gee, I'm sorry I have to take a break now. But come on back after the show," he told the students apologetically. "We'll play some more songs for you."

Jim was relieved that Ken had interrupted, so he didn't have to personally cut the performance short. The students were waiting for more, and he wasn't good at refusing anyone. In his usual humble manner, Jim half-bowed, shook their hands, and thanked them for listening.

The interview with the reporter from the university newspaper went badly from the start. The questions were unprepared and trite. In most cases, Jim gladly accommodated the press with a collection of anecdotes about his life, but this reporter seemed uninterested. Now, on the edge from fatigue, Jim wasn't in a patient mood; he answered what he perceived as inane questions with patented replies.

Usually the jam sessions before the concerts relaxed him. But now the interview had made him more tense and tired than before. He cut the reporter short and walked across the empty locker room, then through the long hallway that led to the stage. Standing behind a temporary partition, he saw the audience through a blue haze of smoke and spotlights. His face fell in disappointment.

The 2,000-seat auditorium looked less than half-filled. The crowd was much smaller than the thousands he had been drawing lately. He felt a pang of guilt. Later, he thought, he would have to apologize to Will and Doug.

He turned back to the quiet hallway to be by himself, lit another smoke, and sighed. Disappointed and exhausted, he felt like being alone. Doug and Ken Cortese appeared and interrupted him again.

"Are you all right?" Doug asked.

"Sure. Hey, doesn't look like I drew much of a crowd tonight."

"Don't worry about it," he said, shaking his head. "It's not your fault. Who would have guessed we'd have to compete with a tennis match?"

Bobby Riggs, the aging tennis pro and hustler, and Billie Jean King, the top player on the women's tour, were engaged in a battle of the sexes. It was being televised that night, and fifty million people were expected to tune in.

As the three men entered the dressing room, Jim did a double take at his reflection in the full-length mirror. He barely recognized himself. His hair was shaggy, his face was deeply lined, and the circles under his eyes were dark.

"Jesus!" he said, his jaw dropping open, "I look like a scarecrow. I must weigh 120 pounds. . . . I'm almost as skinny as Maury." Looking down, he flicked his cigarette and watched the grey and white ashes settle on the toe of his boot. He forced a grin.

"Man, Ingrid would hate that," he said to Doug and Ken. "She would have caught the ashes with one hand and polished my boot with the other." He straightened the collar of his shirt and tried unsuccessfully to smooth out the wrinkles. Then he twisted the long ends of his unruly handlebar moustache and ran his fingers through his thick, curly hair to comb it.

Jim liked to tease me about my frenetic energy and perfectionism. But he was meticulous, too, contrary to his cultivated truck-driver image. It was only lately that he had become too exhausted to care about his appearance.

"Shit, I need to buy another shirt," he said, without looking around. "I should have received some of that royalty money by now. Don't you think, Ken?"

"You mean they still haven't paid you yet?" Ken asked, astonished. "Jim, I've told you before, you've got to look out for yourself. There are a lot of temptations in this business. The money doesn't always flow where it's supposed to."

Jim knew Ken was right, but he hated confrontation. He couldn't bring himself to ask for his money again. The whole financial situation left him frustrated and angry. Staring into the mirror, his mood changed abruptly.

"Fuck 'em, those sons of bitches! I'd like to tell them to shove this fucking business up their ass and just give me my money." Then, embarrassed by his sudden display of anger, he leaned his palms on the mirror and dropped his head.

"Music's my life. But damn it, I can't do this anymore. I'm killing myself, and I don't have a thing to show for it." Ken reached out and put his hand on Jim's shoulder. "I've got no life, man," Jim whispered. "I'm broke, my marriage is falling apart, and I miss my son. He's gonna be two years old next week, and I've hardly seen him since he was born."

Jim thought of Adrian James dressed up in his cowboy hat and boots, riding his tired dad like a horse around the living room. Adrian James liked to strum his toy ukulele and sing "Baa-ba-loooo," imitating Ricky Ricardo on *I Love Lucy*. When Jim was on the road, Adrian James would sing to him in his tiny voice over the phone each night. It was breaking Jim's heart to be away so much, but in some ways it had become as hard to be at home as it was away.

Ken was trying to think of a reply when Maury came sneezing down the hall. Ken let it go and escaped. Jim raised an eyebrow at Maury and then grinned, his mood quickly shifting again, as it often did. Maury was blowing his nose into his huge red bandanna. He finished and stuffed it back into his hip pocket.

"Maury, you look like shit," said Jim. "Where's my scattergun? There must be a cat around here somewhere." Maury wasn't amused.

Jim picked up his guitar and played the opening melody to the new song Maury had recently written for him, "Some Surprise."

"Hey, I like this song," he told him.

His young friend nodded his head in appreciation but said nothing.

"I guess you're still pissed off. No one knows better than you just how crazy I've gotten lately. I guess I owe you some explanation."

"Nah," Maury said. "You don't owe me anything. But you do owe it to yourself and Ingrid to take some time off, man."

"No shit," Jim agreed. "I've definitely hit the wall this time. I've shut out Ingrid and everybody else."

"You need to take care of yourself, Jim," Maury said.

"Yeah," Jim responded, "I've crossed the line, and I'm not sure I know where to go from here. But things are gonna change. I can't keep hiding."

Maury offered a warm smile and spoke a line from his own song: "If I lie, I lose the best part of my mind."

"How did you get so wise at such a young age?" Jim joked.

Just then, Ken returned.

"Elliot, your road manager, just called, and you guys aren't going to like this," he told Jim and Maury. "They've canceled your break again. You're booked through November."

Maury froze.

Jim put down his guitar and aggressively shoved it into the case. After a moment of silence, he shouted, "Fuck them! They can't do that! Next week is my son's birthday, and I promised him I'd be home. I can't do this shit anymore. I'm done.

That's it. I'm calling Ingrid and telling her I'm coming home. That is, if I still have a home."

Ken looked at his watch and said slowly, "Look, you guys, it's time for you to go on."

Without a word, Jim picked up his guitar and walked into the hallway that led to the back of the stage. Maury followed.

When they reached backstage, they stood together in the darkness of the wings. The comedian George Stevens was concluding his act.

Will Mitchell, the committee chairman, stepped up to the microphone and announced:

"And now, ladies and gentlemen, the act you've all been waiting for, ABC recording artist . . . JIM CROCE!" He turned and extended his arm toward Jim and Maury. The audience applauded.

Stepping into the spotlight, Jim delivered his famous grin. He had a unique appearance, not classically handsome but compelling, with features etched too big for his face.

After a few moments, the audience quieted in anticipation. Maury pressed his lips to the microphone and made the sound of a stock car revving up for the race, and the two men, in perfect time, played the opening lines to "Rapid Roy."

> Oh Rapid Roy that stock car boy
> He too much to believe
> You know he always got an extra pack of cigarettes
> Rolled up in his T-shirt sleeve.
> He got a tattoo on his arm that say, "Baby"
> He got another one that just say, "Hey"
> But every Sunday afternoon he is a dirt track demon
> In a '57 Chevrolet.

After the students' applause, Jim stepped up to the microphone. "Hello out there! It sure is good to be here at Northwestern University! I've waited a long time to play this spot. You see, we've been playing some high-society places, like Rome, Paris, Los Angeles, New York City . . ."

He stepped back from the microphone, smiling. Hisses and boos could be heard at the mention of LA and New York.

When the jeering subsided, he began again: "I know what you mean. I feel the same way. And it's true, you know. You can lose touch with real people." He paused.

"So I said to my manager, 'Elliot, when are you gonna book me in a place that has some magic in it? You know . . . a place with real people. . . . When are you going to get me down to Natchitoches, Louisiana?'"

Jim intentionally mispronounced the name of the town, saying it phonetically, and looked offstage, scratching his head as if to ask someone for a little help. "How do you say that, again? Nack-a-tush? Well, it looks like Natch-a-toe-ches to me!" He stepped back as the audience laughed and applauded.

Jim followed his set list. Ordinarily, he would tell a story before singing each of his "character songs," but with his ballads he usually gave no introduction. They were intimate and, he believed, spoke for themselves. He began playing the introduction to "Dreamin' Again," a song he had written for me at our kitchen table in Coatesville, Pennsylvania:

> Don't you know I had a dream last night.
> And you were here with me.
> Lyin' by my side so soft and warm.
> And we talked a while
> And shared a smile
> And then we shared the dawn
> But when I woke up, oh my dream it was gone.
>
> Don't you know I had a dream last night.
> And you were here with me.
> Lyin' by my side so soft and warm.
> And you said you'd thought it over,
> Said that you were coming home.
> But then I woke up,
> And my dream, it was gone.
>
> I'm not the same.
> Can you blame me?
> Is it hard to understand?
> I can't forget.
> You can't change me.
> I am not that kind of man.

Don't you know I had a dream last night.
When everything was still.
And you were by my side so soft and warm.
And I dreamed that we were lovers,
In the lemon scented rain.
But then I woke up,
And I found that again. I had been
Dreamin', dreamin' again.

Forty-five minutes later, nearing the end of his set, Jim finished "Bad, Bad Leroy Brown." As the applause subsided, he backed away from the microphone and turned to Maury. Quietly, he said, "This'll be the last one, okay?"

Maury nodded, and in the hushed atmosphere Jim returned to the microphone:

"I'd like to finish with a song tonight for my new friend, Doug Nichols, who helped bring my one-man-band, Maury Muehleisen, and me here tonight. Take a bow, Maury," Jim announced, motioning to his friend.

Maury smiled and raised both of his arms in the air in appreciation of the applause.

"Yeah, Doug was kind enough to pick us up from the airport today and just about got us killed driving into the city. There was this logging truck 'three times full' that tried to shove us off the road. And I understand where that's comin' from . . . ya know. 'Cause I did some trucking myself for a couple years and met some very interesting people. That was during my character development period. But I'm happy now."

"Yeah. . . . Sometimes drivin' a truck, these guys in the big rigs can get pretty happy too. Because on long hauls you have to get into trying to stay awake a little longer than you can do on the natch, so you can make your haul profitable. The truckers, a lot of them, go into these truck stops, which are like pharmacies on the road. I've seen guys with maybe, ohhh, six or seven thousand pills under their seat in a brown paper sack.

"But I don't take 'em. Uh-uh. I never did. . . . I just like havin' 'em around in case I need 'em. I say, 'What's good for the sick is better for the well.'"

And the crowd laughed and clapped enthusiastically.

"But I'm glad I don't have to do that, 'cause I really like just being able to sing my songs for nice people like you."

Jim motioned to Maury, and in perfect time they played the lead-in to "Speed-ball Tucker" to close their set.

12

I drive a broke-down rig on may-pop tires 40 foot of overload
Lotta people say that I'm crazy because I don't know how to take
* it slow*
I got a broomstick on the throttle, I gotta rope it up and head
* right down*
Non-stop back to Dallas poppin' them west coast turnarounds . . .

When they finished their last encore, Jim and Maury took their final bow. Jim stretched his right arm into the air and waved. "Good night, Natchitoches! Thank you! Thank you very much!"

Jim walked offstage, and Maury followed.

Morgan and Doug were standing at the edge of the curtain, applauding. "Great show," Morgan said, still clapping.

"Thanks. Hey, I've got to make a phone call right away." Then turning to Doug, Jim said, "When I get off the phone, can you give us a lift to the airport?"

"Sure, Jim," Doug drawled, "Whenever you want to go, I'll be ready."

"Morgan, could you please get my stuff together? I'll meet you in the dressing room." He placed his guitar in Morgan's hands and walked quickly down the hallway. Striding up to the pay phone, he lifted the receiver, inserted a dime, and dialed "O."

"Operator," a voice replied.

"I'm calling collect to San Diego. My name is Jim Croce." He gave her the number.

"I'm so embarrassed to ask," she said shyly. "You wouldn't be . . . I mean you're not the same Jim Croce who wrote that song 'Operator,' are you?"

"Yeah, I am. You know that song?"

"Oh, it's my favorite song!" The phone began to ring.

He got more anxious each time the phone rang. Once, twice, three times, then four, then five. I answered and accepted the charges.

"Ing!" Jim exclaimed. "What took you so long? Were you asleep?"

"Oh Jim, I'm so glad you called! No, you didn't wake me. It's still light here. I was just talking about you!"

"Really?"

"Yeah. The deliveryman is here with the roll-top desk. I told him that was my husband singing "Bad, Bad Leroy Brown," on the radio and he said he loved that song. Anyway, where are you?"

"I'm backstage in Louisiana. I just finished the show."

"Are you okay? I'm worried about you, Jim."

"I'm exhausted, Ing. But just three more shows to go and then I'm home. I miss you and Adrian James so much."

"I miss you too, Jim. How's Maury?"

"I'll tell you later. We've decided to leave tonight instead of tomorrow. We're flying out in about an hour."

"Oh! By the way, Jim, that birthday gift you got Adrian James must have been something you dreamed up to drive me crazy. That puppy is peeing on everything. But Adrian James loves him to death."

"How's my little old man?"

"He misses you, Jim. He points to your picture all the time."

"God, I can't wait to see him again! Hey, let's have a big birthday party for him in our new house." He paused. "Listen, Ing . . . I just called to tell you . . ."

Adrian James ran stark naked out the screen door and into the yard in hot pursuit of Spooner, the new puppy.

"Adrian!" I yelled, as the screen door slammed.

"Jim, Adrian's running across the yard after the puppy. I've got to hang up and run after him! He's not safe out there."

"Ingrid, please! Wait!"

"What is it, Jim? I've got to get Adrian! The gate is open."

Pausing, he said, "I love you, Ing."

I hesitated. It had been a long time since Jim had called just to say those words. "I love you too, Jim. Please, please call me later tonight, sweet thing. I've got to go right now. Good-bye."

Jim kept the phone to his ear for a few seconds longer. He placed the receiver back in its cradle. Morgan approached with Jim's guitar in its case. "I packed it up for you, man. Ready to go?"

"Thanks. Yeah, sure, Morgan."

He took the guitar from Morgan and walked toward the exit.

WHICH WAY ARE YOU GOIN'

December 1963

JIM DROPPED THE NEEDLE on the other side of the album. Bob Dylan's plaintive voice filled the room:

> *It ain't no use to sit and wonder why, babe*
> *It don't matter anyhow*
> *An' it ain't no use to sit and wonder why, babe*
> *If you don't know by now.*
> *When your rooster crows at the break of dawn*
> *Look out your window and I'll be gone*
> *You're the reason I'm trav'lin' on*
> *Don't think twice, it's all right*

"Jim, you've got the talent to make it like Dylan," said Joe Salvioulo, Jim's closest friend, whom everyone called Sal. They'd met at Villanova University when Jim auditioned for a student talent show, and now, a year and a half later, they sat listening to records in Jim's living room, as they often did. From the first time they met, Sal's flamboyant wardrobe and unorthodox ways stood out from those of Jim's other, more conservative college classmates. "Besides, if a Jew can make it singing American folk songs, so can an Italian," he joked. Jim grinned.

"That would be great, man. I'd love to play Carnegie Hall! Ya know, Dylan played there last month."

"Yeah, I know. Remember? I saw him here on the same tour, at Town Hall. He was great. He walked on the stage like he owned it. He sang 'Blowin' in the Wind,' 'Don't Think Twice,' and 'Masters of War.' The audience was so quiet when he sang it was eerie."

"God, I'd love to be able to do that," Jim admitted.

"Practice," Sal encouraged, smiling at the old joke, though he really meant it, and added: "You can do it!"

Jim looked at his watch.

"Hey, it's getting late. I better get down to the radio station."

They headed upstairs to get their coats before heading out into the chilly Philadelphia evening.

Jim's father approached the side of the staircase and called after them: "Hey, Jim, I want to talk to you—alone." His index finger was pointed up at his son, his

16

face tense with anger. Sal slowly climbed the rest of the way upstairs himself; Jim hesitated, anticipating his father's wrath.

"Move it. I mean now!" Jim hurried back down. "I've been listening to you boys talk, and I don't like it one bit," his father said, closing in on him. "It's alright to play your music and have a little fun, but you're never to consider it anything more than a hobby. Don't ever get it into your head that you can make music a profession. Leave that for a different kind of people."

He'd heard the lecture before, but Jim was feeling rebellious enough at that moment to taunt his father. It didn't happen often.

"What do you mean 'a different kind of people'?" he said with a trace of sarcasm.

"Listen, mister, you know perfectly well what I mean. Your mother and I don't send you to college so you can grow up and sing songs about drunks and drifters. We won't stand for it!" Jim bit his lower lip and looked away. "You're getting involved with the wrong kind of people. You'll never amount to a thing!" His dad's voice rose, and his finger jabbed the air. "Music is for gypsies, not for my son. You don't know what the real world is like." He took a quick breath. "It's bad enough you study psychology. What the hell do you think you can do with that? I'm not sending you to college to be a bum, and that's final!"

"I'm not a bum."

"Don't talk back to me!" his father shouted, and slapped Jim's face sharply with the back of his hand.

Jim recoiled, glanced into his father's raging eyes, and backed away.

His father, James Alfred, turned and walked into the kitchen. James would never have disrespected his own father. As the eldest son, he had always placed duty to family first, solemnly accepting the role as go-between for his immigrant parents and his American brothers and sisters. The Croces were honorable people who had brought with them the principles of hard work and dedication to family, and James Alfred had worked diligently to overcome the misconceptions and stereotypes of the Italian immigrant.

Jim kept his hand pressed to his cheek to stop the sting and fled up to his room. He gathered his coat, songbooks, and guitar. When he and Sal came back down to leave, his parents ignored them. His father sat reading a magazine in the living room; his mother stood in the kitchen, covering leftover rapini with plastic wrap.

Only Jim's maternal grandfather, Massimo Babusci, whom everyone called Pa, acknowledged Jim. Pa had lived with them since the death of his wife, Bernice, a year earlier. The old man liked to sit in his favorite overstuffed easy chair and sing along at the top of his lungs to old records on his Victrola, re-creating the great

17

Italian operas. Pa had trouble remembering anything that had happened the day before, but he could clearly describe the piazza of his youth and the puppy that had peed on his leg when he was a boy.

Jim loved his grandfather and affectionately squeezed his shoulder when he passed his chair. "The boy," Pa murmured and nodded, patting Jim's hand. He couldn't remember his grandson's name.

Jim and Sal stepped outside, and Jim closed the front door behind him. Turning his collar to the cold, he stood momentarily on the doorstep. His grandfather had put on a record. Jim recognized the opening stanzas to a song by Enrico Caruso. As if on cue, Pa began to sing along.

With Sal ahead of him, Jim ran shivering to his '61 Volkswagen Beetle and jumped in. As they backed out of the driveway, he glanced up and saw his father standing at the living room window, looking out.

"I wonder if he'll ever understand," Jim said aloud.

A light carpet of snow covered the Main Line on the way to the Villanova radio station, WWVU. Jim and Sal discussed various conspiracy theories surrounding the assassination of JFK.

"Everyone's sad around here lately," Jim said. "My mother hasn't let a day go by without mourning. My uncles are upset that the mafia is being blamed."

"The real issue is power," Sal insisted. "It's not so much who did it but why they did it."

Jim dropped Sal off at his apartment and drove on to the campus station. By the time he arrived, he was mentally prepared for his broadcast, a three-hour folk and blues show, including an interview segment that provided Jim the opportunity to meet and talk with a number of the major folk and blues artists who had begun to influence him.

Tonight, Jim was airing a prerecorded talk with Mississippi John Hurt. He'd taped the session earlier in the week. The seventy-year-old black Southern man had generously given him a warm and informative interview, and had brought his guitar.

Jim took his seat alone in the control booth and rolled the tape:

"I heard you played the Newport Folk Festival with Bob Dylan last summer, and that more than 45,000 people showed up to hear you. How did that make you feel?"

"It made me feel real good to be invited to Freebody Park," Hurt said. "That was like real family. Lots of my friends were there, like John Lee Hooker. But Bob Dylan, he sure done brung those folks in."

"Do you believe the Festival marked a comeback in your own career?"

"I certainly don't think it hurt," he answered, laughing. "Of course, my career has seen more comebacks than a Friday night fish fry. I've been around a long time, you know. My first record for Okeh was in 1928."

The recording continued with Jim asking Hurt if he would play some songs. The musician gladly obliged with "Make Me a Pallet on Your Floor" and "Richland's Women Blues."

Jim joined in, strumming his guitar behind Hurt's syncopated rhythms on "Corrina, Corrina" and "Stackolee."

Jim then asked him to tell stories about his past.

Sitting in the booth, listening to the recording, Jim thought that Hurt's emotional, soulful speaking made it seem as if he were still singing. After the interview, Jim had thanked the musician reverently; he knew he had just encountered a legend, a hero of a vanishing period in American history.

Jim closed the program at 10 PM with a final announcement: "Don't forget to make a date for the Giant Hootenanny and Contest on Saturday, January 25, at Philadelphia Convention Hall. This show will be sponsored in part by Villanova, and I'll be joining Tommy Picardo and the rest of the Coventry Lads to perform and do the judging."

He punched in "Irene, Goodnight" by Leadbelly for the last tune of the evening.

Tommy Picardo, a junior and one of his best friends at Villanova, came into the studio, entered the booth quietly, and sat down in a chair, waiting for Jim to shut down. Jim and Tommy had promised to audition local groups at another radio station that night for the upcoming hootenanny. But by now the storm had worsened, and Jim wasn't looking forward to plowing through the snow to get to downtown Philadelphia.

The two hustled outside into the cold and got in Jim's VW. A blizzard slowed the drive down the Main Line. Drifts piled up on the road as the snow swirled in the headlights. Jim eased his way through the storm.

When they arrived at the radio station, Jim entered the parking lot and noticed a car angled awkwardly in a snowdrift, its wheels spinning madly in the snow. A young woman jumped out of the car and pushed against the hood with all of her strength.

Jim caught a glimpse of the girl's shiny, long dark hair and bright eyes, illuminated in the car's headlights. Inside the car, five young men in military uniforms sat cheering her on. Jim slowed down to watch. The teenager gave him an embarrassed smile and waved. He hit the brakes to get a good look at the girl, just as the car full of uniformed boys was freed from the snowdrift. Jim smiled and waved back at her and drove on into the lot to find a place to park.

Inside the station, WDAS, the first two auditioning groups played without much emotion or skill, and Jim grew impatient. Fighting the storm might have been a waste of time. But as he looked through the smoky studio glass at the final group, he changed his mind.

The young woman he had seen in the parking lot battling the snowstorm stood surrounded by the five military cadets. Maybe, he thought, all was not lost. Her petite figure was miniature-mature, but she was still a young girl. Bending slightly at her tiny waist, she shook her long, wet hair free of snow. She had olive skin and wore a short, black sheath skirt, a low-neck mohair sweater, and high, black leather boots.

Sensing someone watching me, I straightened up, glanced through the glass, and caught the intense stare of the man who had smiled at me in the parking lot. I felt as if he were undressing me with his eyes. I tugged on my skirt self-consciously and pushed up the sleeves of my oversized sweater.

I was the new lead singer of the Rum Runners, a band comprised of military cadets and the last group to audition that evening. I had met the group just a few weeks before the audition, when I performed some songs at the Pennsylvania Military College with two high school boys. After our performance at the college, Ty, the leader of the Rum Runners, told me they were looking for a strong female singer and asked me to join their band.

As our group approached the studio microphone, I stole another glance at my judge, absorbing everything about him: starched, light blue Oxford shirt, navy V-neck sweater, neatly ironed khaki pants, and thick, curly dark hair. Most of all, I was drawn to his eyes. They were large, brown, sad, and inviting. I couldn't keep myself from staring at him. Distracted by his gaze, I missed my cue but then picked it up easily.

Jim stared at me attentively. The only discordant notes came from my guitar, which was badly out of tune. After singing a few numbers, the Rum Runners launched into a long instrumental.

Finally, the number ended, and we started to pack up our instruments. The judge got up quickly and rushed into the studio so fast he tripped over a microphone cord, but caught his balance just in front of me and extended his hand. He seemed suddenly tongue-tied and awkward.

"Have you ever considered singing rock 'n' roll?" he blurted out. "I think you'd be great."

20

Before I could answer, he asked my name.

"Ingrid Jacobson," I said, trying to hide my excitement but smiling. "Do you really think so?" I tried to appear as cool as possible. I was only sixteen and didn't even know this guy's name, yet I was captivated by him.

"Come on, Jim," Tommy said, anxious to make the decision on the tryouts and get home. It was already past 1 AM.

"I think you made the cut," Jim said, and winked at me.

One of the cadets put his arm around me and told me I did great.

"See you at the contest," Jim said, leaving the studio, unwilling to fight the military for my attention.

———

The Giant Hootenanny Contest was part of the biggest concert festival of the year in Philadelphia, showcasing folk groups from more than fifty universities and high schools. The official program featured the Coventry Lads on the cover. Jim's clean-shaven face grinned from the corner of the cover photo. He was dressed in a sweater and button-down shirt, and his hair was cropped close. Tommy and the others in the group, including Tim Hauser, who would later go on to form the popular jazz vocal group the Manhattan Transfer, were all dressed the same.

By noon, a large crowd filled the Convention Center. Performers gathered anxiously in the hallways, tuning their instruments and waiting for their turn. Few had ever played in front of a crowd of thousands. The intimidating hall was a theater-in-the-round, and the stage seemed dwarfed by the tower of seats that rose all around it.

The charged atmosphere excited Jim as he sat down at the judges' table near the stage. But as the afternoon wore on, tedium began to set in. Most of the groups played the same songs. By 3 PM he had heard "Lemon Tree," "The Cruel War," and "500 Miles" more than a dozen times. When Esther Halpern, a professional singer and co-owner of the local Gilded Cage Coffee House, played during intermission, Jim ducked outside for a quick smoke and some well-earned silence.

He squeezed through the crowd of musicians and spotted me, kneeling in a corner, frantically trying to tune my guitar.

He approached me, but I didn't look up. He hesitated for a moment, taking a long look at my short white dress. It had black sleeves and black stripes running up the sides.

Jim laughed out loud.

"Hey!" he said, "You look like a little skunk!"

I was terribly disappointed.

I had been unable to forget him after our meeting almost a month earlier and was hoping I would see him at the hootenanny. I had borrowed the dress from an older friend thinking it would make me look grown-up and sexy.

Seeing my hurt expression, Jim knew he had blown it. He looked down and grimaced. "Is everything okay?" he asked weakly.

"I'm just trying to tune this damn guitar," I said, turning away.

His remark had crushed me. I had always been insecure about my appearance. Having grown up with a beautiful mother and voluptuous fraternal twin sister, I never felt I measured up. I took after my father, with my small, muscular frame, slender face, and straight hair.

In a desperate attempt to recover, Jim motioned to my battered guitar.

"Can I help you tune it?" The guitar was a cheap, off-brand Japanese model. He wondered whether it would tune at all.

"No, I can do it myself," I said. I struggled with the strings, but his presence made it impossible for me to concentrate. Distracted and frustrated, I gave up. "There. That's close enough," I said. "I have to go now—everybody's waiting for me."

"Can I see you later?" he asked.

"I don't know. Maybe." I wanted to see him, but I didn't know if he really liked me or just liked making fun of me. I walked away.

As I reached the door, Jim called out, "Hey, Ingrid! You look terrific! . . . Good luck!"

I spun around, beaming, and waved energetically.

Moments later, as the Rum Runners approached the stage, Jim came up beside me. Without saying a word he reached for my guitar, bent on one knee, and quickly tuned it. Rising, he handed it back to me, winked, and disappeared into the crowd.

The audience quieted as we stepped into position. Everyone expected another rendition of a tired tune, but I slowly laid my guitar on the floor and stepped up to the microphone. In a dramatic fashion, mimicking Mamie Van Doren in the movie *Teacher's Pet* with the song "The Girl Who Invented Rock 'n' Roll," I stood between two tall cadets and placed a hand on each of their shoulders. In a breathy voice, I began to sing:

> *You've heard of instant coffee,*
> *You've heard of instant tea,*
> *Well, you just cast your little o' eyes on little o' instant me.*

I turned, looked back over one shoulder, and shimmied seductively, inducing a roar from the audience. Then the Rum Runners played an inspired version of "The Midnight Special," the planned introduction to our set. I picked up my guitar and joined in on the chorus.

Jim later told me that my surprise introduction and strong vocals had earned the Rum Runners first place in the Best Performance category.

After the show, when Jim came to look for me in the post-hootenanny chaos, my father was embracing me warmly, while my twin sister, Phyllis, stood by smiling and admiring the uniformed cadets. Several other guys from the audience, folk singers, and a couple of judges also lingered nearby, waiting to talk to me.

Jim broke through the crowd and waited while I signed an autograph. He asked if we could talk and then led me to a quiet corner, where he looked straight into my eyes.

"I love your voice. Do you think we could sing together sometime? I mean, I think our voices would blend well. I'd love to sing harmony with you. Maybe I could call you and set up a time so we could practice."

I beamed inside but coolly teased him with a shrug.

"I'll think about it," I said with a laugh. Sensing him about to pull away, I quickly added, "I'd love to." My steady voice belied the chills vibrating through me. We exchanged phone numbers and reluctantly said good night.

On the way home, I sat in the back seat with Phyllis, who peppered me with questions about Jim. The only response I gave was a defiant "Hands off."

From the front seat, my stepmother, Florence, asked, "Honey, what kind of a name is Croce? Do you think he's Jewish?"

"Who knows and who cares?" I said, daydreaming about Jim's sexy voice, curly hair, and big brown eyes.

Images of Jim's appearance, sweet smell, and warm smile dominated my thoughts for days. I wondered if he had a girlfriend. Would he want to play music with me if he knew I was only sixteen? When would he finally call?

Two weeks after the hootenanny, there was still no word from him. Finally, I grew impatient and telephoned his home. Jim's mother answered.

"May I speak to Jim Croce please?" I asked cautiously.

"Who's calling?" Jim's mother's voice was quick and suspicious.

"Ingrid Jacobson," I managed to say, twice as nervous as when I had started to dial.

"Jimmy's not here," Flora said icily.

"Will you please tell him I called?"

"Yes." His mother hung up before I could give her my phone number.

I sensed a formidable obstacle, but I persevered. I called his house twice more in the following days. Each time, Flora answered.

Finally Jim called back.

"I've been up in Greenwich Village," Jim said. "My mom's upset that you've been so forward. But I convinced her that you were just calling to talk about music."

My ego was deflated. It hadn't occurred to me that I was doing anything wrong by calling Jim. A few months earlier, my own mother, who had battled a drug and alcohol addiction, had passed away from breast cancer at the age of thirty-six. She wasn't around to teach me the intricacies of social etiquette.

But I also felt disappointed that Jim had to make up a reason for my calling him.

"I'm sorry," I said quietly, uncomfortable and wanting to hang up. Still, unwilling to lose the chance, I forced myself to invite Jim over to my house in Springfield, a suburb of Philadelphia, to rehearse the following Sunday.

"That sounds great," he reassured me.

When Sunday arrived, Jim made the ten-minute drive from his home in Drexel Hill in his VW. He slowly approached the front door of my house with a guitar case in each hand.

When I opened the door, he half-bowed in a bashful sort of way. He looked uncomfortable in his three-piece suit, tie, and heavily starched shirt that cut into his neck.

His face fell when he saw me in a loose-fitting, navy blue University of Pennsylvania sweatshirt and tight, old, faded jeans.

"I apologize for the suit," he said nervously. "I came from my cousin's wedding."

But I smiled and said, "You look great," and motioned for him to follow me. I peered around, putting a finger to my lips, and pointed toward the kitchen where my family sat. I took Jim by the hand and tried to slip downstairs to my room. My stepmom, Florence, intercepted us, followed immediately by my father, Sid; twin sister, Phyllis; and younger sister and brother, Janice and Kenny. I sighed and made all of the introductions.

Finally, I led Jim downstairs to the bedroom I shared with Phyllis. We were alone for the first time. Carefully he laid his guitar cases on my sister's bed, unsnapped one, and took out his twelve-string and some songbooks. Then he unhooked the second case, pulled out a six-string, and sat down beside me on my bed.

I had heard Jim perform at the hootenanny with the Coventry Lads. But now, as he sat on my bed, I heard his true voice solo, so sincere and beautiful. I was mesmerized. As he played the old folk song "Cotton-Eyed Joe," I felt more intimacy with him than I had ever experienced with anyone.

> *Tell me where do you come from?*
> *And where do you go?*
> *Tell me where do you come from,*
> *Ol' cotton-eyed Joe?*
>
> *Well I come for to see you,*
> *And I come for to sing,*
> *And I come for to bring you,*
> *A $30 glitterin' diamond ring.*

Jim finished his song and asked if I would like to try one together with him. He picked up his twelve-string and started to play. He taught me the harmony to Woody Guthrie's "Pastures of Plenty," explaining it was just like the melody "but different." Although I'd been singing all my life, that was my very first singing lesson, and I was excited by how comfortable Jim made me feel.

He had been shy and awkward when he arrived, but with his guitar in hand, he was at ease. He talked enthusiastically about folk music and the history behind each of the songs we sang.

He was pleased at how quickly I learned the words and how good we sounded together. Our voices blended seamlessly, and he smiled at me as we sang.

I was overwhelmed. I liked everything about him: his broad open smile, his strong hands, his slim body, his medium height, his voice. He was seductive but secure. Because I had suffered through my parents' divorce and moved from school to school, I longed for stability. I recognized that playing music gave Jim confidence and liked the feeling of singing with him. He was a good teacher, and I was a good student. I hoped in time to become something more.

After a few songs, I switched on my father's Wollensak reel-to-reel tape recorder to capture the session forever. Jim taught me some traditional folk songs, like Woody Guthrie's "This Land Is Your Land," and then Bob Dylan's "The Times They Are A-Changin'."

We played for almost three hours before he had to leave.

On Jim's way out, my father stopped us in the living room and struck up a conversation. The three of us sat down, and I was pleased that we could all talk together so easily. Jim and my dad found mutual interests in psychology and music.

25

Jim was majoring in psychology at Villanova, and my dad, who loved music and played harmonica, was a family physician who was attending the University of Pennsylvania to complete his psychiatric residency.

I adored my father. My parents divorced when I was only five, and when we were eight, our mother charmed the judge and gained custody of her daughters. My twin sister was content to live with our mother and grandmother. But all I ever wanted growing up was to live with my dad. The fact that my father and Jim took an instant liking to each other was extremely important to me.

"I'll call you this week to schedule a rehearsal," Jim winked as he got up to leave.

"Great," I replied. "And I promise not to call you."

We laughed and then suddenly fell silent, looking at each other with longing. Jim's hands were full of guitars, and my father was still in the room. Jim bowed slightly and backed out the door. He walked to his car, stopping to look back at me. I felt like jumping up and down but controlled my excitement and waved enthusiastically.

Jim called again a few days later, confirming another Sunday practice. He arrived precisely on time, wearing sharply creased jeans and a starched work shirt.

"No wedding today?" I teased.

He laughed. "No. Patsy's the only cousin I have who is old enough to get married, and she weighs about three hundred pounds. But she's got a great personality."

I wasn't quite sure how to take Jim's humor. On the one hand, he was tender and considerate of people's feelings, but when "onstage," he felt free to joke and be boldly coarse.

As a duo, we practiced every Sunday for a month, and our magnetic attraction to each other grew as strong as the improved harmonizing of our voices. We spoke little about our feelings, but our music ignited electricity between us. At first, we gazed into each other's eyes when we sang, but later our feelings intensified, and the intertwining of our voices had become so sensual and arousing that we had to look away.

One day, Jim called and invited me to a party at Sal's house.

"Ing," Jim said, hesitating, "I know this is short notice, but some friends want me to play at a party near school tomorrow night . . . and I was wondering . . . if you could come along and sing with me."

I eagerly agreed, excited to meet his friends. I had longed for a chance to become a part of his world. Then I remembered my 11 PM curfew. I was embarrassed to mention it, but deep inside I liked the fact that my father and stepmother cared enough about me to make rules. While living with my mother after the divorce, I had no restrictions. She often left my sister and me on our own while she was working on South Street at my grandmother's dress store, Mary Greenberg's. My mother also had her own local television show, *The Magic Lady*, in which she played Gershwin and popular songs from the hit parade on piano. Serious and studious, I stayed out of trouble. I worked hard to get good grades and used my boundless energy in gymnastics, field hockey, softball, swimming, art, and music.

"I'll get you back by midnight," Jim promised when I told him about the curfew. "Go see what your dad says."

I came back breathless. "He said yes, but only if you promise to have me home by 12 sharp."

Jim arrived precisely at 7:30 the next evening.

Fueled by nervous energy, I had already been ready for an hour when I heard the familiar whine of his little VW racing up the street.

We drove to Lansdale, talking and laughing, enjoying each other's company. When Jim introduced me to his friends at Sal's apartment, I was really happy to be included but, at the same time, a bit uncomfortable. I was at least three or four years younger than anyone else there, and the obvious interest some of the other girls showed in Jim increased my anxiety.

Jim was quiet with his crowd and didn't seem to notice my nervousness. He left me on my own for a moment and put his guitar case in Sal's bedroom.

The older girls looked my way but made no attempt to make conversation. Then Sal swept across the room to me.

"Don't mind them," he said. "They're just jealous. You must be Ingrid. Jim says you're the entertainment for the evening." I laughed spontaneously. I immediately liked Sal, who seemed as warm and wild as Jim had described. He wore tight black leather pants, a chartreuse shirt, and black Italian boots with exaggerated Cuban heels. Sal had an open, engaging smile, and his black hair was piled high in a pompadour, which accentuated his "blaze" hair—a natural silver stripe that ran through the middle of his head like a streak of lightning.

"You look pretty entertaining yourself," I said. Sal chuckled, but giddy laughter from the middle of the large living room distracted us.

I watched as Jim changed over the course of the party. His shyness evaporated, and a new personality emerged, full of confidence and impishness. Three girls surrounded him and egged him on as he began playing one of his bawdy ballads.

They were members of the Haveners, a female singing group composed of six student nurses from the Villanova University College of Nursing. The music department at Villanova had asked Jim to work with the young women, and they adopted him as their personal music director. He enjoyed the challenge, and within a few months he had developed them into a competent performing group.

The girls idolized him, and although he once climbed through their second-story dorm window during a panty raid, he had no romantic interest in any of them. Still, the attention pleased him, and no matter how unattractive a woman might be, he always found some way to compliment her. He once described one of the nursing students at Villanova to Sal as being built like "a refrigerator with a head." Yet he later confessed to me that when he was alone with her, he had told her what a sweet disposition and beautiful skin she had.

The Haveners kept coddling Jim and giving me hostile glances. Jim continued strumming his guitar. While he played, I sat with Sal on the sofa, taking in the room and the atmosphere. Jim's singing and Sal's easy company made me feel comfortable.

After singing several songs by himself, he motioned for me to join him.

I wanted to sing, but I was growing impatient for the music portion of the evening to be over so I could be alone with him. I had noticed a couple vanish into one of the bedrooms, and the thought of disappearing into the darkness with Jim excited me. But I realized Jim wanted to show off me and our songs to his friends, so I did my best to focus on the music and figured everything else would have to wait.

Jim began the introduction to "Song for Canada," which the folk duo Ian and Sylvia had recently recorded. I sat beside him and in perfect harmony we sang:

> *Lonely northern rivers come together till you see*
> *One single river rolling in eternity.*
> *Two nations in the land that lies along its shore,*
> *But just one river, you and me.*

We looked at each other as our voices entwined, and we were both clearly turned on. I knew the feelings we had kept in check were being played out in our singing. Even the audience seemed to become aware of it. The room hushed. Sal grinned.

"That was hot," he said loudly after we'd finished the song.

I smiled. Jim didn't know what to say, and looked down.

Just then, Jim's younger brother, Rich, stormed into the room, breaking the silence.

"My date wants to go home right now, and I need to borrow your car," he said to Jim. He had come to the party with an attractive Puerto Rican girl from Cabrini University. When one of the guests had made a bigoted joke about Puerto Ricans, she took offense and insisted on leaving immediately.

"Shit," Jim said under his breath. "Look, you'll have to hurry. It's snowing, and I've got to get Ingrid home by midnight."

Rich nodded glumly and left with the car keys.

"He'll be back in time," Jim reassured me.

With the romantic mood we had built now on the verge of collapsing, Jim played just one more song and abruptly ended the concert.

Then he turned on the hi-fi and chose the most romantic record he could find, Johnny Mathis's *Twelfth of Never*. Other couples started dancing, and Jim took me by the hand. He gently led me into the dimly lit hallway, and for the first time we held each other close as we moved to the music. I trembled as I felt his body next to mine and leaned my cheek against his chest. And when "Misty" started to play, he gradually led me through the open door to Sal's bedroom in the turret of the old Victorian home. From the windows of the round room we could see the snow falling softly outside. For a magical moment, it seemed as if we were caught inside a snow globe. I looked up, and he kissed me softly on the cheek; he kissed my lips and deftly shut the door with his foot. I surrendered willingly to his caresses, my breath quickening as his hands moved over my arms, neck, and breasts, where they lingered.

Still kissing me deeply, he gently lifted me onto the bed and slowly reached his hand inside my skirt. I caught his hand, but he persisted, gently breaking my grasp. I relaxed and kissed him. His hand slid upward along my inner thigh. I gasped as his fingers turned upward, but the unyielding seam of my girdle halted his explorations.

Caught off-guard, Jim tried to outflank it but couldn't find an opening. I lay still on the bed, not sure what to do.

He barely heard Sal yelling at us through the door.

"Jim!" Sal shouted, repeating himself. "Sorry to interrupt, but Rich is on the phone. Your car is stuck in a snowdrift."

I popped up like toast.

Jim groaned. Slowly, almost painfully, he got up and started for the living room, then realized he couldn't walk out immediately. He was fully aroused, and Sal would be relentless in pointing it out. "Just a minute," he yelled.

29

Jim pulled out his shirttails and ran to the phone. Rich explained that he was at a gas station waiting for a tow truck, which wasn't going to arrive until after midnight.

Aggravated at the interruption and his brother's bad news, Jim returned to the bedroom and asked me to call my father and explain the situation.

My dad said he understood and told us not to rush on the icy roads.

The lovers' spell had been broken, and both Jim and I cooled off. Shaken by how out of control we had been, we sat together on the couch, as far from the bedroom as we could get.

When we arrived at my house at 2 AM, my father was awake but stayed respectfully upstairs.

When we reached the front door, Jim stared directly into my eyes and kissed me gently. I hugged him, and we remained silent, watching the snowfall under the streetlight, both of us confused and a little embarrassed. He held me gently for a minute and said a quiet good night.

The snow had stopped falling by the next morning, leaving a crisp, clear day. I awakened early with a lover's hangover. I felt horrible, certain that I had ruined my chances with Jim by coming across as cheap and easy. I buried my head under my pillow. A few moments later, I sat up, flooded with the realization of how much I cared for him. I wanted to call and explain how I felt, but didn't have the nerve. Flora might've answered and confirmed her suspicion that I was chasing her son. After the previous night, even Jim might believe that. I collapsed with a groan and buried my head back under the pillow.

Just after breakfast, the phone rang.

Jim said softly, "I want to apologize about last night. I just got carried away. I feel awful."

I wanted to shout my feelings out loud, but caught myself. My words tumbled out in an elated jumble. "So do I. Jim, do you think I'm cheap?"

"Oh no, Ing! It was my fault. Will you forgive me?"

"Yes, of course. Do you forgive me?"

"Yes! Yes!" He paused a long moment, then added, "Wow, that was something."

"Yeah, it was great!"

We were both silent, then began to laugh.

"Jim," I said, in a soft, mocking voice. "I promise I'll never wear a girdle again."

"Oh, yay!" he said.

Two weeks later he invited me to his house for dinner to meet his family.

He picked me up and drove me to the Croces' split-level home in Drexel Hill. "I'm nervous about meeting your mother," I said, staring at the road.

He smiled and placed his hand on my leg. "Don't worry. The Flower will like you, but it might take her some time."

"Who is The Flower?" I laughed.

"That's what we call my mother sometimes. Her name is Flora, or "flower" in Italian. My parents are pretty old-fashioned," Jim explained. "They just don't understand all the changes that are going on today, especially my mom. She thinks the Beatles are destroying the world. Their long hair and music really scare her. And she's serious about it too."

"You're kidding, aren't you? She really thinks the Beatles are ruining the world? That's a riot."

"I know it seems weird," he said, "but she believes it. Both my parents are afraid that I'll be led down the road to hell. That I'll grow up to be a bum or something worse, that I won't turn out to be respectable. You'll see. They're very strict with me. Sometimes they're really overbearing, especially lately."

"I'm afraid your mother hates me already. You know, I thought about how upset she was with me because I called you. I don't think it's a matter of manners. I think women should call men as freely as men call women."

"I agree, Ing, but my parents are first-generation Americans. They believe a woman's place is in the home. Mom is either cooking or cleaning. She doesn't drive, and she's totally dependent on my father. My mother has a way of being short with people. She has a quick, dry sense of humor, but she's really vulnerable. And that's why I call her The Flower."

"Well, what's your dad like?"

"He's a good man. He just has high expectations of me. He doesn't want his sons, especially me, to fall short like my uncles."

"But he must be proud of your music."

"Yeah, my dad loves music for fun. He's the one who bought me an accordion for Christmas when I was six and put together scrapbooks of every concert and school function I ever played. But he would never consider music being anything more than a hobby."

"But music is what you want to do, isn't it?"

"There's nothing I want more . . . but it's hard enough for my dad to accept the fact that I'm majoring in psychology and German, let alone understand that I never want a 9 to 5 job. He'd like me to get a good civil service position with a guaranteed pension or become a doctor or a lawyer. He's a product of the Great Depression, and security is all that's important to him. Can you imagine shuffling papers at the same desk for thirty years? I can't."

He pulled his VW into the driveway. As he opened the door to his house, a din of voices and the rich aromas of roasted garlic and peppers embraced me.

Jim's aunt Ginger stood just inside. "Oh! Here's Jimmy with a date! Hello dear." She kissed Jim on the cheek. He introduced me.

"Oh, Ingi, I'm so pleased to meet you."

Jim seemed relieved by his aunt's warmth and open hospitality, and he walked me into the living room, filled with boisterous Italians. The Croce family was large. Jim's father was the eldest of eight brothers and sisters. Aunt Ginger followed me closely and introduced me to the aunts—Florence, Santina, Evelyn, and Fanny—and their husbands.

Paul, Jim's uncle, walked over to me and introduced himself. Patty and Carmen, Jim's peculiar twin uncles, eyed me up and down from both sides of the room before coming over to introduce themselves. Patty, small, thin, and self-impressed, fashioned himself after his hero, Frank Sinatra. Carmen, in contrast, looked more like Nero: short, round, and devilish.

The rest of the family then crowded around with smiles and small talk, trying to make me feel at home. They had heard I was a Jewish girl. And in an effort to show acceptance, one of Jim's aunts made it a point to tell me, "Italians and Jews are so much alike; sometimes you can't tell them apart."

But I was still uneasy; I hadn't yet passed the acid test. Flora was in the kitchen, ignoring the introductions. I could see her through the open kitchen door. She was a short woman in her late forties and wore a crisp, white, sleeveless shirt, plaid skirt, and hand-embroidered apron.

Finally, she emerged from the kitchen, carrying a relish tray to the table. Jim intercepted her.

"Mom, this is Ingrid," he said, placing his hand gently on my shoulder. Flora glanced in my direction, nodded slightly, and said, "Hello, it's nice to meet you," then turned busily away to place the relish tray in its proper place on the table. Uncle Sam, Ginger's husband, reached for a pepperoncini.

Flora slapped his hand. "*Schifoso!*" she scolded.

Sam was Sicilian, dark, and somewhat sinister-looking, with tattoos of nude women, hearts, and anchors on both arms.

"Watch out for Uncle Sam," Jim leaned toward me and whispered. "He's got a gun."

I forgot about Flora and stared at Sam, who was waiting for her to leave the dining room so he could help himself to the antipasto. I looked searchingly at Jim to see if he was joking, but couldn't tell.

He guided me over to meet his grandfather, Pa. The old man sat off by himself, embedded in a floral-print easy chair. He awoke when Jim gently shook his arm.

With a dreamy smile, Pa patted my hand.

"Oh, the girl" was all he said.

Finally Jim led me to meet a tall, handsome, dignified man standing in the living room doorway by himself. Jim tensed visibly as we approached the neatly dressed, silver-haired gentleman.

"Ingrid, this is my father."

I sensed Jim's intimidation but felt comfortable with his dad as he took my hand in both of his and smiled warmly.

"Welcome," he said, "I'm glad you could come. Jim has said so many nice things about you and your family."

Jim appeared to relax, and I felt a rush of satisfaction. Somehow I had at least momentarily bridged the gap between father and son.

Dinner was served around a long, rectangular table with a full-length clear plastic cover protecting an intricate lace tablecloth.

Everyone knew their seats, and I felt at a loss until Jim's father took my arm and pulled out the chair next to Jim's seat. Jim, smiling broadly, sat on my left.

After Flora served the feast of garlic bread, lasagna, kohlrabi, peas, roasted lamb, and Italian Chianti, Jim got up to tune his guitar. While the women cleared the dishes and began to prepare for dessert, the cousins, the Croce men, and I retired to the living room.

As Jim sang, I studied the room. So this is Jim's house, I thought. It was immaculate—not a speck of dust anywhere. The wallpaper was white with a brocade of gold vinyl, and crucifixes surrounded confirmation pictures of Jim and Rich. The couch and two side chairs were upholstered in dusty-rose brocade, covered with more clear plastic. A china cabinet held small teapots and porcelain statues from Italy.

I watched Flora move intently around the dining room and the kitchen, cleaning up with a sure, single-minded purpose. She seldom spoke to the other women, except to direct chores with her dry sense of humor. In the living room, Jim continued singing.

From the corner, Pa raised his voice and belted out a single line from an Italian opera. Nobody paid attention to him.

Aunt Ginger leaned out from the kitchen and asked Jim for "Charlie Green," a Bessie Smith song about a man who played the slide trombone. Jim obliged, then motioned for me to join him.

We sang three songs, and everyone clapped politely. Flora ignored us, never pausing from her cleaning. "Come on in and sing with me, Mom," Jim called to his mother. "Let Ingrid hear your beautiful operatic voice." Flora laughed off the compliment and continued to clean.

"Come on, Flower," Jim teased, begging her, "sing for us."

"Oh, Jimmy, please," Flora argued. "You know I can't sing anymore. Now don't bother me." She motioned with her hands for him to leave her alone. But Jim refused to take no for an answer. He walked right up to her, tilting his guitar up high in the air near her ear. "Come on, Flower!" He began strumming a familiar tune. "Show Ingrid what a wonderful voice you have. Sing like you sang when you were a girl back in Rochester."

Flora surprised me.

Jim began to play a popular Italian song. All of a sudden, his mother released a soaring soprano voice and sang the song all the way through in Italian.

The family clapped loudly.

"Not too bad for an old woman," Flora laughed nervously, then went directly back to her cleaning.

She's endearing, I thought. She really isn't as tough as she looks.

After several more songs, Jim and I got up to say good-bye. We were off to perform at a student event at Villanova, and afterwards Jim had to do his weekly radio show.

———

Sal had organized a student hootenanny in the university cafeteria below the radio station, and had made himself master of ceremonies. When Jim and I arrived, Sal saw us and waved. He wore a long, black silk cape with fuchsia lining, black boots, and pegged pants, and he carried an antique cane with a red tip. Approaching us, he made a low, sweeping bow.

"Sal," I teased, "you're a little early for Halloween."

"Not Halloween," he intoned. "Tonight, I am dressed for a blind date."

Jim explained that once Sal went on a "blind date" and tapped around with his cane all evening, pretending he couldn't see. Jim laughed and continued: "At one point, he had his date lead him to a piano in a bar where he played for her, mimicking Little Stevie Wonder and Ray Charles. And the asshole never told the poor girl he really wasn't blind—just a *finnochio*!"

The hootenanny began when Sal went up onto the stage and, with a swirl of his cape, grabbed the microphone and introduced Jim, Bill Reid, and the banjo player, Carl Fehrenbach.

The trio opened the show with a couple of Kingston Trio tunes, "Greenback Dollar" and "Tom Dooley." Jim soloed on "Scotch & Soda," and after they finished, he came down from the stage and introduced me to his good friend Bill, a six-foot-two-inch burly Irishman in his late twenties with a big voice and a pronounced swagger. Bill was standing next to an attractive dark-haired woman who introduced herself to me as his wife, Dee. She told me to ignore how rude Bill was for not introducing her. Bill acknowledged her comment by slapping her on the butt and telling me, "I was just saving the best for last!" Dee gave him a look that let me know she was the one who was really running the show. But she let Billy go on that one and started a conversation to get to know me better.

Dee told me that Jim met Bill one summer when Jim took a job painting hallways at the Delaware County Memorial Hospital.

Bill was the foreman on a construction site adjacent to the hospital. During his lunch break one day, Jim went over to watch the construction workers operate the heavy equipment. He was immediately fascinated with Bill, who was reckless, loud, profane, and funny. Though he had no experience in it, Jim told Bill that he wanted to learn to operate the diesel Caterpillars. In good humor, Bill told the kid he was much too skinny to drive the big Cats. Jim was not discouraged. He was persistent and struck up a conversation, bantering with Bill, who simply ignored his requests until Jim revealed that he played the guitar and wanted to be a singer.

Bill loved music and was an accomplished guitarist and banjo player himself, though his predominant talents were brawling and partying.

He told Jim to bring his guitar to the job site, and the following day they played during their break. Bill was impressed and conceded to someday teach Jim to drive the big ten-wheel dump trucks, if Jim would agree to play music with him.

Jim and Bill began to play regularly during their breaks and lunch hours. Bill taught Jim to play bluegrass and some songs he knew by Johnny Cash.

Jim thoroughly enjoyed the robust and unbridled vulgarity that made Bill Reid seem bigger than life. With Billy you just couldn't be sure what was going to happen next—an intriguing quality Jim loved. Jim was a great listener and liked to draw out the exaggerated essence of Bill's personality. Bill liked Jim's attention and felt bigger and rowdier and more important when Jim was around.

Shortly after they met, Bill invited Jim to dinner at his house, where Jim met Dee and their young son, Gregory. As their friendship grew, they played music together almost every night. Bill's volatile marriage to the beautiful, strong-willed Dee, pregnant with their second child, centered on Bill. Dee also took a liking to Jim and often invited him to join them for dinner. Jim thought Dee and Bill were perfect together, earthy and real.

Bill loved to taunt Jim, and the night Jim introduced me to Bill at the hootenanny, Bill immediately began to tell me a story in his booming voice:

"One day Jim comes by to help me put on my new roof. We spent the afternoon up there, drinking wine and hammering tiles. I've got the jug and a hammer, and Jim has a stack of tiles in one hand and a glass of wine in the other. I turn my back to him for a minute when all of a sudden I hear this noise. Whoosh! And I look to where Jim was standing, or where he should have been standing, and I only see him from the waist up! He's falling off the roof! His eyes and his mouth are open wide, but he's still holding on to his wine. Then he disappears. I don't know whether to laugh or not, and I run like hell over to the edge. When I get there, I see this hand holding on to the gutter pipe. Then I see the other hand reaching up and groping around at the edge of the roof. But it's still got the wine glass in it and can't hold on. Jim's swinging back and forth, but pretty soon he slips off and does the neatest back flip I ever saw, still holding the wine glass. I swear he never spilled a drop."

At the conclusion of this hyperbolic tale, Bill winked at me, grabbed his banjo, slapped his wife on the bottom again, and yelled, "It's my turn to play!" He swaggered up to the microphone and belted out a version of one of his favorite country songs: "You Oughta See Pickles Now:"

> *When I was just a little boy,*
> *There lived next door to me,*
> *A little girl named Pickles,*
> *Just as mean as could be*
>
> *Now she ate pickles all day long, she didn't care what kind*
> *Got so mad when I asked her if she grew on a pickle vine.*
>
> *But gee, oh golly, ya oughta see Pickles now*
> *When she walks by, I sit and sigh, all I can say is "Wow,"*
> *But here of late I've got an awful urge to hang around*
> *Gee, oh golly, you oughta see Pickles now*

The audience laughed and clapped along in rhythm. The hootenanny continued with a performance by Villanova University's all-male a capella choir, the Spires. Jim was part of this group as well, and by now I was eager to sing, as I knew that when they were done, it would be time for Jim and me to play our songs.

I was excited to sing with Jim in front of a large audience, and it went well. The applause gave way to demands for an encore, and we sang Ian and Sylvia's "Four Strong Winds."

Sal performed the closing number, an old protest song called "Just a Little Rain." He strummed his guitar meditatively and began to sing, "Just a little rain, just a little rain," and then he sang it again: "Just a little rain, just a little rain . . ."

Over and over it went. The repetition puzzled the audience, who seemed unsure if Sal had forgotten the words or was just teasing them.

Sweat rivulets ran down his cheeks. He kept singing the words with great emotion, but with every line, his face contorted more. His body bent forward, lower and lower, until he was almost squatting on the floor.

"Jesus," said Bill loudly. "He looks like he's going to take a shit."

Jim laughed and doubled over. As Sal struggled on, Jim howled, convinced that he was really putting them all on.

Finally, Sal seemed to remember another line. It was from a different song, but he sang it anyway. To conclude, Sal crossed the stage to where Jim had sunk to the floor, helpless with glee. Sal pointed accusingly at him with his white cane, then burst into shrieks of hysteria himself as the audience broke into laughter and cat calls.

The show was over, and Jim took me upstairs to the radio station to watch him do his weekly show. I took a seat among the boxes of albums and looked around at the posters of Bob Dylan, Muddy Waters, Phil Ochs, Mississippi John Hurt, and others.

Jim's agility with the equipment impressed me greatly. I leaned my elbows on a wooden desk and put my chin in my hands and stayed that way for almost three hours, watching him and listening to his warm, smooth, sensual voice.

When he brought me home, an hour late, my father again waited upstairs. At the front door, Jim and I embraced in a long, passionate kiss.

Jim left reluctantly.

I watched his Volkswagen drive back down the street until it was out of sight, and then listened as the familiar whine faded into the darkness.

BALLS TO YOUR PARTNER

THROUGHOUT THE WINTER of 1963, my life and music were interwoven with Jim's. Almost every day on his way home from Villanova, he stopped at my house after I got home from high school. He'd help me with my homework, or we'd practice new songs or just hang out. Although our physical relationship had gone no further than heavy petting, to me, a virgin, making music with Jim seemed as intense and passionate as I imagined making love would be.

One afternoon when Jim came over and we were on our way to my room, we passed my dad, at work alone in his office. I went over and gave him a big hug and told him we were going to my room to practice.

Jim said hello, and my dad welcomed him warmly.

"Would you like to use the Wollensak?"

"I already borrowed it, Dad. See you later."

"You and your dad have a great relationship," Jim said, as we entered the den, which doubled as the bedroom I shared with my sister Phyllis. It also served as a study and art studio. Phyllis and I had an agreement that we'd never interrupt when either of us had company. "He must really trust you to let us practice in your bedroom."

"He's my best friend," I said enthusiastically as I sat down cross-legged and pulled Jim down to sit beside me. "I love him so much. I can tell him anything, and he doesn't judge me."

"You tell him everything?" He asked impishly, "even about us?"

"Absolutely," I smiled. "He thinks you're terrific! And so do I." I put my arms around him and hugged him.

"If he knows everything, why does he let us practice in your bedroom?" Jim pulled away.

"Jim, we haven't done anything wrong. Not yet anyway!" I laughed. "What we do is natural. Please don't pull away. There's nothing to be ashamed of. He knows I love you."

He didn't say it back. Instead, he unfastened his six-string guitar case and started tuning.

"I can't be open like that with my parents," he said finally. "They're not interested in my feelings, and certainly not my sexual ones. In the Catholic Church, sex before marriage is immoral. Even making out is a sin."

I couldn't help laughing at how provincial he sounded.

"Well, I guess I'd be a terrible Catholic," I said. "Do you feel that way, Jim? Do you feel guilty when we make out?"

"I feel good when we make out. But I could never tell my parents."

"I'm really lucky to have my dad. It's wonderful to have someone who really loves me, no matter what I do. Of course he trusts I won't go too far astray. But talking to him is kinda like going to confession."

Jim placed his twelve-string on Phyllis's bed and opened the case.

"Confession doesn't work that way for me. I don't confess to anything, unless I'm caught . . . and even then."

"I'm just the opposite," I said. "I always try to do the right thing. Sometimes I try too hard. It's probably because of my mom's addiction and the way people used to look down on me when my parents were divorced. I always felt I had to try harder than everyone else just to be good enough."

"I think you're terrific, Ing. I'm amazed at your openness and your sensuality. You don't have to try with me, baby. Just be yourself."

He lifted the twelve-string out of the case, tuned it, and then told me he wanted to sing me a song he just learned from his new Oscar Brand album.

He gave me his mischievous look and started singing an English bawdy ballad:

> I don't want to join the army,
> and I don't want to go war,
> I'd much rather hang around Piccadilly underground,
> living off the earnings of a high-born Lady.
> I don't want a bayonet up me backside,
> and I'd rather not get me buttocks shot away,
> I just want to stay in England, merry, merry, England
> And fornicate me bloomin' life away

"Have you played that song for your mom and dad?" I asked, laughing.

"Not lately," Jim joked.

"I just wish your parents weren't so hard on you. You're so good."

"I'm not really, Ing. I don't try like you do. In fact I'm really belligerent sometimes. I push things to the limit. When I was young, most of the things I got slapped for, I deserved. I tried everything and anything I could get away with," he confessed. "I've always liked collecting guns, knives, sabers, all kinds of weaponry. When I was about eleven, my father took Rich and me to a pawnshop down on Race Street, near his work. While he went to get his mail, I snuck into the store and bought an old revolver. It was a broken-down handgun with bullets that fit another gun. But what did I know? I hid it until I got home. And then Rich and I went into the backyard when no one was around. I put the bullet halfway in the gun, but it wouldn't fit. So I took a hammer to it. The motherfucker blew up in my hand! Man, that smarted. But I couldn't tell my parents. I walked around for weeks with my palm all burnt and bandaged. It was ugly and infected, but I was too afraid to say anything. I deserved a beating. But when my dad found out, all he did was take the gun and bullets away, and he and my mom never said another word about it. But that's when I was younger. He's really tough on me now. It's hard to believe, but he still hits me."

I was very upset that Jim's dad used force instead of reason to guide his son, but Jim Senior still seemed like a good man to me. I recognized that from his old-world point of view, as head of the household, he had the final word, and Jim had better do what he said—or else.

To change the subject, I picked up my guitar and asked Jim if he could teach me some new chords.

"Sure, Ing, but how about if we write a song together, too?'

I put down the guitar quickly and reached into my book bag for a piece of paper with a poem on it that I had written for school. I handed it to Jim to read.

"I like it, Ing. This could work!" Then he began to play some chords and sing the words to my poem:

> *Perhaps I'll never show this world all I can be*
> *I just can't sing to any man the song he wants to hear.*

"That sounds great!" I said, and he continued:

> *And I know that some won't like me*
> *Others try to be my friend,*
> *But I'm all of me,*
> *And that's all that I am.*

We practiced the song with all of the verses a couple times through, and I played my guitar alongside him. Then he put chords to the chorus, and we sang it between each verse. We practiced our parts, and when we got it down just right, I spontaneously put my arms around him and his guitar.

"I'm so excited we've actually written a song together. I can't wait until we play this for my dad!"

"I just wish we had more time together. We could write lots of songs and do lots more things," he said, raising his eyebrows.

42

"You know, things might be different if you moved into the dorms or your own apartment. Have you ever thought about that?" I asked.

"Every day!" Jim smiled. "But it's not that easy in my family. Good sons stay home until they get married or die. My parents are good people, but they drive me crazy.

"You know, when I was five, my parents took me to view the body of an old dead cardinal. He was lying there in velvet robes with these thick fuzzy eyebrows, and his eyes were wide open. I'll never forget my grandmother picking me up and stuffing my face down into the coffin to kiss the gold ring on his cold, dead hand. The ring of a dead man, for Christ's sake!"

"That's disgusting!"

"That's the way Rich and I were brought up, worshiping saints and dead people. Pretty freaky, huh?"

"Do you believe in God, Jim?"

"You know, after reading about the Crusades, inquisitions, and missionaries, and all the millions of people killed in the name of God, I sometimes find it hard to believe in anything religious. But it certainly is something to ponder. I like learning about the Hindus and the Jains and the different beliefs people have. I like figuring things out for myself, and I'm tired of my parents trying to run my life. I wish they'd just trust me to make my own decisions and choose my own friends."

"Like Sal and Bill Reid?"

"Yeah, my parents are suspicious of both of them. 'God forbid,'" he said, imitating his mother, "'you should turn out like them.' Sal's too liberal and educated, and Bill's too earthy. My folks are really tough to please."

"God," I laughed, "I'd hate to ask what they think of me."

Jim didn't respond. His parents had a real problem with my being so much younger than Jim and Jewish, but he didn't want to reveal that to me.

"Yeah," he continued. "My parents find Sal 'questionable,' but at least he's Italian. Bill, on the other hand, is both Irish and disrespectful. He doesn't give a damn what people say about him or think about him," Jim laughed. "Bill's such a wild card. He thrives on causing trouble.

"The first time I met him on the construction site, he wore grimy jeans, work boots, a big straw cowboy hat, and he was wavin' his big gold diamond ring on his little finger. He was the foreman on the project directing all these Caterpillars around the job site. He was so full of himself, laughing and cursing and orchestrating these men on these massive pieces of equipment. He acts like a little boy in a big man's body. But he's good at what he does.

43

"You know, Ing, how I've been hanging out at the truck yard lately and begging Bill to teach me to drive? Well, he offered me a job when I get out of school for the summer. He's going to start giving me lessons on the big ten-wheelers! Then I'll be able to join the Teamster's Union and get around the truck driver's Catch-22."

"What's the truck driver's Catch-22?"

"Well, it's nearly impossible to get a trucking job without a union card, but rookie drivers can't qualify for a union card without first getting a job. So you need to know someone."

"Would your parents be upset?"

Jim shrugged. "As long as I'm making money and it's only temporary, ya know, saving for a respectable future and all, it should be okay with them.

"Hey, Ing, Rich and I wrote a song that I'd like to record sometime. Would you listen to this and tell me what you think?"

He placed his fingers back on the guitar strings and began to play and sing "Sun Come Up," a song he later included on his self-made first album in 1966, *Facets*.

"I really like it, Jim. Did you write the words and music together?"

"Yeah, well, we were just playin' around at home, and it just kinda happened.

"Hey," he said, looking at his watch, "it's almost six o'clock."

I rose from the bed and stood in front of him.

He put down his guitar and wrapped his arms around my waist, laying his head on my chest. "Oh Christ, I hate to go, but The Flower will have dinner on the table, and I'm screwed if I'm late for dinner."

"Yeah, you better go. I don't want your parents mad at me—or you, for that matter."

"Can we meet again tomorrow, Ing?"

"We can meet every day," I told him. He smiled and hugged me tightly.

———

When summer came, Bill kept his word and began to show Jim the ropes at the truck yard. Learning to drive the big trucks stimulated Jim, and listening to the wild stories of the truckers thrilled him even more. Like a drifter, he wandered around the truck yard soaking up the testosterone. While he was at work, he would take a pen and notebook from his shirt pocket and jot down truckers' expressions and stories of one-upmanship. In his truck, he would imitate their lingo on a tape recorder, trying to capture their speech patterns.

Many drivers were tough, angry, and easily provoked. They evinced raw masculinity. The truckers spoke their own kind of truth, offered bluntly, and Jim enjoyed the adventures of the truckers' blue-collar world.

Jim started adding songs to his repertoire by Jimmy Rogers, Merle Haggard, and Lefty Frizzell: American music that he could relate to now that he was doing hands-on labor. He kept gathering the stories of the men he worked side-by-side with and storing them away. The truckers' hard-driving lifestyle, fueled by drink, women, and every sort of debauchery, was not much different from the sailors' lives on the high seas and in distant ports that he had learned about in old folklore books, recordings of eighteenth-century folk songs, and raunchy ballads from England, Ireland, and Australia.

Jim and Bill shared this interest and would sometimes speak in dialect to each other, pretending they were sixteenth-century pirates on the high seas. Like children, they played the parts of swashbucklers.

"Aye, me laddy. The wench needs a good foocking," Bill would bluster.

And Jim would reply. "Aye, and I'm here to give 'er one."

Jim began to portray the lives of working-class men and women in his songs. One of his first efforts was a simple truck driver's ode to his semi, "Big Wheel." For Jim, the perspectives of day laborers and truckers provided a new look at the struggles of humankind. In contrast to his parents' uptight, provincial concern over what people thought, the truckers' unbridled behavior and uncensored speech helped him laugh at himself and his rigid upbringing.

After Jim got to know some of the men better, he asked if he could record their stories. The workers were flattered. Jim's relaxed manner and unconditional acceptance put them at ease. Many talked for hours to the skinny Italian kid, telling tales of wrecks, three-day drunks, and beds full of women.

Excited by the rich, raw flavor of their lives, Jim told me their stories that summer, some of which ended up in the song "Speedball Tucker" and other songs he would later write.

"You should have heard this one guy, Ing," he said, one hot evening as we were walking to Jim's VW on our way to the drive-in.

"This one trucker has more than four million miles under his belt, and I asked him what his most hellish experience was on the road. He told me about the time he and his partner were driving a two-ton sixteen-wheeler down a hill.

"Now, his partner was sleeping. And the trucker put his foot down on the brake, but his foot went straight to the floor. No brakes! He headed into one curve, picking up speed, then another, swerving and screeching with sixteen of those heavy fuckin' wheels roaring right behind him. Finally, he rounded a third curve going so fast he knew he had to barrel off one shoulder of the road or the other.

"On the right was a guy changing a tire on a VW. On the other side was a semi in low-low gear coming up the hill. Then the trucker stopped the story. I yelled, 'Well, what did you do then?' 'I woke up ma partner,' the trucker answered. I asked, 'What did you do that for?' 'Well,' he said, scratching his head, 'Ma partner was young . . . and I know he ain't never seen a wreck like this before.'"

I laughed. I liked that Jim was enjoying hanging around the truckers. He was more relaxed, and even though he was still under his parents' roof and their thumbs, he was becoming his own man, finding his own way. The truckers were shaping his personality and giving him some rough edges that I found earthy and sexy.

When I was alone with Jim that hot summer night at the drive-in, I was more turned on than ever. Though I was doing my best to hold back, he had become more and more persistent, and I dreamed about making love. I wanted to make sure we would be together forever, and I was trying to use my head while every other part of me wanted to "go all the way."

Not all of our dates at the time were to the drive-in. Most included either practicing or performing music.

One Saturday night, when Jim and I were singing at the Italian Club outside Philadelphia, Jim ran into one of his truck-driver friends, Crazy Frank. He was a rugged, lecherous guy with long, slicked-back, black hair and a parade of tattoos up and down his arms. He was known for his free advice:

"Women are sufferin'," he used to tell Jim. "They need you, but they won't tell you that. They'll pretend they don't want you, but they really do. You got to go fuck them. That's what they really want." It was as if Crazy Frank was the real-life version of one of the pirates in Jim and Bill Reid's debaucherous fantasies.

With a wife and three children, Crazy Frank considered himself a good Catholic, but he felt that the collar of the church was a little too tight. Disgusted by the hypocrisy he saw within the church, Frank prided himself in raising hell and stirring things up. Jim introduced Frank to me that night at the Italian Club.

"Nice to meet you, Ingrid," he said, in a brusque voice, shaking my hand. "She's just as good lookin' as I'd thought she'd be." He winked at Jim. "Hey, Jim, I gotta tell you this. I just had a run in with my fuckin' priest." Frank excused his language to me. Jim laughed at Frank's apology and watched me closely, to see how I'd respond to Frank's chauvinistic attitude.

"Now you know, Jim, I'm a loyal parishioner. I take my wife and kids to church every Sunday. I'm faithful. I put somethin' in the collection plate every week. But ya know sometimes things are hard for us truckers. And I ain't got a damn cent right now. So last week I didn't put nothin' in his collection box.

"Now the father, he knew the way to my house because he had eaten our food and drunk my whiskey lots of times. So he rings the buzzer," Frank said, imitating the priest pushing the doorbell. "And I tell my wife, 'Don't you answer that door.' She's cryin' and doesn't want to open it because she's ashamed we don't have any money.

"You know my wife. She's a good woman, right?" Jim agreed with a nod. "Yeah, she's good . . . too good for me," Frank admitted. "So anyway I get this crazy look in my eye. You know the one, Jim. And she gets scared. I start for the front door, which makes her cry even harder because she's afraid of what I'm gonna do. And when I open the door and that son-of-a-bitch is standing there waitin' for somethin', I don't invite him in. I make him stand there. So he tells me he's noticed that the collection plate's been a little short lately. By this time, I'm ready to strangle the motherfucker. But I'm nice. I say, 'Father, you can see my wife's with child. You know work's been slow, and we can't put money in right now.' And then the son-of-a-bitch has the balls to tell me I'm not a good Catholic because I can't put fuckin' money in his plate.

"I say, 'FUCK YOU, Father!' And the priest goes white, his jaw drops, and he runs away like he's seen the devil. Well, maybe he had. The way I figure it, none of that shit has anything to do with religion. What does putting money in his fuckin' plate have to do with being a good Catholic? I'm not buyin' that shit, Jim."

"You're a character, Frank. I'm gonna write a song about you someday," Jim told his trucking buddy. Frank smiled. "I'd like that, man. Make it a fun one!"

I wasn't as impressed with Frank as Jim was. His chauvinism and disrespectful comments made me feel sad for his wife and kids. I hoped the violence and attitude of guys like Frank didn't rub off on him too much.

When the summer was over, Jim took a break from trucking and returned to Villanova as a junior. Though he needed to attend classes to please his parents, his focus was mostly on his music and our time together.

———

In addition to performing at local coffeehouses and colleges, Jim continued working as a DJ on his WWVU radio show. But he was always looking for a way to play in front of an audience. He wanted to get more practice and earn some extra money too.

His hopes were answered one night, when Bill asked Jim to meet him at the Riddle Paddock, a steak house thirty miles from Jim's home in Drexel Hill. "And bring your guitar," Bill insisted.

The Paddock was an old converted racetrack stable in Lima, Pennsylvania, on the highway near the sheep and horse pastures that surrounded it. Inside, gathered around tables draped with red-and-white checked tablecloths, a raucous crowd ate, drank, swapped stories, fought, and stomped to the music. In the center, where the horse corral used to be, was a floor-level stage. Folk, country, and bluegrass musicians played to an unlikely and volatile mix of ranch hands and cowboys; Royal Air Force personnel from a nearby training facility; Australian and Irish sheepherders who had come to Pennsylvania to work on the up-country ranches; wealthy doctors and lawyers with and without their wives; students and professors from the surrounding colleges—Villanova, Penn, Temple, Cabrini, and Swarthmore; construction workers; and anybody else who lived within a thirty-mile radius.

The Paddock was a haven for the wealthy to get down and dirty, for students to find refuge from teachers and parents, and for working guys like Bill to be their unabashed selves.

Carrying his guitar case, Jim entered the Paddock for the first time. He saw Bill playing the banjo onstage and took a table close by. Before Bill completed the set, he invited Jim to join him.

Jim took out his guitar and took the stage, and the two finished the set taking turns singing lead and harmonizing. Bill played bluegrass, and Jim threw in some popular country tunes.

One of the owners, Dolores Meehan, liked what she heard. When Jim stepped away for a break, she hired him as a solo performer on the spot.

"You'll get a free prime rib dinner," she said. "Plus $25 a night and all the drinks you want." Dolores was a small woman with short blond curls and a starched shirt-waist dress emphasizing her big bust. She was sophisticated, businesslike, and a bit uptight, especially compared with her husband, Paul, an Irishman who remained relaxed and easygoing under any circumstance. He did the cooking, and she booked the acts and took care of operations. They seemed an unlikely couple but did a great job making the Riddle Paddock a busy and successful club.

"Well, thanks," Jim replied shyly, surprised but very pleased to land the job. "I guess we have Bill to thank for this."

"Just don't drink as much as he does," she grumbled.

Little did Dolores know that Jim could hold his own when it came to liquor. But to his credit, no matter how much he drank, from bottles of beer to martinis in beer glasses, his control over his actions and his ability to sing remained intact.

From that night on, Jim became a regular performer at the Paddock, singing several nights a week. Landing his first regular gig was just the boost he needed. It was a world apart from entertaining at colleges and his parents' church functions. He was eager for me to see him perform professionally and to join him onstage.

One Saturday night, we entered the Paddock through a back door off the small kitchen. The delicious smell of rare prime rib and hot baked, buttered potatoes caught Jim at once, as it usually did.

His gaze rested on a rare slab of beef lying on an old wooden plank, kept warm by a red heat lamp.

"No! No!" Dolores screamed. "Don't you dare serve it like that!"

"Why not?" exclaimed her husband. "It looks downright appetizing!" Dolores pursued Paul through the doors from the dining room.

"What's all the commotion?" Jim asked. Dolores kept close behind Paul, who was carrying a huge, freshly prepared family-style salad.

"A mouse got caught in the exhaust fan," she said, gasping for breath, "and it landed in pieces all over the salad. Paul wants to take it out to get a rise from the guests."

With a comically ghoulish look, Paul swung the salad bowl into Jim's view. It was strewn with odd bits of mouse.

"Yum, I'll take a drumstick," Jim laughed. He picked out a tiny, bloody leg from the lettuce leaves and Roquefort dressing.

"Oh my God!" I blurted out.

Dolores slapped Jim's hand. "Shit, you men disgust me. Jim, go out there and entertain the crowd, and Paul, make another salad!"

But before she could stop him, Paul took the mouse salad out for the guests to admire.

Exasperated, she grumbled about Paul's exploits for a moment, then turned to walk away when she noticed my wide-eyed expression.

"Who is this, Jim?" she asked, changing from demanding wife to a gracious host. "Aren't you going to introduce us?"

"Of course," he replied.

Paul came bounding back into the kitchen, puffed up with pride from the rave reviews his salad received.

"Dolores and Paul," Jim said politely, "I'd like you to meet my girlfriend, Ingrid." Jim squeezed my hand. "She's going to sing with me tonight."

"Glad to meet you," Paul said, slamming the salad bowl down on the edge of a steel sink.

"It's not always like this here," Dolores apologized. "I'm going to clean up this mess, but I can't wait to hear you sing later, Ingrid. You must know the crowd goes crazy for Jim."

Jim settled me in at the front table near the stage, and I watched him take command of the room. He looked happy and confident. Then, when his first set was almost over, he asked me to join him onstage. The audience quieted as we began to sing together, taking in the close harmony of our voices and no doubt sensing the desire we had for each other.

After we finished the set, I went back to my table, and Jim asked a Royal Air Force officer in the crowd, whose music he'd grown to enjoy, to join him in "The Doggy Song," an old bawdy ballad. The Irish and Australian sheepherders always argued about whether or not Jim had the lyrics right, and he knew the song would stir things up. Each faction taught Jim their own version, and he sang each side's lyrics separately. He nodded to the officer, and they began:

> The doggies had a meeting, they'd come from near and far,
> Some by motorcycle and some by motorcar.
> Each doggy passed the entrance, each doggy signed the book
> Then each unzipped his asshole, and hung it on a hook.

Jim loved embarrassing his crowd with profanity and boyish humor. He sang a couple more versus and ended with the punch line:

> So that's the reason why, sir, when walking down the street
> And that's the reason why, sir, when doggies chance to meet,
> And that's the reason why on land and sea and foam,
> Dogs will sniff each other's asshole to see if it's his own.

The crowd roared and clapped. "Another one!" they shouted. "More bawdy ballads!" the Australian sheepherders demanded. Jim continued with one entitled "Cats on the Rooftop."

Bill Reid came into the Paddock and sat at a table near me, chugging down a couple beers with a woman he had just met. Her name was Chris Sigafoos, a beautiful, shapely blonde. Bill had eyed her from across the room and immediately strode over to her table and challenged her to a beer chugging contest. This was Bill's usual method for impressing the opposite sex.

Chris laughed and accepted without hesitation. She had recently emigrated from Germany after marrying a medical student who was attending the University of Pennsylvania. To her, the pale American beer was like drinking water, and she liked Bill's brashness and bold, broad smile. Eager to win the bet, she drank her drafts down with ease, one right after the other.

One of the Irish sheepherders yelled to get the officer off the stage and bring me back up to sing. "I don't want some bloody Englishman slobberin' all over the microphone!" he shouted.

The Englishman insulted him back, and between the amplified argument and the din of voices and clinking glasses, the audience scarcely noticed that a fistfight had simultaneously broken out between a country redneck and a black man who was sitting with a white woman.

Jim kept playing until a rather intoxicated waitress started pulling on his guitar, trying to get him to dance with her. Trying to get away from her grasp, Jim accidentally poked one of the guitar's tuning pegs through her hoop earring, then pulled her around in a circle and shouted, "Why doesn't everybody just sit down and be nice?"

Nobody was paying much attention to Jim now.

A beer bottle bounced off a chair, and I scrambled toward the kitchen for shelter. Like a scene in an old Western movie, more fights broke out, and more bottles and chairs began crashing around the room.

Bill had lost the beer chugging contest to Chris and was stomping around in a drunken sulk, enraged that he'd lost to a woman. Chris was laughing and teasing him unmercifully.

"I'll pull my dick out and chase you around the room with it," he shouted.

"Go ahead!" she shouted back. "Flip it out right here on the table! I'll bet you $10 you can't find it!" He glared and then grinned, his anger giving way to admiration.

To save face, he went and wrestled the redneck who had started the near-riot to the floor and threw him out of the bar. Gradually people began to sit back down, and the Paddock's vague sense of order seemed momentarily restored.

"My foot!" Paul suddenly shouted.

It was pinned to the floor by a butcher knife.

Blood pulsed out, and Paul stood transfixed, staring down at the huge knife stuck in his foot.

Jim ran and found me, and we joined the crowd hovering around Paul. The brawny Irishman stood proudly until everyone had a good look. Dolores insisted that he pull it out so she could take him to the hospital. He yanked the knife out of his foot, and Dolores cleaned and wrapped his foot with kitchen towels. They quickly left for the hospital.

Jim headed back to the stage to finish his set for the crowd, who acted as if nothing out of the ordinary had just happened. As he passed one of the regular patrons, whom he knew as the owner of a nearby dog kennel, the old man grabbed his sleeve and tugged on it. Jim nodded to him, picked up his guitar, and began playing "Old Blue," a sentimental ballad about a hunting dog:

When Old Blue died he died so hard
He shook the ground in my backyard.
We lowered him down with a golden chain
And with every link we called Blue's name . . .

Just as he did every week, the old man listened to Jim sing "his song" and drank his beer with tears streaming down his face.

When Jim finished "Old Blue" the old man stuffed Jim's shirt pocket with a couple dollars. "Thanks," Jim said quietly. And indeed, he was grateful for the old man's regular tips.

The Riddle Paddock was Jim's longest-running gig ever. From the beginning of his junior year, his performances at the Paddock gave him a great audience for trying out new songs and monologues.

By spring, I had become a regular feature in Jim's show. At first, I only sang a song or two with him. But in time, I had begun to take requests for solos, with Jim standing off to my right, accompanying me on guitar. I felt comfortable onstage.

With all the practicing we'd done, performing was easy, especially without having to play an instrument. I was able to follow Jim's lead, and our repertoire grew quickly. I loved singing with Jim, but it was different for me. I wanted to sing with him forever, but I wasn't ambitious about becoming a professional musician.

I loved singing with Jim as I had with my late mother, since some of my best memories of her are of when she accompanied me on the piano. I often thought that I would be a performer, as she was, and that I might even have the talent for it. But deep down I believed my true calling lay elsewhere, and what I wanted now, more than anything, was to help Jim become a star.

While I loved making music with Jim, there was one part of our performances that made me really uncomfortable. Singing bawdy ballads was one of Jim's favorite aspects of performing at the Riddle Paddock. But I was embarrassed to sing those tunes, and Jim knew he could get a rise out of me. As I'd seen him do with his mother the night I'd met her, he'd put me on the spot. He'd interrupt our set with a bawdy ballad or two. Jim's way of impishly cloaking the vulgarity of the words by immortalizing their classical place in history was fun for him, but I had been brought up around foul language when I lived with my mother and grandmother, and the cursing and swearing I heard in arguments at home, and down on Philly's rough South Street, made me want to be more proper. Singing vulgar lyrics in public was not something I wanted to do at all. It just felt wrong.

Though I would complain to Jim under my breath that I didn't want to sing those songs, he'd ignore my protests and say I was way too serious. Then he'd pause mid-song, waiting along with the audience for me to sing a verse.

Although it seemed merely a part of our act, Jim truly embarrassed me and used my embarrassment to make the act funnier. The longer I hesitated to sing the verse, the more cheers we got from the crowd, especially on the wild nights, when the audience called out for their favorites.

On one such wild night that spring, I was fortunate to be in the audience and not onstage as Jim did his thing.

"You know," he began, "some of the greatest songs in our language came from the English tradition. You go down into the Appalachians, start digging around, and you'll find that a lot of tunes that became our folk songs originally came from England, Scotland, and Wales. And then, if you really get a chance to sit around in some of these countries, you'll discover pub songs, originally sung by the British army and navy."

Jim started to play the introduction to a popular hymn on his guitar and continued: "Ya know, in those days they used to just kind of pick up a melody. Most of the time the only songs they knew in common were ones they'd learned in church. So they'd write new words and convert a hymn into a common song. This is one that must have brought the wrath upon them. It's an old piping tune, and I'll just do a bit to show you how it happened. Then we'll lead you to that great world of traditional bawdy English ballads." With a twinkle in his eyes, Jim launched into:

Oh, her name is Diamond Lily,
She's a whore in Piccadilly,
And her brother's got a brothel on the Strand.
And her father sells his asshole round
The elephant and castle,
They're the richest bloody family in the land.

"Well, that's how it all started," he explained. "And then there were some great English poets who decided they'd couple their brash wit with their church tunes and create tunes of their own. Rudyard Kipling wrote a few and promptly lost his position as Poet Laureate of England when he wrote the song, 'God Bless the Bastard King of England.'

"And Robert Burns, the Scottish poet and rake," Jim went on in rich brogue, "used to attend parties in the Highlands and related how a particular lyric was inspired by one of the most famous tunes in the English language. At a great party many years ago, it was told, some fellow sprinkled itching powder on the floor. Now in this part of the country the locals wore 'ken underwear,' which in Scottish stands for 'no underwear,' so when they began to dance, they kicked this itching powder onto their legs and up their skirts. And at the same time, somebody put an aphrodisiac in the punch. Soon, everybody's giving each other that lean and hungry look, that lewd and lascivious stare that meant, 'You're going to be the recipient of my long anticipated glee.'

"Then somebody put the oil lamp out, and, as is recorded in the Library of Congress, what happened next, lad, was an orgy of such great magnitude that forty acres of corn were fucked completely flat."

Over his audience's shrieks of laughter, Jim leaned into the mic and sang:

Four and twenty virgins,
Came down from Inverness,
And when the Ball was over
There were four and twenty less.

While he continued playing, and still in brogue, he told them, "Remember this chorus because I want you to sing it with me after each verse." He sang it once through and had them repeat it with him:

54

Singing, balls to your partner
Your ass against the wall,
If you never been had on a Saturday night,
You've never been had at all.

The crowd expressed their enthusiasm with cheers and whistles. "If that's tickled your fancy, listen to the next eleven verses," Jim continued:

There was doing in the parlor,
And doing on the stones,
But you could not hear the music,
For the wheezing and the groans . . .

The audience joined in stronger, shouting the first line of the chorus, "Singing, balls to your partner," after every verse, but then instantly hushed as Jim began the next, and then the next, each more outrageous than the last, until the song came to its crescendo with the final verse, followed by the final chorus, with everyone screaming the words at the top of their lungs:

The village magician he was there,
He gave us all a laugh.
He pulled his foreskin over his head,
And he vanished up his ass.

Singing, balls to your partner
Your ass against the wall,
If you've never been had on a Saturday night,
You've never been had at all!

As Jim stood there onstage, beaming at having succeeded in leading the entire audience into an X-rated frenzy of song and laughter, I couldn't help thinking that in spite of his family trying to stifle his true ambition, he was doing exactly what he was meant to do: expressing himself through his music.

ALABAMA RAIN

ONE NIGHT IN THE SPRING of 1964, Jim had called to say he was on his way over, and I sat in my bedroom listening, as I always did, for the hum of his VW bug. He lived in Drexel Hill, just a short distance away, but that night the fifteen minutes it ordinarily took for him to get to our house in Springfield felt unusually long.

When he arrived, I ran downstairs. He and my dad were already in conversation when I reached the living room. Before I could greet him, my stepmother came over and gave Jim a big hug and said, "Jim, I prepared a delicious, traditional Shabbat dinner with brisket and kasha and *varnishkas*. Let me get you a plate."

"I'd love to try some, but I just finished dinner with my family. How about next time?"

My twin sister interrupted their conversation with another hug and told Jim that her friend had a crush on his brother, Rich.

"Can we set up a blind date for them?" Phyllis asked. "It would be fun if all of us could go out together."

Janice, my younger sister, and Ken, the youngest and only boy in the Jacobson household, each took one of Jim's hands and pulled him downstairs to the rec room. They had just gotten new pets and wanted Jim to see their gerbils.

As Jim stepped off the bottom step, he heard a squeal under his shoe and saw that he had stepped on a gerbil's head. The rodent began to run around and around in circles to the right. Jim picked it up carefully to make sure it was okay, and told Janice and Kenny, "I think he's gonna make it," but joked, "If he keeps circling to the right, let me know. We might need to step on the other side of his head to straighten him out." Jim spent some time with the kids to make sure their new pet was okay while I went to my room to start my homework.

It seemed as if he were taking forever with the kids. When he finally joined me, I gave him a quick hug and said, "Jim, I have so much homework tonight—would you please help me? I just wish I could remember facts like you do, but unless I can sing things, I can't remember anything. Besides, the sooner I get my homework done, the sooner we can practice."

"Or do something else," Jim suggested.

"Jim, I'm serious. I really do have a lot of work to do, and I want to make sure I do well so I can get into a good college."

"I know you do, sweet thing, but Ing, it's only 6, and we have plenty of time. Besides, it's Friday night, and we have all weekend to get your homework done." He wrapped his arms around me, and I relaxed. "Let's take a ride to the Dairy Queen, or maybe we can go to the drive-in," he said. "Peter Sellers's new movie, *A Shot in the Dark*, is opening tonight."

"That sounds like fun, sweetie, but actually I don't have all weekend to study. Tomorrow I'm going with my dad to the University of Pennsylvania Hospital to see about a possible job. You know how much I love doing my art and spending time with my dad. He found out there's an opening this summer for an assistant art therapist. If I get the job, it would give me the opportunity to do both, and I could learn so much."

"Okay, Ing. What's the capitol of Budapest, and what countries border France?"

"Oh Jim, I'm not joking."

"I know, Ing, but I've waited all week to be with you, and I need to hold you and feel you next to me."

"I wanna be with you, too, but I need to study."

As always, we compromised. Jim quizzed me on geography and history for about an hour, just in time for us to make it to the drive-in.

Most of our time together was like this. We played music whenever we could and made out every night we were together. By April, we were inseparable.

Jim had begun sharing his private thoughts and stories of his childhood with me, and one afternoon, at the end of our rehearsal, he began to open up about his relationship with his father.

"When I was young, he used to take me down to South Philly every Saturday morning for accordion lessons."

"Oh Jim, you must have been so cute. I can just imagine you at five with your little knobby knees, trying to hold up a big accordion. Did your dad encourage you to play then?"

"Yeah, he really got me going on my music. He used to play Fats Waller and Bessie Smith records—jazz was his favorite. And mine too. When I was little, he always supported me. When I was about seven or eight, I'd go down with him to his office on Race Street in Chinatown. I'd wander around with him while he picked up the mail and did a few errands. Rich and I would look into the hock shops, tattoo parlors, and alleys and watch out for each other. I was blown away by the characters I saw down there. I've been fascinated with people ever since."

He picked up his six-string and said, "Listen to this song by Bessie Smith. A songwriter named Jimmy Cox wrote it for her during the Depression." He began to play, "Nobody Loves You When You're Down and Out."

At the end of the song, he repeated the last lines of the chorus twice and said, "You know when I sing this song I just picture what it must have been like back then. Can you imagine that Bessie Smith and Louis Armstrong couldn't find a gig?"

"I'm glad things are changing. I don't think that there's ever been a better time to make music."

Jim put down his guitar and kissed me. This usually meant rehearsal was over.

Excited and aroused, we left the house and climbed into Jim's car.

"What should we do tonight, Ing?" he asked with his big grin. "Would you like to get a bite to eat, or take a walk, or catch a movie?"

I quickly interjected, "What do you think?"

Jim drove to our favorite parking spot: at the Presbyterian Church on the corner near my house. Once there, he pulled out a tattered map.

"It's time for your world geography lesson," he joked. "Come over here and sit on my lap." I sat on his lap and faced him. While his finger traced the outline of the boot of Italy on my thigh, I slowly unbuttoned his shirt and ran my hands across his chest. I felt him stir beneath me, and pressed against him.

I heard the map drop to the floor.

After the windows were covered with steam and we had gone as far as we could without going all the way, Jim dropped his seat back, and I lay in his arms.

During those chilly spring nights in 1964, the Volkswagen became our sanctuary. We spent hours in it, making plans and making out. We shared our dreams and fears freely, becoming two halves of a whole, neither complete without the other.

"I hate my nose," he said. "Even when I was little, it was too big. When I first started school, they made me the lead in the Christmas play. You know what part I played? Rudolph!"

"I'm so sorry, Jim," I held back my laughter. "I hate mine, too."

"And I wish I had more muscles." His scrawny appearance embarrassed him. I thought he was adorable.

"I think you look just like my hero, Maynard G. Krebs, from *The Dobie Gillis Show.*"

"Gee, Ing, thanks a lot."

"I think he's cool and funny like you. I'm sorry you feel bad about the way you look, but I'm not as pretty as a lot of the girls at school, and I don't let that stop me. I went out and competed in cheerleading against these adorable blonde, blue-eyed Anglo Protestant girls, and I won. I don't even know if I like cheerleading, but I wanted to be the first Jewish cheerleader they've ever had!"

"You're amazing, Ing! You stand up for the things you believe in, and I'm so proud of you. Besides, I think you're pretty, and I bet none of those girls have an ass like yours!"

———

Our choice not to go all the way that night was a mutual decision, but it was getting harder and harder to hold back. He worried that I was too young, and he didn't want to get me pregnant. I was also concerned about pregnancy, but even more, I feared losing Jim's respect. In the early 1960s, virginity was an important virtue. Until now, I'd been the forbidden fruit, and I wondered if my allure would wear off if I gave in to Jim's and my desires.

When I was young, my mother had shown me that being seductive, secretive, and sexy was powerful, even magical. Although she never talked to me about sex, I understood that Marilyn Monroe's and Ingrid Bergman's allure and permissiveness were something to be admired. In my mother's apartment, I rarely wore clothes. I loved the wonderful, sensual feeling of being naked. On the other hand, my voluptuous sister was modest and never undressed even in front of me.

In my father's home, I was always dressed, of course, except in the privacy of my bedroom, but love, sex, birth control, and other intimate matters were openly discussed.

Since the age of eight, I had known the details of sex. My father had once matter-of-factly shown me a medical book in his office about sexual reproduction. I studied the book's fascinating transparencies and drawings of the sexual organs. He calmly explained intercourse.

"You mean it just fits inside like that?" I marveled. "That's neat!"

Over the next few months, Jim's and my resolve melted under the constant sexual heat we generated.

On April 27, 1964, I celebrated my seventeenth birthday, and Jim spent every penny he had to buy me presents—S's, he called them, for "surprises." On this occasion, he gave me a jade ring and a pair of handmade sandals. Most importantly, he told me that he loved me and one day he wanted to marry me. The ring symbolized his commitment.

"This is the best birthday I've ever had," I told him that night, as we sat in the VW. The talk quickly turned to the subject of making love. This time, we could no longer find a reason why we shouldn't. I was now seventeen; we were deeply in love and would undoubtedly be together forever. Of equal importance was the timing of the event. My parents were leaving for a week's vacation, and I was in charge of the house.

The night they left on their trip, Jim arrived for our rendezvous. It was very late, and my brother and sisters were already sound asleep. I waited for him at the door, wearing only a robe. Holding hands, we slowly climbed the stairs to the big bed in my parents' room. Nervously, I closed and locked the door, then seductively slipped out of my robe and let it slide to the floor. He leaned back against the pillows and gazed at me.

"Isn't this great?" I whispered. "I've never been naked in front of you before."

He grinned and silently motioned for me to come to him. Together, we unbuttoned his shirt and pants and slid them off. Then Jim lifted me onto the bed and kissed me deeply. We began to make love, slowly, gently. He took his time, searching my body with his strong, delicate fingers.

After exploring each other's bodies and turning each other on for as long as I could stand it, I drew him toward me. "I want you so much, Jim," I breathed. As he entered me, I gasped. Our bodies moved together with heat and instinct.

The telephone rang, shattering the delicate balance of our passion like crystal. I reached over to the nightstand and automatically clutched the receiver before the first ring was complete. "Hello!" said my stepmother, Florence, her voice sounding urgent. "Ingrid?" she asked. "Is that you?"

"Yes, Mom."

"Are you alright? You sound funny."

"I'm fine, Mom. Everything's good." I could feel Jim slipping away from me.

"Well, I just wanted to call, honey, and tell you we made it to Beach Haven.

"That's good. I'm glad you're there safe and sound."

"Why don't you go back to bed and get some rest?"

"Okay, I'll talk to you tomorrow. I love you. Say hi to Daddy for me."

I hung up the phone. Jim was pulling up his pants and looking as guilty as if he'd been physically caught in the act. We stared at each other for a moment and then began to laugh.

———

In June 1964, Sal encouraged Jim to compete in a folk singing contest sponsored by the National Student Association. The NSA, representing four hundred college and university student governments, was headquartered in Philadelphia. Through a nationwide search, four student musicians would be chosen to represent the United States at an international student cultural festival in Istanbul, Turkey. They would also tour throughout the Middle East and North Africa, playing for heads of state, business organizations, student assemblies, and public festivals.

Contest applicants had to not only possess musical talent but be politically astute and speak at least three languages. The letter Jim received stated that applicants had to be "intelligent people with a fairly good basic knowledge of American politics and life." Those students chosen needed to have "compelling stage presence." The NSA wanted good instrumentalists, willing to undertake a vigorous schedule and learn new material and being capable of performing music that could be communicated across language barriers.

On Sunday, July 28, Jim auditioned at the Main Point, a popular coffee house on the Main Line in Philadelphia's suburbs. He held out little hope for winning, even though he qualified. He'd studied political science and German at Villanova, and he spoke Italian with his grandfather.

Three weeks later in July, Jim received word that he had been selected. The tour was to leave the United States in one week. Initially he was thrilled, but his joy quickly turned to grave apprehension.

At first, he wouldn't say what exactly was worrying him about the trip. Finally I coaxed him into telling me.

"I'm afraid of catching some exotic disease, especially malaria," he said, embarrassed. He admitted that his concerns about his health were obsessive. "I get that from my mother," he explained. "When I told her about the trip last night, all she could say was 'God forbid the diseases you could catch over there!' She's got me paranoid."

"But the vaccinations you'll get will protect you from diseases," I reassured him.

"Oh God, the shots are just as bad!"

With more coaxing, I finally convinced him to get the vaccinations. Although I tried to be supportive of his trip, I was nervous about how the separation might affect our relationship. Jim's parents had been pressuring him to stop seeing me. He had finally confessed to me that his parents still hoped he would find a nice Italian, Catholic girl. To Jim's mother, relationships weren't about the sort of romance and passion her son and I felt.

"Love is sex and sex is love," Flora would say, "and it all wears off."

Distracted with trip preparations, Jim didn't notice my anxiety about his leaving. The six weeks he would be gone seemed an eternity to me.

Once the vaccinations were out of the way, Jim became excited about the tour.

"I can't wait to walk the old city streets of Istanbul and take in all those exotic sights," he said. "I'll finally get to see the places where history I've read about actually happened!"

Jim was an avid reader, and Lawrence Durrell was one of his favorite authors. Jim had first read *Justine* and then became absorbed in the entire *Alexandria Quartet*. He fantasized about the romantic societies of the Mediterranean, and the forthcoming trip inspired him to read some of Durrell's most erotic passages to me.

A week before the tour got underway, the quartet met at the Main Point to practice for the first time. They named themselves the Philadelphia Choir. Jim first met Bob Knott, a twenty-two-year-old tenor from Stanford who played the banjo, mandolin, and guitar. When Bob walked into the club, Jim was playing, "Charlie Green: Won't You Play That Slide Trombone," an obscure song by Bessie Smith not usually played by guitarists. When he finished, Bob extended his hand and said, "Hi, I'm Bob Knott, and you just played one of my favorite songs."

"Well, unpack your banjo," Jim replied. "Do you know 'Any Old Time' by Jimmie Rodgers?"

"Of course," Bob said.

Next, a twenty-two-year-old, sandy-haired Gene Uphoff, unpacked his homemade rosewood guitar and joined them. A staunch liberal from Minnesota and a champion of equal rights, Gene had been selected for his passion for politics and his quiet charm. Though guitar was his first instrument, he was told he'd be playing the banjo in this group. With only a week to practice he was glad to see Bob could fill in wherever needed.

Last to join the group was Suzie Levin, a round, bouncy, blue-eyed, twenty-two-year-old from Champaign, Illinois. She walked over, pulled out her washboard and kazoo from her knapsack, and joined in on the chorus. Her strong voice harmonized wonderfully with theirs. She introduced herself and gave Jim and Bob a big hug. Her braless, cheeky, hippie style and bold laugh were intoxicating. She was an artist, a cartoonist, and the only woman in the band. Jim liked her enthusiasm immediately.

Suzie put down her knapsack, kazoo, and washboard and began to chant a cappella. In her rich contralto voice, she sang the spiritual "Let Me Fly to Mount Zion." The four began to harmonize. They had only a week to blend their styles and master their repertoire before leaving for the tour.

By the time the Philadelphia Choir left New York on August 4, 1964, Jim had read several books on exotic diseases. Bob was becoming an expert on malaria just from listening to Jim ramble on.

"Malaria is caused by the protozoa of the genus *Plasmodium*," Jim told him during the flight to Europe. "It's transmitted only by the female anopheles mosquito, recognizable by her long legs trailing low behind her in flight."

When Jim stepped carefully off the plane in Rome, watching intently for a low-flying, long-legged female mosquito, Bob burst out laughing. He began to wonder if his new friend was a hypochondriac.

Jim's first glimpse of Italy did not impress him, even though it was the country of his heritage. In his diary he wrote:

> *Rome airport very flat; country very hot, looks like south Jersey with less trees.*

But it was Istanbul that provided his first real culture shock. On the way to the youth hostel, the cab driver, Najib, continually beamed a toothy smile at the students, while ignoring the road. A luckless goat wandered into the roadway, and despite Jim's frantic hand signals to Najib, who spoke little English, the cab flattened the poor animal. Najib never slowed down, but simply shrugged and said, "God's will."

The youth hostel itself was another surprise. Sixty beds, infested with lice, were crammed into one room. The bathrooms were little more than closets with holes in the marble floors. When they arrived, Jim entered one of the bathrooms. He came out laughing and then dragged Bob in for a look. "Shit, someone stole the toilets!" he laughed.

That first afternoon in Istanbul, the four Americans tried to take naps, but the bed bugs bit with a vengeance, covering their bodies with tiny red welts. Unable to sleep, Jim wrote the first of his daily letters to his family:

> *Dear Mother, Dad, Rich and Pa,*
> *This has really been some experience. (Pardon my writing. I'm in a 60-bed room in Istanbul and being attacked by bed bugs.) Wow! What a city. Very nice people from all over the world, many from Germany. Dad, those German lessons are finally coming in handy.*
> *I have rested up and feel good. We have seen quite a bit of the city in the past few days. The city is divided in two halves. The old half is really different,*

with mosques, temples and castles all around. The bed is not like home but I suppose it'll have to do. The toilets are, well, let's just say interesting.

Yesterday we went to the funeral of the head of the festival, who was killed in a car crash. They carried the body through the narrow streets of the city for several miles to the mosque. The Swedish group led the procession with their band. It was very sad.

Mom, my clothes are going far. There are plenty of sinks for washing them and they dry in several hours . . . dungarees in three hours, underwear in about two.

Dad, I will not be able to send many cards because they cost about 60 cents to mail. It's just too much. Well, it's time to eat so I'll leave. Beautiful breeze blowing thru the city and the courtyard of this big palace sized building we're quartered in.

Say hello to everyone.

Love,

Jim

Searching for a place to eat, the young folksingers wandered through the narrow medieval streets until they found a restaurant with local music, shish kebab, and Lebanese dancers. Over dinner, Jim gave another dissertation on malaria and convinced the group they needed to find some quinine.

The following morning, the foursome searched for a drugstore. As they walked through Istanbul's bustling streets, Jim noticed people staring at him.

"What's the matter with them, Bob?" he whispered. "Haven't they ever seen cutoffs before?"

Bob choked back his laughter. He couldn't believe Jim's naïveté. Besides the knee-length cutoffs, Jim wore a polka-dot shirt, mirrored sunglasses, knee-high black nylon dress socks, and shiny, pointed Italian shoes. He stood out like a neon sign next to Bob's khaki pants and tan shirt.

"It may not only be the shorts, Jim," he said, but Jim just shrugged.

Later that morning they found a druggist, but the man spoke no English. Suzie knew the Turkish word for "prevention," and the druggist grinned and seemed to understand. Reaching behind the counter, he pulled out a box of condoms. Jim laughed and bought them. Suzie tried again. Finally, the druggist understood "malaria" and sold them the medicine. He also gave them instructions that they took to mean "Take the quinine once a day."

He charged them $25. As they left the drugstore, Jim popped one of the pills in his mouth immediately. His constant talk about disease had begun to worry the group, and the pills boosted their spirits.

By the next day, they felt fully rested, rehearsed, and protected. The quartet of students performed their first show at a castle once belonging to a sultan of the Ottoman Empire. Guarded by the straits of the Bosporus Sea, the castle and the stage itself hung off a cliff riddled with ancient caves overlooking the water.

The exotic adventure of Istanbul and the enthusiastic reception from the audiences excited Jim. Although few listeners spoke English, he was thrilled by the way he could communicate through his songs. He saw firsthand that music was indeed a common language.

Although Jim soon got into the swing of traveling, he began to suffer from both constipation and diarrhea, which he dubbed, "the Turkish trots." During one stretch, he wrote an entry in his diary about this dilemma:

I must be approaching a world record,
six days and no shit!

They traveled on to Belgrade, Yugoslavia, where they performed for Russian and Czechoslovakian exchange students.

By the time they'd arrived in Beirut, Lebanon, everyone's stomach problems worsened. They assumed they had contracted a virus. Jim blamed it on the Middle Eastern drinking water, which smelled like sewage. Bob was bedridden, and Gene had to be taken to the hospital.

"This is pretty bad, but thank God we haven't contracted malaria," Jim reassured the group. "Just make sure you take your quinine every day."

As Jim waited for Gene and Bob to recover, he wrote his first letter to me. Most of it centered on his excitement over a Persian carpet he had just purchased "for our first apartment." As he typically did when a subject interested him, he had read half a dozen books on Persian rugs before he went to a factory in Beirut to pick one out. He boasted in his letter that he had bargained with the merchants until he had been able to purchase an $800 rug for only $200. His letter was short, and it was the first of only two he sent me during the entire trip, even though he continued to write his family daily. From Beirut he sent home a note written on toilet paper.

Dear Family,

Excuse the writing paper. Rich, can you believe this is toilet paper? I guess it means we've arrived in Beirut. Actually, it's one of the prettiest places I've ever seen. Yesterday our two student guides took us to a cave in the mountains. Tiny mountain roads with drop offs of about 800–900 feet. It was beautiful. Our lunch consisted of about 15 different types of food. It was amazing! Last night we had dinner at Casino Nasr on the Mediterranean. Our group consisted of 8 people. First they brought out 55, Yes 55 plates of Lebanese hors d'oeuvres, everything you could imagine. Then a huge fish dinner!

I'll write again soon.

Love,

Jim

In Beirut, a guide took Jim to the Purgatory Dance Hall, a dimly lit club full of overweight and unattractive dancers and prostitutes. The guide pointed to the women with pride and boasted in a Lebanese expression of good luck, "I think we have just hit a cat!" Jim laughed so hard he had to hold his stomach.

Later he wrote in his journal:

I met a girl named Fatima at the Purgatory Dance Hall. I'm lucky I met her before Ripley did. She had split level chins!

When Bob and Gene had recovered from their mysterious illness enough to move on, the tour continued to Cairo and Tunisia. On the plane Jim and Bob met a young airline steward named Hussein Hussein. He had noticed their instruments and eagerly told the musicians he played the harmonica. He gave Bob brandy to soothe his stomach and invited Jim and Suzy into the cockpit. Hussein proudly showed off his skills by playing "Sweet Georgia Brown" on his harmonica, while Jim, Suzie, and the pilot sang along.

During their travels, Jim and Gene talked at length about Marxism and Gene's desire for social change and the redistribution of wealth in America. Jim listened intently, absorbing much of what Gene had to say. Gene had been hopeful about the voter registration drive in the South, but the recent race riots flaring up across the nation discouraged him. Now the news that Congress had overwhelmingly passed the Gulf of Tonkin Resolution, giving President Johnson carte blanche to officially enter the war in Vietnam, further depressed him. He related his concerns to Jim, who empathized with Gene's sense of humanity. At home, Jim buffered himself against the passions of politics by poking fun at them, much as he did with organized religion. Here, away from home, he openly engaged in political and philosophical discourse.

At the same time, Jim developed a close friendship with Suzie, who, in addition to being an accomplished musician, was an excellent artist and cartoonist. One of the traveling group's responsibilities was to report to the NSA about their experiences and people they had met during the trip. The obligation to provide detailed reports fueled a rumor that the CIA was behind the tour.

Suzie's reporting style was to draw cartoons on the hard, brown toilet paper they found in Istanbul and send them back to the NSA, which, according to some students they had met, turned them over to the CIA.

Susie was bold, with a strong belief in the values of her American generation: women's rights, peace, and free love. She recognized that the Tunisian culture frowned on her behavior, so she tempered herself to an extent, but it didn't stop her. Once Suzie went for a camel ride, shocking the Tunisians, who had never seen a woman straddling a camel before. When she finished the ride, Jim and a number of fierce-looking Tunisian soldiers came to help her down. Laughing, Jim told Suzie to "take it easy."

Suddenly one of the soldiers drew his knife against Jim's throat and began to scream at him in Arabic. Their guide rushed over and convinced the soldier to put away the dagger. The host explained to Jim, who was pale with fear, that "teasy" meant "ass" in Arabic. The soldier thought Jim was insulting Suzie. Later, Suzie captured the event on the brown toilet paper and gave the cartoon to Jim.

The tour continued back through Italy, with the group giving daily concerts.

Jim clipped a report written by the American Consulate General of Istanbul inside his travel diary:

> *The four folk-singing American students brought down the house at the Ninth International Youth Cultural Festival. The three serious young men and vivacious girl delighted the local citizenry who applauded them for playing in the streets of the exotic 2,600 year-old city.*
>
> *The foursome is the only folk singing group besides a chorus from London. The United States N.S.A. gave each musician complete transportation costs and a $14.00 per diem for their talents in singing and playing Negro spirituals, Hillbilly tunes, Blue Grass and Grand Ole Opry melodies, Ragtime, the Blues, old and contemporary folk songs.*

The consulate's report went on to explain how Russia, Yugoslavia, Israel, and Lebanon had sent colorfully costumed folk dance ensembles to the friendship festival. Student theater groups from England, Belgium, France, Germany, Switzerland, Italy, and Norway performed pieces by classic and contemporary masters, including Shakespeare, Becket, and Sartre.

The Americans gave their concert in the afternoon, when the Turkish air force was making flying raids over Cyprus. They couldn't read the Turkish papers, but there was excitement in the streets about the raids. The Philadelphia Choir thought the commotion was about them and didn't realize there was a war scare.

At the end of that week, the tour reached its final stop near Lagos, Nigeria. There Jim met Razak Salijah, an energetic Nigerian student representative from a nearby university, who wore a perpetual smile. Jim liked him immediately and hoped to spend time with him learning about the local culture.

However, the humid African climate was stifling, and Jim began feeling even sicker than usual. The mosquitoes were thick, and he was covered with bites— a sure sign, he thought, that he was coming down with the dreaded disease.

Within days, the entire group complained again of stomach problems. Concerned, Razak took them to an American doctor at the university. The doctor examined them but was unable to diagnose the problem.

"Are you sure we don't have malaria?" Jim asked nervously.

"Have you been taking quinine?"

"Once a day," Jim reported.

"Once a day? No wonder you're constipated! You're only supposed to take it once a week!"

Chagrined, Jim and the others in his group put away the quinine pills, and on the advice of the doctor, Jim shed his anxiety over malaria.

The group recovered from quinine poisoning, and Jim spent afternoons with Razak, who told him about local folklore and religions, which included stories about superstitions, witches, and human sacrifices. Jim was intrigued. He loved folk stories, especially when they could be put to music.

Razak was a political activist and shared with Jim his fears about the future of Nigeria. Fighting had broken out among rebel factions, and the friction seemed about to escalate into civil war.

One evening, Razak took Jim to an open-air nightclub where musicians wailed on electric guitars plugged into a gas-powered generator. Jim joined the Nigerians, drinking the local banana beer and trying to imitate their dances.

The American singers gave daily performances around Lagos and were invited to perform in a ceremonial arena before a local king.

At the performance, Razak told Jim, "This arena has been used for centuries by the tribes to sacrifice dogs to Ogun, the god of iron."

"I hope they like the show," Jim joked.

————

On September 13, 1965, the students spent their last day in Nigeria. Jim and Razak went for a long walk and expressed their feelings of friendship for one another. Jim hugged his new friend and wished him the best of luck. He worried for Razak's life and found it difficult to say good-bye.

In Philadelphia, I awaited Jim's return with growing trepidation. The two letters he'd written me lacked any expression of his love for me. I was afraid that my going all the way with him had been a mistake. I didn't know what else it could be.

He returned on September 14 but didn't call.

"I can't believe I haven't heard from Jim," I told my father. "I hope he's okay. Maybe he's still recovering from the trip." Days went by, and still no call came. I thought of every reason I could for his neglect.

"He doesn't know we moved while he was away—that's it!" I told my dad, trying to convince myself. "He must have not gotten the message I left with his mother that we moved. Maybe I should call him."

While Jim was out of the country, my father had purchased a home in Wallingford, about forty miles west of Philadelphia, from Dick Clark, the local disc jockey and host of *American Bandstand*. A little over a week after Jim returned, I finally called him myself.

"Hello." It was him.

"Jim," I asked anxiously, "is that you?"

"Oh, hi, Ingrid," he said as if I were a casual acquaintance. "How have you been?"

"Did you have a good time?" I asked back, more anxious than ever. "I wish I would have heard from you more."

"I had a great time," Jim said coolly, expressing no remorse or concern that he hadn't called since he'd returned. He was polite but didn't ask to see me before he hung up.

The conversation left me devastated.

"He acted as if we had never been in love," I cried to my dad. Although I felt confused and hurt, I told myself that sooner or later, Jim and I would be together again. Maybe he just wasn't ready to get so serious yet. I tried to convince myself that it would work out better this way.

Out of loneliness, I began dating John Grant, a military cadet I'd met at a performance at the Pennsylvania Military College when I'd sung with the Rum Runners. My friendship with John, however, was platonic. Though the cadet had strong feelings for me, I was still in love with Jim.

In January 1965, John got orders to head out for South Vietnam. In February, a year to the day after Jim and I had had our first real date, I learned that Jim was dating my closest friend, Peggy. Humiliated and depressed, I shut myself off in the attic and worked in solitude on my art. For months after Jim's return from the tour, I felt the pain of his rejection.

In the spring of 1965, I decided that even though I loved Jim deeply, I had to put him out of my mind.

I started by immersing myself fully in ceramics and painting and by performing as a solo artist at folk contests. Two ceramic pieces I constructed were selected for the Craftsman 65 exhibit in New York City, and with more confidence in my art, I applied to both the Rhode Island School of Design and University of Pennsylvania. I decided if I was good enough to get into RISD, I'd go there. If not, I'd study psychology and work with my dad as a lay analyst.

On a Friday night just after my eighteenth birthday, I performed as the opening act for Len Chandler at the Main Point. Jim had seen an ad in the *Philadelphia Inquirer* announcing the performance.

That night he sat in the audience, smiling sheepishly. When I first noticed him, I was filled with raw emotion. I looked away, purposefully not setting eyes on him throughout my set. When I finished, Jim came to the stage.

"Uh, hi, Ing," he said. "How have you been?"

I could hardly contain myself. My heart ached so badly. I still loved him, but my feelings were intense and confused; my throat tightened, and I could barely speak.

"Okay" was all I could muster.

"Your voice sounds wonderful," he said with a forced smile. "But your guitar is a little sharp. Can I tune it for you?" He put out his hand to reach for it. I quietly passed it to him. He braced one foot on the stage and placed the guitar across his knee. Cocking one ear, he tuned it.

"Can you sit down and talk for a few minutes?" he asked. I wanted to talk to him but felt torn and needed to pull myself together.

"Can you stay for my second set?" I asked, trying to buy time.

"I'm sorry. I've got to go. I'm driving up to visit a friend in Maine tonight."

I felt sick all over again.

He tried to smile, and then walked away.

Suspicion overcame me. Was he going to visit another woman?

That night I stifled my cries in my pillow. The following morning, my father handed his red-eyed daughter a large envelope from the Rhode Island School of Design. I had been accepted for my freshman year of college.

"Daddy, I can't believe it!"

"I'm thrilled for you, honey," he said, hugging me.

"By the way, Daddy, I'm going out tonight. A classmate asked me out to the movies, and I said yes. It'll be my first date since John left."

Less than an hour later, my dad called me to the phone.

"It's Jim," he said.

"Hi, Ing." He sounded urgent. "I'm calling from a phone booth near Maine, but I just had to let you know that I thought about you the entire time I was driving up the coast. If I drive back right now, can I see you tonight?"

I paused, trying to know what to say.

"I'm sorry, Jim. I have a date tonight." My heart sank, but I knew I couldn't put my life on hold for him anymore.

"Well," he asked, panic in his voice, "can I see you after your date brings you home?"

"No, but you can see me tomorrow."

"Oh, okay, sure. How about 9 AM?"

"That's fine, Jim. We can have breakfast at our house."

The next morning I heard the familiar whine of his approaching Volkswagen. I waited anxiously inside until he rang the bell. Reluctantly, I opened the door. He grinned, shrugged his shoulders, and lifted both eyebrows.

"Let's talk," I said, and led him inside and up to the attic, which had been converted into my art studio and bedroom.

Over the next few hours, he told me about his trip and the weeks following his return. He covered a lot of ground but left out that he'd dated my best friend. He had convinced himself it meant nothing.

"My parents increased the pressure on me to break off our relationship as soon as I returned," he said sadly. "I guess I gave into them. But when I saw your name in the newspaper, and it said you'd be performing at the Main Point, I knew I'd made a mistake."

He hesitated. I said nothing.

"And when I saw you singing Friday night, I realized how much I missed you and needed you." He pulled me to him and wrapped me tenderly in his arms. "I'm so sorry I've hurt you, Ing. Please forgive me." He kissed me on top of my head. "I promise I'll never do this again. I love you, Ing. I'll always love you."

———

Years later, when Jim wrote the song "Alabama Rain" for his second album, *Life and Times*, he captured the innocence of those days in the early '60s, when we were young and had our ups and downs in love. He set the song in Alabama to give it the feeling of the sultry South. But it is those steamy nights in Jim's little green Volkswagen that I remember whenever I hear his song.

Lazy days in mid-July, country Sunday mornings.
Dusty haze on summer highways,
Sweet magnolia's callin'.
Now and then I find myself
Thinkin' of the days,
When we were walkin' in the Alabama rain.

We were only kids but then,
I've never heard it said
That kids can't fall in love and feel the same,
I can still remember the first time I told you,
"I love you."

Drive-in movies Friday nights,
Drinkin' beer and laughin'
Somehow things were always right,
I just don't know what happened.
Now and then I find myself,

Thinkin' of the days,
When we were walkin' in the Alabama rain.

We were only kids but then,
I've never heard it said
That kids can't fall in love and feel the same,
I can still remember the first time I told you,
"I love you."

FACETS

I
N AUGUST 1964, WHILE JIM was on the international student tour, a spontaneous uprising in response to police brutality had broken out in North Philly. Close to a thousand people were arrested, and the community businesses were trashed.

Sal, who was completing his graduate work in folklore at the University of Pennsylvania, phoned Jim upon his return that fall to fill him in about the riots and to discuss the other major events of that pivotal year: the obscenity trial of Lenny Bruce, the Johnson/Goldwater presidential race, the student response to the escalating "police action" in Southeast Asia, and the Warren Report's conclusion that Oswald had acted alone in the murder of President Kennedy.

Jim was eager to tell Sal about his trip outside the country and how it had reinforced his belief in the power of music. They laughed together about Jim's malaria phobia and the unintentional overdose of quinine. And Sal saved the best for last.

"How does working on the soundtrack of a television documentary grab you?" Sal asked him.

"Great."

"Finally, being a folklorist is paying off. I got a contract to produce the soundtrack for *The Miner's Story* and thought you'd be a natural for it. It's a profile of American coal miners. It highlights the boom times after World War I and the decline that followed. Channel 10's camera team filmed the miners' families at home and then went down into the mines with the men. Jack Palance is the narrator."

"So where do I fit in?"

"Well, you know, Palance was born in the coal country. He comes from one of those northeastern Pennsylvania towns like Carbondale, Hazelton, Pottsville, or something. Anyway, he's the driving force behind this documentary, and he's passionate about the story. He's been overseeing every detail of the show, including the music. He's even checked you out, Croce."

"That's scary. What's he checked out?"

"Well," Sal continued, "probably everything he could. He was impressed that you were chosen to do the NSA tour, and when I played him a tape, he liked your voice and your repertoire. What he wants to hear now is the music you'd suggest for his soundtrack."

"Are you for real, Sal? He wants me to write the soundtrack?"

"He wants us to write it and you to sing it."

"That's great! When do we start?"

"How about this afternoon? Can we get together at your house? I've missed The Flower's home-cooked meals."

"Sure, come over after your class, and stay for dinner." He knew his mother and father would be gracious at dinner in spite of their disapproval of Sal. The reality was that in spite of Jim's newfound independence from traveling, he still lived at home, and it frustrated and embarrassed him that he couldn't entertain his friends without judgment from his parents.

Behind Sal's back, Jim Senior derided both Sal's flamboyant appearance and his status as a full-time student.

"Tell me: What can he do with a degree in folklore?" he would argue. "As far as I'm concerned, what he's studying is a total waste of time."

Still, the Croces were always generous and hospitable, especially if the friend was Italian. His parents often invited Jim's classmates, like Tommy Picardo, Mike DiBenedetto, Bruce Bartollini, and, reluctantly, Sal, over for a good meal. The students were happy for the chance to be in a home instead of a dormitory and enjoyed Jim's mother's delicious Northern Italian home cooking.

When Sal joined the Croces that night for dinner, Jim waited until dessert to tell his dad about the documentary.

"Dad, while I was away, Sal got me a job cowriting and singing the soundtrack for a nationwide television show. And I'm getting paid for it."

"As long as it doesn't interrupt your studies, it sounds okay by me. What do you think, Mommy?" he motioned to Flora.

"Uh-huh," she said, while vigorously clearing the dishes from the table.

———

Jim spent weeks researching material for the soundtrack. In addition to their original compositions, he and Sal chose the song "Coal Tattoo" by Nashville songwriter Billy Ed Wheeler as the theme song. It depicted the short, oppressed lives of the coal miners, symbolized by the coal dust that permanently embedded itself in the miners' cuts and scratches, forming a blue, indelible "coal tattoo."

Jim's work on *The Miner's Story* gave him confidence and a sense of legitimacy. After viewing the show just once, Jim was able to come up with songs and music for the score. He and Sal completed the soundtrack in a couple of weeks, well before deadline, and for the first time in his life, Jim was paid as a songwriter. The show was a critical success, and there were royalties to follow.

———

Before Jim left home one winter night, when he was scheduled to play a gig at the Riddle Paddock, he received news that his Nigerian friend, Razak, had been killed in a student uprising.

Razak's death saddened and alarmed Jim. On his way to work, he stopped by my house to tell me about his loss. We sat on my bed, and I consoled him. He also admitted he was troubled about his draft status and the escalating war in Vietnam. President Johnson had increased the number of military personnel in South Vietnam to 35,000 men, and there were now daily air strikes against the North.

"Tommy suggested that I join the National Guard, like he did, to avoid the draft. What do you think, Ing?"

"What do you have to do if you join?"

"Well, I'd have to go to boot camp for about six months, and then I'd be required to attend weekend meetings for five years. But it's highly unlikely they'll send me overseas."

"Six months apart," I lamented. "But it's better than the alternative of your being drafted."

———

On May 22, 1965, Jim joined the Army National Guard. The preliminary meetings bored him, and the impending boot camp left him hanging. He waited nervously for the call that would take him away.

Besides playing regularly at the Riddle Paddock, and at the Main Point as an opening act, Jim was invited by residents of Philadelphia's elite Main Line region to play their private parties.

Twenty-five dollars a night wasn't much, but he took the jobs graciously, happy to get whatever paying work he could as a performer. Jim was sorry to see that many of the wealthy residents "with at least four hyphens between their last names" were offering him less money to play than he was receiving at high school functions. But he hoped that if they liked his music, in time he could ask for more.

On one occasion, the famous artist Andrew Wyeth hired Jim and me to perform for an outdoor party. When we arrived at the Wyeths' house in Chadds Ford, we were directed to wait in the kitchen with "the help." It was interesting to see that musicians had their place alongside the cooks and maids, but I felt quite comfortable among them. While preparing for the picnic, the chef offered us a savory chicken soup with a variety of hors d'oeuvres and a multilayered omelet. It was the fanciest home cooking I'd ever tasted, and I was enthralled by the presentation and amazing flavors.

The party was taking place on a great lawn near the house, and horse-drawn carriages transported the guests to the picnic. The Wyeths' teenage son, Jamie, already an accomplished artist who was following in his family's footsteps, loved music and invited Jim and me to ride with him in his carriage to the party. Jamie was very gracious, and when we finished the performance, we were asked to play several encores.

Jim and I were invited back to perform at the Wyeths' home and again at a philanthropic fundraiser they held on the Main Line. The pay never got better, but the experience was an eye-opener. I was surprised that in modern America there was still such a sharp division of the classes. This experience also reinforced Jim's deep conviction that we needed to make a record in order to succeed.

———

When Jim invited me, the proverbial tomboy, to the Villanova University junior prom, I bought a fancy, pale blue dress and my first pair of heels. I was taking another step toward being womanly and hoped it would please both Jim and my father. The night of his college prom, Jim arrived wearing a stylish three-piece suit and carrying a corsage. Hearing the doorbell ring, I hurried to greet him, wobbling as I navigated the stairs in the new heels.

"You look like Minnie Mouse in those pumps," laughed Florence. I was flooded with insecurity.

"Should I wear something else?" I asked anxiously.

When I opened the door, Jim stepped inside and came to my rescue.

"You look amazing," he said, pausing a moment to stare. Gently, he slipped his hand under the bodice of my strapless dress and pinned on my corsage.

———

Students packed the dance floor at Villanova. Jim found a table with two vacant seats, introduced me to a few of his classmates, and then escorted me to the center of the room.

I loved to dance and enthusiastically took his hand. Jim let my hand go, and his face grew serious with concentration. Dramatically, he stepped away from the crowd. Bending forward, he grabbed his right elbow with his left hand and started to rotate it. Simultaneously, he lifted his leg like a dog about to pee and gyrated it again and again. In spite of the beat, he was dancing his own bizarre dance to his own rhythm.

The others stood by in amazement. At first, I was embarrassed for him. I didn't understand what Jim was doing. *Could this be Jim's idea of a dance?* I wondered. In fact, it was. Jim continued to gyrate his elbow, lift his leg, and turn slowly in circles, at all times gazing into my eyes. Suddenly, I couldn't contain myself. I began to laugh harder and harder, as did others around us, exactly the response Jim wanted.

———

In the summer of 1965, I graduated from high school. At eighteen, I felt independent and talked eagerly of my future as an artist and my excitement at attending the Rhode Island School of Design and Brown University for my core classes. Though Jim felt threatened by my leaving, he was pleased for me, even to the point of assimilating my goals as his own. To be a part of my artistic world, he took up photography, haiku writing, and painting with Japanese bamboo brushes. That spring, he graduated from Villanova with a degree in psychology and a minor in German. But now that he was out of school, he had no idea how to apply these skills to get a job.

During the early evenings and on every weekend, Jim and I practiced and performed together and added many songs to our repertoire. We learned covers by Gordon Lightfoot, Ian and Sylvia, Simon and Garfunkel, and the Lovin' Spoonful, and we performed at two folk clubs in downtown Philadelphia, the Second Fret and the Gilded Cage. We were becoming well known as a duo and played as many as three or four nights a week together. Music making and our impassioned, if somewhat cramped, lovemaking in the front seat of the Volkswagen also kept us busy.

"Ing, we need to find a better place to make love," Jim joked. "Otherwise, you're gonna have VW from the steering wheel permanently imbedded on your butt."

———

One afternoon in late August, as I packed for college, Jim told me in a melancholy voice, "I sure wish you didn't have to go away."

"Jim, you know how much I love you," I reassured him. "But this is my dream, just like making music is yours."

82

"What about those college guys up there, those artistic lechers?"

"I only want you. You know that."

"Well, maybe we should get engaged." he said. "Then as soon as you finish school, we can get married."

"I know we're going to get married someday. But I need to complete my education first."

"I can't wait that long," he pleaded. "Come on, Ing, let's get married next year. You'll have a year of college behind you, and you can finish school as Mrs. Croce."

"Why don't we just live together first? Move up to Rhode Island with me! And then next summer, if I survive my freshman year, I'll come back, and we'll get married."

"Yeah, that would be great, but you know how my parents are. They'd disown me. And anyway, I want you to be my wife."

"I want to be your wife more than anything, Jim. But don't you think it would be fun to be lovers first? Wouldn't it be great to get a place of our own in Providence? We could spend every night together in a real bed, and you'd never have to go home."

"Ah, baby, that would be great, but you know I can't."

His relief in having my word that I'd marry him lasted only until the day I actually left for school. Alone and without career direction, he felt miserable. But he continued to play the Riddle Paddock, sometimes solo but often taking Rich or his young musician friend Carl Fehrenbach to play with him for company.

Alone in his room and motivated by loneliness, Jim began to write short stories and love songs. He recorded them on his father's reel-to-reel tape recorder and mailed them to me, always accompanied by a long romantic love letter. He wrote every day, sometimes twice a day, and telephoned at least once a week.

His first love story and letter awaited me when I arrived at RISD.

THE LOVE STORY
(A ribald classic, a fragment of a Chaucerian-type tale)

It is believed that this series of tales is an autobiographical one written by a young man during adolescence and middle years dealing with a great, wondrous love affair with a maiden believed to be Super Girl.

In years long past there lived in a beauteous shire a fair enchantress who was courted by a young gallant. She enjoyed his company, his singing and the music of his lute. They soon were deep in love and dallied in carriage, loft or when her parents were away, in the great bed of the royal chamber . . .

The story went on to tell of our first night together, cloaked in mythology. Jim's romantic fable revealed his lofty expectations for our relationship. The letter he enclosed with the story further expressed how much our love meant to him.

My feelings, though equally intense, were down-to-earth, honest, and open. I was flattered by his embellishments but afraid I might not live up to his expectations.

In another letter Jim wrote to me while I was away at RISD, he used Japanese brushes to paint a motif that matched the poetic opening lines:

Dear Ingrid,
As the bamboo grows straight & tall
So grows my love for you.
I've been painting with my new Japanese brushes and I just had to write. I spent the day hunting, hiking and riding.
(I didn't get anything) Nothing much else is new except I love you more. I can't wait to see you. We have lots to do (ha ha)
that's my sexy laugh, so take note.
I may take on some private Mainline Parties on Friday and Saturday, but I can't even sing straight everything sounds to me like Ingrid, love, love, love making . . . Well, I'd better stop thinking like that before I attack my pillow. I've been really jumpy and restless . . . this oriental painting is just the thing I need. It embodies not only the form but a philosophy of simplicity and symbolism, and beauty that is an experience both aesthetic and visual. I'll show you some of the things I've done when you come home for Christmas. You probably see so much art work though, that it won't interest you but I'll show it to you anyway. I'd love to hear all about your work please write me about it. Well, I'll talk to you on Wednesday so goodnight. Think of me when you sleep for I will think of you, and every moment will be a moment of love.
I love you Ingrid.
Jim

I read the letter with a subtle sense of surprise. Jim's artistic attempts touched me deeply. He was trying so hard to please me, even to be an artist like me.

Our separation was causing Jim's insecurities to continually resurface, and another letter quickly followed:

Dear Ingrid,

I don't do much without thinking about what you're doin' and about how nice it will be when we do see each other. Last night I went night fishing down by the shore. It was really breezy. I got there at dusk (I went alone), the beach was deserted and covered with all sorts of junk. It was kinda weird you know empty knowing that nobody was gonna be there swimming or just messing around. The real season is over and only a few people passed by on evenin' walks. The water was warm, but the spray and the wind made it seem colder.

My mother made a thermos full of hot coffee, which really hit the spot. I only wish I had you there with me. But don't worry 'cause there'll be time. You'd never believe how many people tell me how perfect we are for each other. I just smile (or grin) and say, "[Yay]."

Love
Jim

As much as I enjoyed the sentiments in Jim's love letters, I found just as much pleasure in his humor, as in this adorable letter in which he described his effort to save money:

Dear Ing,

You'll also be proud that I'm resisting all temptations to spend money. I'm saving all my money for your wedding ring. So far this week I almost bought: a) a big motorcycle; b) a quick draw pistol and a hand tooled Mexican holster and belt; c) a model 'A' Ford, completely restored.

Love,
Jim

After four months at art school, although I missed Jim terribly, I was deeply engaged in my studies and enjoying my independence. My father supported my educational expenses, but for extra money I worked as a maid and cook for three college seniors from Brown. I enjoyed cleaning their home and preparing meals for them and felt it was good practice for marriage. For the first time, I felt in control of my life. The academic instruction at Brown and art education at RISD weren't easy, but I loved the challenge. There were so many great artists at RISD, and the beatnik milieu of the students was exciting.

Although I didn't partake in RISD's extracurricular drug scene, my first roommate was expelled for drugs. Fortunately, my new roommate, Margie, and I had a lot more in common and became fast friends. I shared Jim's tapes and letters with her and couldn't wait to introduce them to each other.

The following letter, one of his most romantic, arrived a week before Jim's Christmas visit:

Dear Ing,

You can't imagine how I'm just dying to hold you (only a few days, thank God) and I'm eagerly awaiting next weekend. Right now it's raining. It's one of those cold rains beating against my bedroom window and that just makes me feel worse; cause it's times like this that I wish all the more that we were together and warm. Someone once said that fires in fireplaces are only to look at and not to sing or make love in front of, but I'd like to tell him a thing or two. The way I feel now I could make love in a fire and still feel cold. But, it won't always be like this. The nights of hearing cold rains hit the windows and winds rattling panes and snow falling and us together in a nice warm bed are just around the corner. I think of lying still in your arms and listening to your heart beat and hearing your breathing and whispering, "Ingrid," and you answering, "Yes," in such a soft tone that I can almost feel velvet and then I say, "Ingrid, I love you, and I love to hold you, and at last we're alone for real and for good."

Goodnight Sweet Thing.

I love you,

Jim

———

That fall, Jim's parents had grown increasingly impatient with his lack of a career direction. Feeling the pressure, he'd applied at several radio stations hoping for a job as a disc jockey or advertisement writer, both of which he'd done at Villanova's campus radio station. He was finally hired as a sales representative selling airtime to business owners in the impoverished black neighborhoods of West Philadelphia. The station owners joked that if Jim could survive selling airtime on the streets, he could move up to the glamour of writing radio commercials.

He didn't see it as a joke but as a real step up. And although he didn't enjoy sales, and the pay was miserable, it eased the pressures at home. Working at the station gave him an excuse to get out of the house during the day and a way to earn more money for an engagement ring. Getting married had become the most important thing on his mind.

While I was away at school, Jim became even closer to my father. He visited my dad in his office several times a week. They engaged in long conversations about psychology, philosophy, music, and religion. They discussed Freud and Jung, Nietzsche and Buber, and the various religions Jim was exploring. My dad showed him a personal diary he had kept while he was the doctor in charge of a German prisoner of war camp in World War II. My father's compassion for Nazi POW patients overwhelmed Jim. He had come to admire and love my father deeply.

Although Jim had always been intensely private, hiding his real feelings behind his humor and facades, in my father's company he opened up about his problems at home.

"I wish I could talk to my father the way I talk to you," he confided to my dad on one of their visits. "No matter how hard I try to reason with him about making music my career, he doesn't want to hear it."

"You need to make your own decisions, Jim," my dad suggested. "You know, I was raised by a domineering mother, and even now she calls me every day to tell me what I should do. If you continue to try pleasing your parents at the expense of your own dreams, you'll wind up disappointed and angry."

Jim pondered my dad's words for a moment and then spoke in a low, serious voice: "Sid, I've been thinking a lot about death lately. You know my cousin Steve and my uncle Ralph both have cancer. I've been taking turns driving them to and from the hospital for chemotherapy and radiation treatments. Seeing them suffer makes me realize that life is so short."

My dad clenched his jaw in pain. Several months earlier he had been diagnosed with pancreatic cancer, and the doctors had given him less than a year to live. But only Florence knew. He had lost a lot of weight, he felt tired often, and his color was jaundiced. He hoped no one else knew what was wrong.

"Does it scare you, Jim?"

"Well, it makes me wonder. But as a Catholic, I'm not supposed to doubt."

"What do you doubt?"

Jim bit his lower lip and tried to formulate his answer.

"Well, I still have a lot of questions about spirituality. God seems speculative to me. But I want to believe in something, and I want the freedom to question."

My dad was still a skeptic, too, in spite of his knowledge of his impending fate. He said, "I encourage you to keep up your search, Jim, and let your conscience be your guide."

———

A week before Christmas I awaited Jim's arrival, eager to show him how much I had matured. My new bohemian art school forms of self-expression were much more colorful than the buttoned-down style of Jim's conservative friends at Villanova. I had bought an Indian madras bedspread in beige, yellow, blue, and red at a head shop for under $10, and made a sack dress and matching scarf. I also found a pair of black, netted stockings covered with a rose pattern that made me look as though I had tattooed flowers up and down my legs. Sexy, I thought.

Standing in the lobby of the dormitory, I heard the little green VW chugging up the enormous hill that led to RISD. Unable to contain my excitement, I ran out and waved wildly until he spotted me. Jim stopped the car, jumped out, and raced toward me. I bolstered myself, expecting a passionate embrace, but suddenly Jim stopped short and stared at my legs.

"Oh my God, Ing!" he said, pointing at my stockings. "Hurry up and take them off! We need to burn them before they multiply."

I stepped back, startled and hurt. I knew Jim was only trying to be funny, the way he'd been about my skunk dress at the hootenanny, but his timing was awful, and just like that time, when he saw I was hurt, he realized what an ass he'd been.

"I'm so sorry, Ing. I know you must have looked all over the place to find those stockings. I didn't mean to hurt your feelings, honest. It's just that your legs surprised me." I started to laugh and figured I was being too sensitive. Jim hugged me and lifted me off the ground in his embrace. When we touched, it was as if we'd never been apart.

———

Much of Provincetown was closed for the winter. Searching the lonely town, we found a quaint but inexpensive boarding house with only one room available. It was perfect. We signed in as Mr. and Mrs. James Croce and hurried across the street to the only open restaurant. A freezing Atlantic wind blew in off the ocean. Portuguese fishermen sat around the tables at the family-owned waterfront café. After a dinner of delicious hot tuna stew, we walked through the deserted street to our cozy room.

Jim sat on the bed and played his guitar. Inspired by the gusty winds rattling the windows, he sang his favorite sea chantey, "Blow the Candle Out." I loved the way he sang it. It was one of the first songs he'd ever played for me. As I looked around the little rented room, I realized we had no time restraints and could be together without fear of interruption.

When Jim finished the song, he reached into his suitcase, pulled out a small, dark blue velvet box, and opened it slowly, revealing a full-carat, white-gold diamond ring. He looked at it with pride. Saving money had always been difficult for Jim. He'd rather have spent it on impulsive gifts for his friends and family. The ring represented not just his love but three jobs, endless nights at the Paddock, and a difficult exercise in restraint.

He slid the ring onto my finger and asked me to marry him.

"Yes!" I said enthusiastically, again and again, and hugged him close. We undressed slowly, and as the wind roared outside the window, Jim caressed me and whispered in my ear, "I love you, Ing, and I always will. I want to make love to you like never before, all night long. I'm so happy you're going to be my wife, Ing. I can't believe you're all mine."

————

The next morning, we went back to the fisherman's café and shared half a dozen hot blueberry muffins fresh from the oven. Jim poured me coffee from a large thermos. I wasn't a coffee drinker—in fact I'd never even tried it before—but to appear grown-up, I drank the thermos dry as we discussed wedding plans and how to break the news to our parents. Naturally hyperactive, I was rendered comically speedy by the caffeine. By the time Jim paid the bill, his animated hummingbird had checked out of the inn, had packed the car, and was sitting and fidgeting in the front seat ready to go.

On our way to Wellsfleet, I reviewed my last four months at RISD, speaking at breakneck speed. When we reached the sand dunes, Jim pulled off the road, parked, and grabbed his guitar. Taking a blanket and picnic basket out of the trunk, we walked hand in hand. In the shelter of a secluded dune, we spread the blanket and huddled together out of the wind; having been on the Cape before, Jim had anticipated this moment. Several weeks before, he'd composed a haunting melody he called "Ingrid." Now he played the song for me. I was seldom sentimental, but the music made me cry.

When he finished, Jim put down his guitar and embraced me. Our tenderness turned to passion, and on the cold New England sand dune, we fervently made love again.

———

On Christmas Eve, Jim and I joined my family for a small Chanukah dinner.

"Are you going to tell them now?" I whispered in his ear. He nodded and cleared his throat.

"You know," he said to my father and Florence, "Ing and I have been talking. It's been really hard for us being away from each other. So we've decided to get married. Show them your ring, Ing," he said proudly. And I showed my family the ring I had kept hidden until that moment.

"And next semester I'll apply to school in Philadelphia," I said.

"Wonderful! Wonderful!" my dad said, happy for us and glad we'd be near him and the family.

"Mazel tov!" Florence said, rising from her chair to kiss us both. "I'll call Rabbi Kaplan first thing in the morning."

"Mom, I don't know if we need a rabbi for this ceremony."

"I think it's a great idea, Ing," Jim responded.

"Why do you think a rabbi is such a good idea?"

"I'm going to convert to Judaism," he said.

I was stunned.

"Jim, that's great!" Florence exclaimed. "I'm delighted! But have you told your parents?"

"I'll let them know after I tell them about our wedding plans—one shock at a time."

———

On Christmas Day, the Croces invited my family to dinner in Drexel Hill. As usual, the house overflowed with Jim's relatives. Jim sat next to Aunt Ginger at the long dining room table. Toward the end of the meal, holding my hand, he whispered to Ginger, "We're getting married."

"Hey, everybody," Aunt Ginger announced loudly, interrupting everyone, "Jimmy's going to marry Ingi!"

For a moment, the room was silent. His father's face froze. His mother glared. Jim's aunts and uncles toasted their congratulations and hugged Jim and me.

Jim sighed in relief. He had planned everything perfectly. His parents would express their disapproval and concerns later in private, but for now their opposition had been muted.

"I hope your parents don't stay mad at us forever," I whispered, and kissed my fiancé on his cheek.

———

Though his parents were less than thrilled about Jim's engagement, his new attitude about work at the radio station pleased them, and slowly they began to change their minds about the marriage. Sensing he was maturing and was getting serious about earning a living, his father surprised him one evening after Jim returned from work.

"Jim, I'd like to talk to you for a minute," his father said. "You know, before you get married, you need to put a little money away for you and Ingi, a little nest egg."

"I know, Dad. I'm trying to save," he said honestly, hoping his father wouldn't start pressuring him again.

"I can see you've been trying. That's why I'd like to give you a hand. I've got an idea, and I think you're gonna like this one. How would you like to make a record album? I was talking to a client last week who owns a recording studio. He can get us the studio time at a reasonable price. And once you've recorded, we can have the album pressed and packaged ourselves."

Jim stared in shock at his father.

"I'll front you the money to rent the studio time and get the album packaged. Then it's your job to sell the records. I penciled it all out, and I figured it will cost about $750 to make five hundred albums. You can sell them for whatever you think you can get, and the profit, after the expenses are taken out, is your wedding gift."

"Geez, Dad, I don't know what to say. Thank you. It's a great idea!"

"Do you think you can sell that many albums, Jim?" his father wondered.

"Absolutely," Jim responded, ecstatic that not only was he going to cut his first album, he would be able to do it with his parents' blessing.

His father's lesson in economics was invaluable. Jim assembled a group of musician friends to back him: his brother, Rich', on guitar and percussion; Bob Knott on harmonica; Karl Fehrenbach on banjo, guitar, dobro, and tambourine; Mike DiBenedetto on guitar, piano, and electric accordion; and Ken Cavender on bass and banjo. And Sal would be the producer.

In the winter of 1966, the young men gathered at the Croces' house to rehearse the songs that Jim and Sal had selected for the album. Although the musicians had played together on many occasions, they only had one night to arrange and practice their song list before going into the studio to record. "I know professional studio musicians do this all the time," Jim Senior worried out loud, "but you guys are just college students. I hope one practice is enough."

Early the following morning, they met at the recording studio in Wilmington, Delaware. Their enthusiasm couldn't be squelched even by the chilly reception from the studio engineer, angry at having to work so early in the morning with another novice group. His mood didn't change until the group performed their first song. They played flawlessly and cut the entire first side with only one or two takes on each song. Impressed, the engineer became wholeheartedly involved in the rest of the session and encouraging.

"He's got the talent to become a star," he told Sal. "He can definitely do it!"

Jim named the album *Facets*. He wanted the songs to represent a variety of styles, and Sal thought it was important to show Jim's versatility. He hoped they could use this album as a demo to get Jim a real record deal. With more than 2,000 songs in Jim's working repertoire, they had a difficult time narrowing it down to only 11.

The final cut included three of Jim's originals: "Sun Come Up," which he had written with Rich; "Texas Rodeo," which he had written on his own; and one of my favorites, a Rudyard Kipling poem that Jim had set to music, "Gunga Din." Also featured were "Coal Tattoo" from the documentary, "Steel Rail Blues" by Gordon Lightfoot, and "Charlie Green," a song Bob Knott thought was important for the album. For his family, Jim included "Hard-Hearted Hanna" and "Big Fat Woman," songs he had learned from listening to his dad's 78s. Also included were "The Blizzard" and "Running Maggie," which featured Karl's banjo picking, and "Until It's Time for Me to Go" by Buffy Sainte-Marie.

Jim wished I hadn't been away at school so I could sing on the album too. Instead, he asked me to design the cover. But at the last moment, Jim's father got a "deal" from the album presser on the record jacket. The background album cover was a gaudy coppery-gold with a garish chartreuse sticker that read "Facets by Jim Croce" in black print, hand-pasted almost in the center of the cover. Jim was appalled when he saw it. But in spite of the horrendous cover, Jim sold *Facets* for $5 each, and most of the albums sold the first week. They were all gone in a month.

Jim paid his father back, leaving us a $1,750 dowry.

"You did a good job, Jim," his father said. "But this is small time. It's not the same in the big league. The people in the entertainment world are thieves and worse. Don't get mixed up with them, Jimmy. That life is no good for you."

———

When I came home for spring break, we announced our wedding date of August 28, 1966, at our engagement party. I had been accepted to Moore College of Art in Philadelphia for the fall semester, and Jim and I planned to live in nearby Media.

During the months before the wedding, Jim took classes from Rabbi Louis Kaplan in preparation for his conversion. At the rabbi's encouragement, Jim candidly asked questions about Judaism. When I returned to my family's home in Wallingford after I completed my first year at RISD, Jim came over to tell me he discovered he had to go through a ceremonial circumcision that included a slight cut on his foreskin. He was in a panic. He walked around in a stupor for days prior to the ceremony, scared of the procedure.

The ritual took place at a ceremonial bath with other Jewish men as witnesses. Much to Jim's relief, the small cut healed overnight, and the next day he made love to me as a Jew.

Of all Jim's friends, only Sal openly discussed the conversion. Jim and Sal shared a bizarre sense of humor that often centered on each other's illness, misfortune, or embarrassment. This was Sal's turn.

"How was the *moil*?" Sal asked Jim after the ritual.

"I'll tell you, but let's never discuss it again," Jim said definitively. "It had to be one of the most embarrassing moments in my life, not to mention the scariest. First, I went to the baths and waited around for a group of male witnesses to check out my penis."

"That sounds like fun," Sal joked.

"I felt like I was going down to the River Ganges for phallic worship and, God forbid, the water. You know I've come close to drowning in every body of water I've ever been in. I was sure I would drown by submersion. But all they did was dip and cleanse me and say some Hebrew prayers. Then I had to go to the '*moil* department' and reenact my circumcision. I was expecting this big knife to come down on my dick. But out of the *moil*'s pocket came this dinky little knife. He pricked my penis, and it was all over. I was officially stamped kosher."

"Why did you do it, Jim?" Sal asked seriously. "You must love Ingrid a lot to take a chance with your dick."

"Ing had nothing to do with it," he protested. "I never was very good at being a Catholic with all the questions I have. And besides, the rabbi had a great record collection."

———

The weeks prior to the wedding, my father's health took a turn for the worse. In constant pain and bedridden much of the time, he could no longer hide the seriousness of his illness. Florence finally admitted to the family that he had cancer but, on the advice of his doctors, didn't divulge that it was terminal. The family was told that a new procedure performed at Mt. Sinai Hospital in New York City could cure him. In reality, the procedure would only help alleviate some of the pain. Unfortunately, the operation didn't work as well as they had hoped. Although his pain was temporarily lessened, it left him partially paralyzed.

Jim and I spent as much time with him as we could. When his condition worsened, he asked to see Jim alone.

"Jim," he said slowly, "you know how important education is to me. Will you do your best to help Ingrid stay in school?"

"Of course, Dad," Jim said. "I know that her art is as important to her as my music is to me. I promise I'll make sure she graduates."

———

In mid-August, just two weeks before the wedding, Jim's orders from the Army National Guard finally arrived. After a year and three months of waiting, he was now required to report to boot camp in Fort Jackson, South Carolina, just one week after we were to be wed. By this time, the United States had nearly 400,000 troops in Vietnam. And there were rumors that the National Guard might be called up soon.

We had planned to hold the wedding ceremony at my family's house in Wallingford, so my dad, who continued to weaken, could attend the ceremony. Jim wasn't sure whether his own parents would be there. After he'd revealed he was converting to Judaism, they had stopped speaking to him. He avoided their intense silent treatment by staying away from home as much as possible. After a couple of weeks of alienation, their relationship was terribly strained.

On the morning of the wedding, I had no one to help me dress. Upstairs in my room, alone and naked except for a pillbox hat, I was totally excited about marrying Jim but depressed about the brocade dress I had picked out with my stepmom at Loehman's Discount Department Store. I hadn't wanted a traditional wedding dress, but now, looking in the mirror, I frowned—until Jim's grinning face suddenly appeared in the reflection.

Startled, I turned. "Jim! What are you doing here? Don't you hate this dress? Isn't it just awful?"

"Here let me help you," he said, laughing as he pulled it away and dropped it on the floor. "Now, that's better. Just leave your hat on."

He frantically pulled off his wedding suit, and we fell on the bed laughing.

Minutes later, Rabbi Kaplan knocked on the door. "Ingrid, it's time to go over the ceremony."

I popped up, and Jim stifled his laughter in the pillow. "I'll be right down, Rabbi," I managed to say. I dressed hurriedly and ran down to meet Rabbi Kaplan, while Jim crept out of my room.

Jim and I stood in the gazebo in my parents' backyard as the music began. Suddenly Jim's parents appeared at the gate. My stepmother, Florence, whom I considered my second mother, welcomed them in. They stood uncomfortably on the side as the traditional Jewish wedding proceeded.

At the short reception that followed, my father thanked Jim's father and mother for coming. Rich had come too. My dad told them it meant a lot that they came. The strain on both families was still intense, and coupled with my dad's illness, the party was subdued and ended quickly.

Jim and I changed into jeans and threw one small suitcase and a guitar into the VW. We drove off eagerly to our honeymoon in Saint Augustine, Florida.

I didn't care where we were going as long as we were together. But Jim, the historian, was always interested in the olden times. On the drive down, he explained to me that on our wedding day in 1565, six hundred soldiers and settlers had come ashore at the site of the Timucuan Indian village of Seloy. It was founded forty-two years before the English colony at Jamestown, Virginia, and fifty-five years before the pilgrims landed on Plymouth Rock in Massachusetts. Banners were flying and trumpets were sounding when they went ashore and named their conquest Saint Augustine.

"It's the oldest settlement on the North American continent. Isn't that cool, Ing?"

"It's very cool," I told him. "I like when you tell me stories. Tell me some more—it's a long way to Florida."

For much of the way I drove, so Jim could play his guitar, and we could sing together. We were happy but felt the dark cloud looming: Jim had to leave for boot camp in less than a week.

He wanted to spend as much time in bed with me as he could. His sexual appetite was insatiable, and we managed two days of nonstop lovemaking until I finally protested.

"The only thing I'm going to remember from our honeymoon is the ceiling and the floor and the flashing neon pizza sign across the street. I can't do this anymore, Jim." I began to cry. "We can't make up for six months of your being away in only seven days!"

"I'm so sorry, Sweet Baby. I never want to hurt you. I love you so much, and here I am being an animal," he apologized. "Let me take you out for a nice dinner. How 'bout pizza?" he joked.

That night after dinner at a small romantic café, we took a long walk. Jim bought me my first pair of bell-bottoms, a pretty white blouse, and a discounted, heavy, navy-blue pea coat for winter.

The next night, when we were ready to dine, Jim said to me, "Please wear the new clothes I bought you, sweet thing. I like getting you S's, and you look so pretty in them."

"I love the outfit you bought me, sweetie, but the pants are way too long."

"I'll hem them for you," he said.

"Are you sure you know how?"

"Absolutely," he insisted. "Take a shower and get ready, and they'll be done when you are."

While I showered, Jim took a needle with dark blue thread and awkwardly began to sew my new blue-and-white striped bell-bottoms. The result of Jim's loving efforts was comical. My new pants were transformed into stovepipes. The basting of the thread was so tight I could barely get my foot through the pant leg. But Jim was so proud of his work he didn't notice. And eager to please my new husband, I just wore them anyway.

Three days later, we reluctantly returned to my parents' home in Wallingford. The following day the entire Croce clan of aunts, uncles, and cousins came over to the Croces' home to see Jimmy off to boot camp. He was even more distraught than I.

Rich drove us to the station.

"I've never seen you look so sad," I told Jim on the train platform.

"I'm going to make a terrible soldier," he lamented. "And how am I going to live without you, Ingrid?"

He stood silently holding my hand. When it was time for him to board, we hugged and kissed; then Jim shook his brother's hand and hugged him strongly. Jim slowly took a seat next to the window and waved forlornly as the train pulled away.

OPERATOR

JIM WAS MISERABLE IN BOOT CAMP. September in Fort Jackson was hot and humid. His stomach ached, his head pounded, and his body was covered with hives. Having to take orders irritated him. Worst of all, he yearned for home.

He could call me only once a week, but from the start he wrote every day, sometimes twice. The letters varied in length from a few quick lines to six-page sagas. Though the majority of correspondence to his family dwelled on his hateful experiences in boot camp, his letters to me were saturated with desire.

September 7, 1966

Dear Ing,

Here I sit in a deserted barracks, in love, lonely, yet certain of something deep within me that makes me feel better than anyone else. Here I lie in my saggy, broken bed, certain that your body waits for my touch to electrify it. Here I sit thinking. My mind dwells on each and every pleasure we've given each other—remember the night I gave you the jade ring? The night we danced in Sal's room while it snowed? The church parking lot? Each of these carries memories of a thousand pleasures all entwined in you.

Tonight it is getting cold and windy, but the memory of you is the fire within that keeps me warm. I love you very much.

Your husband,

Jim

When officers did allow "grunts" like Jim to call home, recruits lined up at the pay phone bolted to the side of the PX. He usually had to wait more than an hour in the long line, sometimes in the pouring rain, to make his call. He could hear other men ahead of him speak longingly with their loved ones back home. There were also the sad conversations, when some unfortunate soldiers learned that the "Dear John" letters they had received were true.

When it was Jim's turn one rainy September night, he pulled his raincoat over his head, cloaking his conversation.

"Yes, operator, I'd like to call collect to Ingrid. Would you put me through, please?"

"Sorry, the number is busy."

"Ah, geez, I only have a few minutes." He stalled for time, unwilling to give up the phone. "Hey, where are you from, operator? That accent sounds familiar."

"Philadelphia, sir."

"Me too," Jim explained. "It's a nice city. Sure beats Fort Jackson, South Carolina. I miss it. Wish I was there right now. Listen, would you mind trying one more time? I need to talk to my wife, and I've been waiting in line an hour to use this phone. We just got married, and I haven't seen her in a month!"

"Sure, sir . . ." In the background he heard faint clicks on the line.

"This is the operator with a collect call for Ingrid."

"This is Ingrid."

"Go ahead, please," said the operator.

"Ing, how are you? I miss you so much."

"I'm fine, sweetie. How's my sweet thing doing down there?"

"I hate it here, Ing! How the hell can we be separated and be expected to live? Today, thank God, I got a break. My truck driving paid off. The sergeant had me drive a truck all over Fort Jackson; it was easy, and I sure needed the break. I'm sore as hell from those exercises. Everybody is. Shit, this is worse than living at my parents' house."

"Oh, Jim, I'm so sorry you have to go through this. It sounds awful. But I want you to know I'm working really hard at school. I can't wait to show you my new work."

"I can't wait to see it, sweet thing. I wish we had more than three lousy minutes to talk." He looked at the second hand ticking by on his watch. "I just want you so much I can't stand it. Just know how much I love you and miss you."

I lowered my voice. "I love you, too, Jim. Don't worry, my love. We'll be together soon."

Someone rapped on the wall next to the phone, and Jim heard grumbling.

"Well, the guys behind me are getting restless. I'd better go. Remember to keep writing me. Good night."

Jim kept his word, and his letters kept coming every day. Although the letters were filled with longing and loneliness, his stories about life in the barracks reassured me that he hadn't lost his sense of humor:

October 3, 1966

Dear Ing,
Last night we snuck into a beer hall. We got back early, but some of the country boys stayed and ended up in a big brawl (massacre) with a bunch of Puerto Ricans. We could hear it two blocks away. One of the boys in our

barracks, a tobacco farmer with a wise look and one squint eye, lost four teeth. He sat on the porch saying, 'Gawd dayum, that old boy sure hit me, I reckon.'

I laughed myself to sleep. You wouldn't believe the people down here. I met one guy that doesn't have heat in his house. He just got emergency leave due to a death in his family. He's from Kentucky and his wife has 23 brothers and two sisters. REALLY, the army checked—his father-in-law was 82 years old—married four times to four sisters. This guy's wife's brothers were her cousins! It's unbelievable!

Write me soon.

Love,

Jim

When Jim arrived at boot camp he weighed 140 pounds, but within a few weeks he put on 20 pounds of muscle. His new body was one of the only positive aspects he could admit to in the entire experience. He hated the discipline that went along with it.

"The exercises are a ball-buster for me," he wrote, "especially since my whole platoon is composed of farmers who look at this as just a place to come to get out of shape."

"No kidding, Ing," he wrote in another letter, "this one guy is so strong he could stick his finger up his ass and hold himself up."

He lamented the strenuous regimen further to his brother:

October 8, 1966

Dear Rich,

Last night my sergeant got drunk and came over to me and said, "Croce, as strong as you are, why cain't you do those exercises?" (My sore shoulder kept me out for a while.) And I told him, "At least I'm not fat." He got pissed, I laughed, and man am I in the shithouse now. Then the other day we had to get our shots (for diseases). In moving down the line I was wincing (like everybody else), but I made the mistake of saying, "Goddam." Well, this S.O.B. with the smallpox needle said, "Do y'all cuss in Latin, boy?" then jabbed my arm for about 30 seconds straight, laughing with that goddamned redneck grin sayin', "That'll teach you to cuss in line."

Rich, never, never go into the Army, it's a needless pain in the ass.
Jim

Jim didn't take directions easily, not at home and not from his sergeant, a caustic loudmouth he described in a letter to me as looking like an "egg with teeth" and having the "mentality of a goat."

One afternoon, Jim tacked a sign on the bulletin board outside the mess hall:

"Half the Army reads comic books," it stated; "the other half just looks at the pictures." The sergeant rounded a corner and caught him.

"So you think you're a comedian, huh, Croce?" he asked, his voice rising in anger. "Well, not in my platoon. I guess I'll just have to let you suffer the consequences." He jabbed Jim in the chest with a forefinger and moved closer. He pressed his nose in Jim's face and shouted, "Kid, you've got an attitude problem! And guess what? You just flunked basic training!"

The sergeant reassigned him to Company D—the Dumbbell Platoon—where he had to start boot camp all over again.

Jim wrote to me about it on October 12:

I'm beside myself! I'm in the dumbbell platoon! It's like being sane and being put in an institution. That goddam Sgt. sent me here just to get a laugh! I went to the captain and said I passed all my tests and asked why I was being sent to Company "D." He just said that was one decision that all Sgts. can make unquestioned. I can't get out of here no matter what I do. I'm in a slow learner platoon. IT'S UNBEARABLE!"

Almost everyone in Company "D" is a college graduate. They're just messing with our minds. Some of these Sgts. are really unbalanced and the officers stick up for them. Our Sgt. kicked a boy in the head (with a helmet on) at the rifle range the other day. The boy's head rang for an hour. But the worst part is that this screws up our plans for you to come visit in a few weeks. My visit might be revoked. I miss you terribly.

I want you.
I love you,
Jim

His reassignment to the dumbbell platoon wasn't a complete disaster. His new sergeant, Leroy Brown, was a huge, swaggering black man with a shrewd sense of humor, and he enjoyed Jim's jokes. At Jim's prodding, he rapped nonstop in black street jive. Jim wrote to Rich about Sergeant Brown:

"He looks like Sonny Liston, Yesterday in joking around, (he's really nice), he said, 'Ahm Bad. You know where I lives all the bad people live on one street, and the further down you go the badder they is and I live two miles down that road. Now, I ain't saying Ahm bad, but when all them bad peoples get together, they all call me boss.'"

Fortunately, Sergeant Brown didn't believe Jim belonged in the dumbbell platoon and gave him a special pass for my visit. Elated, he wrote:

November 13, 1966

Dear Ingrid,
Where there's a will there's a way. I've succeeded in obtaining something which will answer our hopes and dreams. I've become one of the few men in the history of this company to get a semi-pass. Next weekend you can come down! I've made arrangements at the Port Guest House (about $1 a night) and I got permission from my Sgts. (they really feel sorry for me) to be with you Saturday night and Sunday 'til your plane leaves. I can't wait!
Love,
Jim

In spite of that glimmer of brightness, Jim hated everything about boot camp.

The only thing positive about it, other than his enhanced physique, was his new sense of independence and self-confidence. He even began to overcome his preoccupation with germs and diseases, in part because Sergeant "Egg with Teeth" had stopped allowing infirmary visits whenever Jim complained.

Jim expressed his growing skepticism of and disgust with the army in letters written the following month to Rich and me:

November 16, 1966

Dear Rich,
They really brainwash these young kids here. Everything is directed toward, 'being a man'. Go Airborne Ranger Special Forces, if you're good enough to get in. (Yet the statistics show that 67% of the Green Berets get killed in Vietnam.)

My new slogan is "Join the ranks of the civilians, if you're smart enough to get out."

Brother Jim

November 18, 1966

Dear Ing,

How can I like it here? Men talk of easy ways to kill. One of our sergeants said he'd killed men with rifles, pistols, his bare hands, and with a knife, then went into detail on what each method entailed. I've not heard a wise thing since I've been here.

Love,

Jim

November 20, 1966

Dear Richie,

I went for dinner in a little place in town that's supposed to be good. I had a half-decent chicken-fried steak, french fried potatoes and a brown lettuce salad. The guy next to me ordered spaghetti and meatballs. He got a plate of cold spaghetti with half of a hamburger and ketchup poured all over it. Can you believe it! There was a sign on the wall, sayin', 'This establishment reserves the right to refuse service to people detrimental to business.' It was dated one day after the passage of the Civil Rights Bill. A Negro is still a second-class citizen in the South. Yet, the owner came over to us and said, 'Soldiers, we close on Sunday in respect for God and Baptist traditions.'

It's a riot of incongruity down here.

November 21, 1966

Dear Richie,

It's not too bad down here—I haven't had the urge to run away recently. Oh yay! Everybody but about two of us went on pass last night. I stayed in. It was nice to be alone—no jingling 5,000 dog tags no squeaking bunks, (some

guys hitch-hike under the covers), no farts, no shaving cream in the face
while you sleep, nobody turning your bunk over while you're in it. It was
a treat.

See you,
Jim

———

The weekend before Thanksgiving, I finally flew to South Carolina to visit.

Confined to Company D, Jim couldn't leave the base, so Sergeant Brown picked me up at the airport in an army jeep. When we arrived on base, the sergeant parked at a drab green building that served as headquarters for Jim's unit. As I climbed out of the jeep, I noticed several men in army fatigues leering at me from under a tree. I searched among the soldiers for Jim but didn't see him. I noticed one soldier in the crowd waving at me, and it made me a little uncomfortable. Thank God I have an escort, I thought.

Suddenly, the waving soldier pushed through the crowd and jumped directly in front of me. Startled, I backed away and then recognized the grin and the eyes. "Jim!" But he didn't look at all like the Jim I knew. He seemed enormous and stood so straight. He was muscular and almost bald! This wasn't the skinny, gawky man I'd fallen in love with. His big, deep-sunken eyes looked even sadder than the day he had left.

I stood there, feeling shy and uncomfortable. Jim quickly took me by the hand and pulled me toward the Port Guest House, fifty yards away.

As we walked across the parking lot, other soldiers hooted and whistled. Jim grinned from ear to ear.

"I'm sorry the guest house is so seedy," he apologized. "But since I'm confined to base, this is our only choice." The moment we were through the door, he buried his face in my neck, kissing me hungrily and pulling at my blouse.

While I still had half of my clothes on, I insisted: "Wait, wait—please Jim, wait! I've missed you so much. And I've dreamed about being with you every day. But please slow down. This scares me!"

"Oh Ing, I'm so sorry. I'm being a goat. See what the army has done to me? I'm an animal!"

"I know how lonely you've been, sweetie. Some of your letters are so sad they make me cry. But even if we only have a little time to be together, I still need time to talk with you. I want to tell you about school, how different it is being a married woman, and about my dad. He doesn't look good, Jim. He really worries me. They say the operations are helping him, but I can't tell."

Jim sat down on the bed next to me. "I'm sorry Ing. I didn't mean to make you feel uncomfortable." He put his arms around me, and I pressed my head to his chest. "I couldn't help myself. But I'll try."

I tried to put aside my discomfort, and we held each other tight for several minutes until we both relaxed.

He listened to my stories about my dad, home, school, and visits I'd made to his family. He filled me in on his latest hardships. Then gently, he began to kiss my neck. He unbuttoned my blouse carefully and guided me back onto the bed.

"I guess we can talk in the morning." I sighed with pleasure as I unzipped his fatigues. "I need you so much, Jim. I can't tell you how much I've missed my best friend. And I've missed making love with you, too," I laughed. The rooms of the guest house were filled with other soldiers and their wives, girlfriends, or prostitutes. All night long, I heard a chorus of moans, thumps, and creaks from adjoining rooms.

Four days after I left, Jim wrote home to his family:

November 23, 1966

Dear Dad and Mom,

It's Thanksgiving eve and with a big pan of Ing's delicious brownies next to me, I sit down to write. Things were fine until yesterday, when I was selected with six other boys from our company (250 men) to be an honor guard and firing squad member at a military funeral.

This morning we left sharply dressed and proceeded to Manning, South Carolina, about 50 miles away. The dead soldier was one of three boys in a family currently in Vietnam. His body was accompanied home by his brother, a huge, stone-faced, bemedaled, Green Beret.

The small Negro community turned out in force. The little white-washed Baptist church was filled. The cemetery was in the back of the church. The ceremony was short and so sad that I'm at a loss to describe it. All of us stood at attention with tears in our eyes until we fired the volleys over his coffin.

Then the tears ran down my face. The flag was folded and given to his brother, who gave it to his mother. The people were so plain, so simple as only rural Southern people can be, that it added an extra note of tragedy to the whole funeral. Their grief was so deep, so real that everyone, even our Sgt., who's going to Vietnam in December, cried. The whole thing in Vietnam is just a waste. Of all the useless ways to go, in some rice-paddy. You'd be surprised how many Army people feel that way too. It's a shame. I can't wait to leave the Army life. As short a time as I've been here (compared to some of the other people) I still say I don't care for it. Even better I don't like it! But soon I'll be home for good. Then I can forget about this. I can't wait to see you all again. I miss home more and more each day and exist for Ing's letters. They keep me going.

Just thinking civil thoughts (like working) makes my night easy. The days are all the same. We run, run, then run some more. I've cleaned my rifle so many times only to have a young Lt. with a Christ complex find a grain of sand in an inaccessible place! I think I'd like to buy an army rifle someday just to fill it with sand and put it in the rain to rust. Now we spend our days shooting. From early to late, we shoot, and shoot and run. Well Mom and Dad, I'm going to go to sleep now I've had a rough day.

Take care of yourselves and have a nice Thanksgiving.

Love,

Your son,

Jim

Before starting boot camp, Jim had sent Tommy Picardo a cassette of his *Facets* album. Tommy had moved to New York City after graduating from Villanova a year before Jim, and he was establishing himself in the music business as a jingle singer and upstart producer.

While Jim was in Fort Jackson, stranded from his music, Tommy was working at Command Records, a subsidiary of Paramount. Tommy's letter encouraged Jim:

At Ease:

I've held off writing to you because I think I have good news. The 'Clique' (that's what we call ourselves now) will have a record out within the next ten days. It will be on Laurie Records, and A side will be "Drifter's Medley." . . . Now here's where you come in, I figured it would do your morale some good if "Sun Come Up" could be included, so we recorded it . . . Naturally you'll receive writing credit. The song will be published by myself and Marty Foglia (Martrick Music). The best thing that could happen . . . Columbia heard our version and wants it for The Brothers Four. If it can be arranged, after our version comes out, maybe I'll work out a deal to see they receive and record it. If they do, maybe you won't have to work at all.

Sweeter words could not have been written. "You won't have to work at all." Jim read them again and again. He trusted his friend to take care of business for him.

> . . . *Enclosed are the contracts, which you should sign and send one [sic] back to me as soon as possible. I'll have records done within two weeks . . . Work on new material. If the Drifter Medley clicks, we'll be doing another session soon, and you know I'll push to record your stuff*
> *Get hot, and take care,*
> *Tom*

As Jim endured his final weeks at boot camp, I spent much of my time with my father. My stepmom and I took turns caring for him. He was embarrassed to need our assistance in changing position to alleviate the pressure on his bedsores. Most humiliating, he had lost control of his bowels. I hated seeing my father so helpless; he had always been my strength.

One evening, while I was gently cleaning him, to alleviate our mutual self-consciousness I talked about my art classes, the latest letter from Jim, and the house Jim and I would rent when he returned.

As I talked, my father's eyes filled with tears. Suddenly I too was flooded with emotion. My dad had always hidden his problems from me, but now the physical and emotional pain had exhausted him. I saw a vulnerable side of him I had never known before. When I'd finished helping him, I carefully leaned over the bed and held him.

"You and Jim are my best friends," I confided. "I don't know what I'd do without you."

He looked very tired. He whispered, "I'm so glad you and Jim have each other. I love you, Ingrid."

I had prayed that he would get well. But at that moment, and for the first time, I wasn't sure he would. Although he had been weakening every day, I didn't want to believe his illness was terminal. Before the cancer, he had never missed a day of work. This isn't fair, I thought. We've only had three years since my mother died. We both deserve more than this. After all, Florence told me he would get better. I wanted to believe it was true. I told him I loved him too and, through my tears, thanked him for everything.

———

As Jim's release date from boot camp neared, I searched in earnest for a house to rent. After scanning ads and driving all over town, I went to a real estate agent in Media near my family's home in Wallingford, forty miles west of Philadelphia.

Both Jim and I had always enjoyed the historical town's quiet atmosphere and heard it had reasonable rents. One street we liked in particular was West Front Street, with its tree-lined brick sidewalks and slim three-story town houses that were over 150 years old.

I asked the agent about renting there.

Sizing me up, he said, "I can't believe you're old enough to take out a lease. Anyway, there isn't a house available in that area."

I took my marriage certificate and driver's license out of my purse to prove my status and age. The agent pursed his lips and studied them. Serendipitously, a young man came into the office and dropped a set of keys on the desk. "For 12 West Front Street," he said.

"I'll take it!" I cried out.

The agent replied sarcastically, "You don't even know how much it's renting for or what it looks like." But I was persuasive, and though he was reluctant, he escorted me to the historic house.

It was located on the plaza next to law offices and across from the old courthouse. The rent was $100 a month. I wrote a check on the spot, signed the lease, and then rushed home.

Florence met me at the door. "Your father has just been taken to the hospital in an ambulance," she said. "He isn't doing well."

Swallowing my excitement about the house, I went inside quietly, trying to take in what my stepmother had said. It didn't sound good. Yet the doctors had been so reassuring all along, and my father had an iron will to live. I wanted to rush to the hospital but was told I would have to wait.

The following day I tried to lift my stepmother's spirits by taking her to 12 West Front Street before we went to see my dad in the hospital.

"I can't wait for Daddy to visit our home," I said as I guided Florence up the steep steps to the second floor. She stopped on the landing.

"Ing, he'll never see this house." Her voice broke.

"What do you mean?"

"He's dying, Ingrid," Florence said softly.

I caught my breath.

"But he went to New York for treatment!" I yelled. "Why didn't you tell me?"

"The doctor told me not to tell anyone," my stepmother admitted in a whisper. "He has only a few more days to live."

I picked up the phone and called Dan Mason, my father's friend and physician, and he helped me to get Jim home immediately.

———

On emergency leave, Jim arrived at my father's bedside with me within twenty-four hours of my contacting him. In extreme pain and under heavy sedation, my dad struggled to sit up when he saw Jim and me come into the room. He held my hand and managed a weak smile as Jim related some anecdotes about the army.

"I love you both," he told us. The following day, my father passed away.

Jim's parents attended the funeral.

"I'm glad I got the chance to know Sid before he died," Jim's father told his son after the funeral. "I went to visit with Sid a few times while you were away. What a good man he was. I will miss him," he said with tears in his eyes. What Jim's father didn't say was that talking to my father had helped him understand his son and himself better. Although he still didn't approve of Jim's conversion to Judaism, his anger had diminished.

Later that day I told Jim, "I can't believe he's gone. It still feels like he's here with me. My dad was the most important person in my life. He taught me to believe in myself. Thank God I have you."

Jim held my head to his chest and took a deep breath. For the first time he sensed his responsibility as the head of the household. He wanted to do the right thing, to care for me, and to be there for my stepmom and the children when they needed him.

"I need to be closer to you, Ing. I've got to find a way to get a transfer," he said. "I don't want to leave you alone, not even a couple of months."

With the help of Dr. Mason, Jim received a transfer to Fort Dix, New Jersey, only an hour's drive from our rented house in Media. There he worked on gaining a hardship discharge, which the army approved two months later. On March 3, 1967, Jim was released to the National Guard Reserves. He was still obligated to attend monthly Guard meetings but was free to go home.

Reunited with me at last, Jim got back his old part-time job selling radio airtime to black merchants in Philadelphia's inner city. His determination to be serious was exemplified by his new business style of dress. "I got me a new suit, a new tie, and

I even went out and got myself a pair of those funky black shoes, those ones with the funny little holes punched out of them," he joked.

After a short time at the job, Jim was promoted to translating commercials into the language of soul.

"I'd sell airtime to Bronco's Poolroom, and then write the spot. Something along the lines of a James Brown refrain, 'You wanna be cool, you wanna shoot pool (dig it),'" he told an interviewer years later.

To supplement our income, since I was busy studying at Moore College of Art, he also worked as a substitute teacher at Palansky Junior High in a rough neighborhood in the small, industrial city of Chester, Pennsylvania. Most students he taught in special education had either learning disabilities, police records, or both. Jim used to joke that he "taught in the only grammar school anywhere where half the pupils had draft deferments." At the same time, his old friend Sal was teaching special education at another school in South Philly. He and Jim often got together to try to top each other's stories.

"One day I walked into class wearing a new suede coat," Sal said. "So I asked my class if anyone knew where suedes came from. None of them knew. So I told them suedes were small rodents, like rats, that lived in the nearby Tinicum Swamp. I even took them on a field trip to the swamp. I had them wading through that polluted, murky water, searching for suedes."

"Shit, Sal," Jim said, shaking his head. "How many did you lose?"

"I can't tell. Attendance is always low. But for weeks afterwards the kids would go by the swamp after school looking for suedes." Sal laughed. "When they couldn't find them, I told them the suedes were probably migrating."

Although he had always shunned hard work, Jim was doing great juggling his jobs and still finding time to play music.

Each morning he rose early and brought me a cup of espresso in bed, just as his father had done for his mother. Then I made breakfast, and he took me to catch the train to Philadelphia for school. In between substitute teaching and radio work, he shopped and prepared elaborate dinners. He always made sure our evening meal was ready before he picked me up at the train station.

After dinner, Jim would play his guitar and light up a joint, a practice he'd begun at boot camp. I was uneasy with Jim's indulgence.

"Don't worry, Ing: smoking grass isn't addictive," he said. "It's safer than drinking. Everybody does it." I wasn't convinced but let it go. While he played and we sang together, I washed the huge stacks of dishes, pots, and pans he had used preparing our meal.

As soon as he was discharged from the army, we resumed playing at the Riddle Paddock several nights a week, from 8 until midnight. Not only did Jim get the chance to try out new material, but we also began to develop our social life as a newly married couple.

By 1 or 2 in the morning, we'd crawl into bed exhausted.

Our house at 12 West Front Street soon became a gathering place for artists and musicians in the area. Friends came over to our place for home cooking and to listen or join in while Jim and I sang. Around that time, a young student who had met Jim at Villanova visited us to jam and play some of his new material. His name was Don McLean.

"Starry, Starry Night" and "American Pie" were among the acclaimed songs Don would later compose, but back then he was a young student seeking feedback and intelligent criticism. Jim became somewhat of a mentor to Don, who eagerly sought his approval.

Along with many other musicians, Don would drop by the house to jam, trade songs, and speculate on how to get an album deal. Some, like Don, were interested in making music their career but weren't sure how to get started.

At the same time, I set up a gallery in our home called "The Hundred Little Pot Shop." I constructed a window box to display one hundred miniature pots that demonstrated the different glazes and shapes of my pottery.

I also sold my paintings off the wall. Jim was creative with his hands too. On one wall hung unusual works of leather—"Little Uglies," he called them—purses, wallets, and belts Jim had created. He wasn't sure whether to be proud or embarrassed by their crude appearance and unsophisticated design.

When we could, we sold our work. What wasn't sold would usually end up as a gift or an S for someone special to us.

Several afternoons a week, after class, Janice, age ten, and Kenny, now nine, walked over to our house. They attended a private Quaker school in the neighborhood and enjoyed visiting Jim, who sang for them and told stories of his most recent teaching escapades. Jim was their surrogate father and rarely put off seeing them, in spite of his heavy schedule. He felt he owed it to my dad, but he also truly loved them and wanted to help them get a good start in life.

During the summer of 1967, Jim and I accepted jobs at the Lighthouse, a camp for children who faced challenges: some came from disadvantaged homes, and some had disabilities.

Many of the campers came to Jim with rigid classical training and played music by rote. Some of them were close-minded to any music other than classical.

"I know they don't play the guitar like this in the orchestra," Jim would tell them, "but the guitar and the style of music I perform do have a great place in our history. Listen to this song by a man named Woody Guthrie. It's called, 'Click, Clack, Open Up the Door, Boys.'" He would start tapping his foot and deftly picking the strings. With a sly, funny grin he looked at each of the children until they smiled, and only then would he begin to sing.

In ceramics, I taught the campers to make coil pots and how to attach slabs of clay with slip. The pottery the children made was charming and very creative. They seemed to have a great experience and were proud of the work we displayed at the end of the summer. I was also thrilled to teach several young blind children who could see more with their hands than some sighted children did with their eyes.

In time, with perseverance and imagination, Jim managed to spark interest and get a laugh from even his most serious-minded kids. He prepared an act as a one-man band, adding more instruments and sounds as needed to impress and surprise his young students. Jim was determined to use his music to communicate. And by the end of the summer he felt he had been successful. Some of the campers asked if they could take private guitar lessons from Jim.

When camp was over, we were both asked to return as camp counselors for the following year.

In the fall, when I was a junior at Moore College of Art, Jim returned to teach at Palansky Junior High. Three days into the new school year he was offered a full-time job teaching special education.

"It's no coup," he told me. "Fourteen other teachers have quit this position within the first three days! The class is supposed to be uneducable. I don't think the administrators expect me to last either."

On his first day in class, only eighteen of the thirty students on the roster appeared.

Even though they were in junior high, most had flunked several times, and some of the seventeen- and eighteen-year-olds were well over six feet tall. Jim admitted to me that he was intimidated by them, but he knew he couldn't show it.

"You wouldn't believe it, Ing," he said one evening over dinner at the end of his first couple weeks at school. "They need a referee, not a teacher, to handle these kids. Today, I tried to break up a fight between two of my girl students, Wanda and Joyce. Wanda is a promiscuous fifteen-year-old, and Joyce Elizabeth Taylor Carter-Potter-Brown must outweigh me by at least 150 pounds. She knocked me to the ground. Then Wanda, the little over-sexed one, comes and presses up against me sayin', 'Jim, I had me a black baby last year. How 'bout you makin' me a white one this year?'

"I told her, 'Be nice now, Wanda. You know I can't do that. Besides, don't I teach you to do your history and geography so you can go to high school next year? You don't want another baby, do you, Wanda?' and she pouted and strutted on her way.

"Then Joyce shoved me back against the wall, and said, 'Well, fuck ya, then!'"

Later that month, a seventeen-year-old cross-dresser named Harold showed up at school wearing a dress, packing a pistol, and proclaiming he had come to "kill Mr. Croce."

For more than a week, Harold had been promising Jim, "I'm gonna kill you, man," but Jim hadn't taken the threat seriously. Then one day, in a burst of violence, Harold tore down a thick wooden fire door to the entrance of the school, searching for his teacher. Jim was alone in his classroom, and over the loudspeaker he heard the principal saying, "Mr. Croce! Mr. Croce! Lock your door! Harold has a gun. He's looking for you!"

Jim locked his door, but that afternoon when he met up with Sal to swap stories, he was still tense.

"They got Harold before he got me," he said, after relating the whole incident to Sal. "In the first three weeks I've had my tires slashed five times and the driver's door of my VW bashed in. My car has so many dents in it now, we call it the Raisin. Ing and I spray-painted it basket brown last week to kinda hide the dents, but I don't know how long I can take this."

———

One morning, Jim put his guitar case in the car.

"Are you going to play at school?" I asked as I climbed in the passenger side.

"Yeah, I'm gonna try somethin' new," he said. "If I can get the kids to pay attention to the songs they like, maybe I can teach them to read. It's worth a try."

"That's a great idea," I said.

"Yeah," Jim said laughing. "And next week I'm gonna give them a math lesson. Teach them long division. I'll bring in Italian bread, salami, cheese, and peppers and see how long it takes them to make a sandwich. Then I'll have them do the math, and if they figure it out, we'll have a party." Jim paused as he maneuvered the car through traffic.

I GOT A NAME: THE JIM CROCE STORY

"Did you know," he continued, "according to my class, Camden and Willowgrove, New Jersey, were part of the thirteen original colonies? Ing, we've finally found people who know less about geography than you do."

"Yeah," I said grinning, "but just don't teach them the way you taught me!"

We pulled into the parking lot of the train station. I gathered my books and portfolio and leaned over to kiss him good-bye.

"Keep up the good work. You're doing a great job with those kids. Just don't get killed while you're doin' it."

"Well," he said, before pulling away from the curb, "I think they're liking me more now. Yesterday a kid named Maurice, who never really talked to me before, came up in the hall and asked, 'Mr. Croce, who do you like better, your wife or your woman?' I said, 'Hey, wait a minute, Maurice, I'm a married man.' He gave me a blank look. 'I know you're married,' he said, 'but all men have their women.' And I told him, 'Maurice, my wife is my woman.' He shook his head in disappointment. 'Jim,' he told me, 'it's a mighty poor rat only got one hole.' And the little guy strutted back down the hall."

"That's quite an education they're giving you," I laughed.

That morning in class, Jim handed out copies of sheet music to songs by the Drifters, the Supremes, and other Motown groups. Even though the students were functionally illiterate, they studied the pages with an interest he hadn't seen before. The singing went well. One girl smiled shyly when she proudly proclaimed at the end of class that she could now spell "I love you, baby" and get every letter right.

That night Jim told me about his success with a new sense of enthusiasm. "I heard administration doesn't like me bringing my guitar to school," he said, "but they're not saying a thing for fear I'll quit. I hope next year something happens with our music before they fire me."

———

In the spring, I received a fellowship to study painting and ceramics for a semester anywhere in the world. Jim and I talked it over, and I chose San Miguel de Allende in southwestern Mexico. Its ceramics program had an excellent reputation, and Mexico was inexpensive. The $1,000 award seemed like a fortune to us. Based on the budget I put together, Jim would be able to join me for two months of the trip. I paid our bills, bought the plane tickets, registered at the school, and still had spending money left over for the trip.

Mexico excited me. I had never been outside the United States before. But I was unhappy that the art program began at the end of May, more than a month before Jim would be finished teaching. He was apprehensive about his bride traveling without him and being in Mexico alone for a month. I finally talked my closest friend, Deborah Warner, into accompanying me and insisted on buying her ticket.

The two of us flew to Acapulco for the weekend before classes started.

The day we arrived, we sat down at a juice stand near the beach and ordered a tropical fruit drink.

Two young Mexican men approached.

"Are you ladies from the United States?" the tallest one asked in good English. He wore a crisp blue shirt and cardigan sweater. "My name is Miguel. And yours?"

"I'm Deborah," my friend replied. "And yes, we're from the East Coast."

"I'm Daniel," the other man added, smiling broadly. "We're students at the University of Mexico. Are you studying down here?" He, too, was also impeccably dressed and had a cute, boyish look.

"I'm here on a scholarship to study art for the summer," I explained in Spanish. I had studied the language in high school and spoke well enough to make conversation.

"*Bien!*" Daniel replied. "You can practice your Spanish, and I'll practice my English."

"Hey, would you like to go and watch the cliff divers perform?" Miguel asked. "You won't want to miss it if you've never seen them before."

"Thanks for asking, but I'm married," I said.

"That's okay—this isn't a date," Daniel replied. "Just a little Mexican hospitality."

"Well . . . I don't know." I looked away, embarrassed.

"Ah, come on!" both students pleaded.

Deb shrugged her shoulders.

"Why not?" she asked happily.

"Alright," I agreed, naïvely. I liked the idea of a Mexican tradition, and I wanted to see and learn all I could about Mexico.

Both Deb and I enjoyed the divers' precision and grace, and found our student escorts to be perfect gentlemen. On the way back to the hotel, we stopped at a seaside café for dinner.

"Wow, isn't this beautiful," I said as we got out of the car. "Look at that amazing sunset!" I wished Jim could be with me to share the romantic nightfall. The colors of the sky were magnificent, and Acapulco was a paradise.

The café was filled with American tourists and Mexican students, all fueled on rum and tequila.

"Try the specialty of the house," Miguel suggested. "It's rum, mango, and lime. You'll love it!"

"Oh, I don't drink," I told him. But he insisted, and the beverage was so delicious I drank it quickly before our food arrived. I rarely drank liquor, and felt dizzy and sick right away. "Excuse me," I said. "I'll be right back." I asked the hostess where the restroom was.

"*Afuera*," the woman said, pointing outside. "*Por alla.*"

I walked several hundred feet out onto the beach. I felt queasy, but the cool night air helped me get my bearings. I used the toilet, splashed water on my face, and combed my hair. When I came out of the restroom and walked back across the beach toward the restaurant, before I knew what happened, someone grabbed my shoulders from behind and, overpowering me, threw me violently to the ground. With one hand, he covered my mouth, pinning my head. With the other, he yanked my skirt up to my waist, then fell over me from behind. All the breath was crushed out of my chest. He dropped his trousers and forcefully raped me. Gasping for breath, speechless and powerless, I was no match for his size and weight. Scrambling to his feet, he disappeared into the night.

I lay motionless, my heart and head throbbing. Terrified, I opened my mouth, trying to scream, but no sound came out. I forced myself to sit up and brushed the gritty sand off of my face, chest, and arms. Horror and anguish engulfed me. Oh God! I thought. I can't believe this happened to me. I held my stomach. Tears rolled down my dirty cheeks. I thought of Jim and was suddenly filled with shame. Slowly I got to my feet and walked back to the restaurant. Still stunned, I headed inside, eager to just grab Deb and get back to the hotel.

Within a few feet of the table, I knew my assailant was sitting there. Daniel stared at me, forcing back a grin.

"Hey, what took you so long?" he asked.

I wanted to scream but felt paralyzed.

"Let's go, Deb," I managed to say. I wanted to heave in repulsion. Deborah sensed the urgency.

"Okay," she said.

"Why so suddenly?" asked Miguel.

"They must need to get their beauty sleep." Daniel laughed.

"We'll call a taxi," I said.

"No, come on," Miguel insisted. "We'll drive you back." He got to his feet.

I leaned against Deborah.

"What's wrong?" she whispered. I couldn't reply.

116

The students drove us back to our hotel and let us out. The minute I got to my room I bolted for the bathroom and threw up. Frightened and angry, I lay trembling on my bed.

I was furious this man had raped me and then acted so cavalier. At the same time I wondered if it wasn't my fault. If we hadn't gone to see the divers and then out for dinner with these students, it wouldn't have happened, I told myself.

Finally, vacillating between feelings of rage and guilt, I fell asleep. I dreamed a dream that had haunted me ever since the court forced me at the age of eight to move from my father's home to my mother and grandmother Mary's apartment in Center City.

In the dream, I'm in an alley on Savoy Street, behind the Rittenhouse Claridge apartments, where we lived. It's very dark and very late at night. Suddenly a man jumps out from the shadows and comes after me. I'm running away, and I try to scream, but no sound comes out, no matter how hard I try. I keep running and trying to get help, but I never get to the end of the dream without waking up—until that night in Mexico.

I woke up scratching myself all over my body and intuitively jumped out of bed. I looked over at Deborah, who was already on her way to the bathroom down the hall, saying that there were bedbugs everywhere. We ran to the showers, where we stayed the rest of the night, huddled on the hard floor.

My body was full of welts and scratch marks, but all I thought about, while lying there in the corner of the shower, was Jim. *How could I ever explain this to my husband?* I thought. I didn't say a word about the attack to Deborah. And I was too ashamed and frightened to report the rape to the Mexican authorities.

All at once, every man in Mexico, including the police, seemed threatening. I didn't know whom I could trust. Confusion overwhelmed me. I decided not to tell Jim right away, not until I had had time to sort things out in my own mind. The next morning Deborah and I caught the first bus to San Miguel.

Although the routine of school helped me not to think about the attack every waking moment, I lived in anguish. I wanted to explain everything to Jim, but not over the phone or in a letter. Before he was scheduled to arrive, I wanted to be certain I wasn't pregnant. Right before Jim came, I had a test performed at a local doctor's office. The results arrived: I wasn't pregnant and had not contracted a venereal disease. Relieved, I resolved to tell Jim exactly what had happened when he arrived that week.

Jim flew to Mexico City with Deborah's boyfriend, Bill. We met them at the airport Saturday morning, and the four of us spent the weekend touring Mexico City.

"Being away from you has been awful," Jim said, hugging me as we walked to the car on Sunday to head to San Miguel. "I'm so glad we're finally together. I never want to be without you again."

"Me too," I said in a whisper.

"What's wrong, sweet thing?" Jim asked. "You don't seem yourself."

"I'm okay, Jim."

"No, something's different. Aren't you feeling well?"

"I'm fine, really," I insisted. My stomach churned at the thought of telling Jim the truth. "I'll be fine," I said, trying to drop the subject. Once we reached San Miguel, I knew I had to tell him everything.

He had always been extremely jealous and possessive, but as much as I dreaded his response, I had to be honest with him. I prayed he would be understanding but feared how it might hurt him and our relationship.

That night, I refused sex.

"What's the matter, Ing? We've been separated more than a month, and you don't even want to make love to me. Don't you love me anymore?"

"I'm just tired, sweetie. You know how much I love you. We can be together in the morning." I turned my back to him, and he cuddled up to me and held me through the night.

The next morning, I haltingly told him the story. He initially reacted with detached curiosity. Like a reporter, he pressed for all the details. Quietly, he listened very closely to each response and then prodded me on. Slowly his demeanor changed.

"Why were you with those Mexican guys in the first place?" he demanded. "How stupid could you be to go with them? You were just asking for it! You put yourself in such a damn stupid position! You've ruined everything! You're a whore!" he shouted. "An adulteress!"

I tried to tell him that I didn't do anything wrong, that I was raped. It wasn't my fault. But he stepped toward me and slapped me across the face. I recoiled, sobbing. His face filled with pain and hatred, and he stormed out of the room.

WHAT DO PEOPLE DO?

THE SUMMER IN MEXICO took its toll on Jim and me. When we returned for my senior year at Moore in the fall of 1968, I was still in pain and knew Jim was hurting too. He manipulated our conversations, constantly shifting the attention away from our problems. His judgments and almost quarrelsome lovemaking left me feeling ashamed, alone, and ugly. I wanted to get counseling, but Jim refused.

One morning, after taking a shower to get ready for class, I walked naked from the bathroom into the bedroom as I always did.

"What the fuck is the matter with you?" Jim demanded. "Don't you see those guys trimming trees right outside the window? What are you trying to do, get them up here too?"

I was stunned and struggled to ignore his accusation. His behavior seemed cruel, and it was growing more unbearable with each new incident. He was considerate and supportive one moment and then turned scathing the next. What had once been erotic to him was now tainted. It was obvious he blamed me for the rape and considered me branded with a capital *A*.

That night, while we were eating dinner, the phone rang. Jim grabbed it.

A familiar voice made its way through the long-distance haze. "It's Tommy. I've been trying to reach you. Where you been?"

"Oh," Jim replied with a sigh, "Ing and I just got back from a couple of months in Mexico, and I'll tell ya, my stomach wasn't right the whole time. I got Montezuma's Revenge, with the runs so bad I couldn't make it from the hotel to the taxi cab. It was embarrassing as hell."

"That's very funny, Jimmy."

"Yeah, about as funny as a monkey fucking a football. So what's going on with you? How's Pat doin'?"

"Pat's fine," Tommy said flatly; then his voice lifted. "Hey, I'm working on a Coke campaign now and a few other things. It's not bad money. It'll bring in about $50,000 this year with residuals."

"That's incredible, Tommy. I didn't know you could make that much bread singin' oohs and ahhs."

"I wish I could get you in on this too, Jimmy, but it's cliquish. Mostly the same twenty to thirty studio singers get to do all the big commercials. And I'm just starting, but I'm working on some pretty big accounts."

"Sounds like it," Jim said. Tommy always downplayed issues of significance. By comparison, Jim felt he must have been doing something wrong if Tommy could make that much just singing backup.

"Listen, I've set aside some money from my job at ABC. I met some guys there, and we've put together a little company to produce an album or two. We need some talent. I thought maybe you could come to New York, and I could help you out."

"Oh, I don't know," Jim said. "Ingrid's just back at school, and I'm . . . well . . ."

But he couldn't resist the glimmer of opportunity. "Ya know, maybe we could come up and check things out."

"Good—how about this Friday? You guys can stay at our apartment."

"Ah, okay . . . ah sure, we'll see you then. We'll call before we come."

Jim hung up and headed toward the refrigerator. "That was Tommy," he said, reaching for a beer. "He wants us to come to New York and stay with him and Pat. It'll be fun to spend some time away. What do you think?"

"I have so much work to do for school this weekend, and I was really hoping we could spend some time alone, just talking."

"Sounds fun."

"Jim, I'm not saying we can't go, but we really do need to talk about all this. It's been over two months since the attack, and we have to get our feelings out in the open. We can't keep being miserable like this."

"Come on. Don't be so serious—it's not that bad. Anyway, Tommy wants us to come up to New York. He's formed a new company, and they want to make an album with us! This could be our chance."

"Tommy doesn't give a damn about my singing, Jim, you know that."

"Well, I do! And besides I like singing better than talking anyway."

"Well, that's a fact. But please, Jim, just listen to me. I promise you: I didn't do anything wrong. It wasn't my fault. But when you look at me, I feel like you think it was."

"Ing, please, let's not get into this again. Listen, I've got this new song I want you to hear." He went and got his guitar and brought it back to the table.

I sighed heavily, wishing I could just scream at him for changing the subject, for playing music every time I wanted to talk things through, for shutting me out.

Damn it! I thought. *What can I do to make him open up and talk to me?* My heart sank. There was a distance in our relationship now that I didn't know how to bridge. I hated myself for what had happened to me and hated Jim for what he was allowing to happen to us.

While he picked out the melody to the new tune, I was deep in thought: *Was it my fault? Did I subconsciously lead my attacker on, the way I saw my mother taunt men?*

Then my thoughts turned to the opportunity Tommy had just offered us. Like Jim, Tommy related to people through music, but he seemed to have even less capacity than Jim to express his feelings in conversation. Though I wasn't looking forward to spending time with Tommy in New York, I wanted Jim to be happy. Maybe things would be better if Jim could finally devote time to his music. I was willing to do whatever it took to get back to where we were before Mexico.

"Okay, Jim, let's go to New York Friday. I want you to have the chance to make this record. And besides, I really like Pat. I wonder how she's doing and if she's still singing."

Jim put down his guitar, got up, and came over to hug me. "Thanks, Ing. This means a lot to me."

———

I bought a new top for the trip to New York and wore one of my two pairs of tight-fitting jeans. While I was checking myself out in the mirror, Jim complimented me on how pretty I looked, how sexy, but I wasn't comfortable with the "sexy" comment. Was he being honest, or was he mocking me?

The New Jersey Turnpike was a monotonous road with uninspiring industrial towns most of the way.

"Jim," I said, looking up at his eyes, which were transfixed on the road. "I feel so alone. What can I do to make you forgive me, to make you talk to me like you used to?"

"There's nothing wrong."

"Nothing wrong . . . I can feel how angry you are when you look at me sometimes, even when you make love to me."

"Oh, you know you like making love as much as I do, Ing."

"I do, Jim, but you're obsessed with it, and you're forceful, like you're trying to punish me!" I was spilling out my feelings, but I couldn't help it.

"That's bullshit!" He glared at me. "I said there's nothing to discuss."

I recoiled and swallowed hard to hold back tears.

Several minutes passed.

"Jim, can we please get counseling?" I asked cautiously. He didn't answer.

"If my father was here, you'd talk to him. Wouldn't you? Come on, Jim—you studied psychology. You know this won't just work its way out. Please talk to me."

He changed the radio station.

Miles and minutes passed before he broke the silence.

"Don't worry," he said. "We're going to have a great time this weekend. We'll go to the Village to Ferrara's for some cannoli and espresso and to the Bitter End. Maybe we can sit in with Bob Dylan," he joked. "I wonder who's playing there this weekend?"

"I don't care who's playing there, Jim. All I care about is us. You know that once we get with Tommy, all you'll do is music."

"That isn't true, Ing. We'll eat too."

"Please stop avoiding me. Please talk to me."

"I can't, Ingrid! Don't you get it? I can't." He turned up the radio loud, shutting down the conversation. A little over an hour later, he maneuvered the old VW through Manhattan's West Side.

Tommy's office building was at 40 West 55th Street, right in the center of the city. Jim was impressed. Tommy really was doing well if he could afford to have an office and an apartment in Manhattan. We went up to the fifth floor and were met by the receptionist, who looked up from her typewriter when we stepped off the elevator.

"Hi. How ya doin' today?" The blond receptionist, chewing her gum loudly, greeted us with a heavy New Jersey accent.

"We're good, and how about you?" Jim smiled. "We're here to see Tommy Picardo—oh, I mean, Tommy West." He smiled again.

"Oh, you must be Jim and Ingrid. I'm Joni, the secretary. Tommy told me you were comin'."

She buzzed Tommy's office and then told us, "I'll take you back."

We followed Joni through a maze of offices. Jim had expected Tommy to have a broom-closet–sized office somewhere and was surprised at how spacious it was. Tommy got up from behind a huge desk. He wore bright new jeans and an Oxford button-down shirt, starched to perfection. He extended a hand.

"Hey, Jimmy. Thanks for coming up."

Tommy was only a year older than Jim, but his demeanor and Manhattan surroundings made him seem almost ten years his senior. His thick, short, curly hair was meticulously cut and fingernails freshly manicured. As Jim stood there in his faded clothes and home-cut hair, I couldn't help noticing how "establishment" Tommy seemed in contrast to Jim.

"Sure, man," he said, and shook Tommy's hand. "Looks like you're doing pretty well for yourself."

"Yeah, things are good. I just got back from a trip to the West Coast with my business associates. We met some artists who want us to produce them. We also went down to Nashville to talk to Bobby Goldsboro. Remember Goldsboro? He had that hit 'See the Funny Little Clown' and 'Honey,' that came out pretty recently."

"Yeah, I know who Bobby Goldsboro is. And you're going to produce him?"

"Yeah," Tommy said. "Well, at least we're thinking about it."

"Who's 'we'? How many partners do you have?"

"Three—well, kinda four. Come on," he said, finally acknowledging me with a glance. "You can meet them too." He led us out to one of his partners' offices. "Hey, Phil, I want you to meet my old Villanova buddy, Jim Croce."

Phil Kurnit's office was lined with vintage mahogany bookcases packed with law books. Boxes of papers were stacked everywhere.

"Phil's our attorney. He used to do the contracts for ABC Paramount. That's where we all met."

Phil looked up through dark-rimmed thick eyeglasses that were gigantic for his face. "Heard a lot about you and your music, kid," Phil said with a strong New Jersey accent. He forced a thin-lipped grin as he stood up from behind his desk.

He was about five-foot-five and a good twenty pounds overweight. Again, although Phil was only three or four years older, Jim thought he looked like somebody's middle-aged parent.

"It's Elmer Fudd," he whispered to me as we walked over to shake Phil's hand.

Phil looked at me with a big crooked smile and said with a patronizing tone, "I understand that you can sing too?" and then he winked.

Keeping my eyes on him, I nodded cautiously. Attorneys made me feel uneasy. I learned early on that they rarely meant what they said. Having spent a decade of my childhood in the middle of my parents' custody battle, with promises that I could live with my father that never proved true, I didn't trust lawyers. I instinctively felt suspicious of Phil Kurnit.

Tommy escorted us all down the hall to Terry Cashman's office. As we entered the office, Terry was talking with the third partner, Gene Pistilli. Tommy made the introductions, and Phil added, "Terry used to play pro baseball, but now he just plays hardball here." Phil laughed in a high, uncomfortable giggle, as if he was sharing a private joke.

Terry was Phil's childhood friend, and they complimented each other's style and philosophy of work. Standing together they made a comical pair. Terry was tall, lanky, and awkward for an athlete. As he was making a comment to Phil about other business matters, Jim whispered to me, "Hey, it's da wabbit!"

Gene Pistilli was concentrating on tuning his guitar. He was sitting on top of Terry Cashman's desk with one foot bracing the floor. "We just got one of Gene's songs recorded by Spanky and Our Gang," Tommy said flatly.

I finally spoke up. "Which song is it?" I asked.

"'Sunday Will Never Be the Same,'" Gene answered, with a warm easy smile. "Have you heard it yet?"

"I sure have—it's all over the radio! You wrote that song?" I looked at Gene with admiration. "That's great!"

"We wrote that song," Terry interjected. "And it's on the charts with a bullet. It's gonna make us a bundle."

I liked Gene immediately but wasn't comfortable with the rest of the partners. Gene seemed as if he actually enjoyed making music, as if he was having fun writing and playing songs.

He was wiry, dynamic, and handsome, with jet-black wavy hair, a thick moustache, and dark expressive eyes. He was dressed in faded jeans and appeared less impressed with the business than the other partners.

"Wanna play?" Gene asked, getting up and handing his guitar to Jim.

"Sure!" Jim took the instrument and started playing "Wear Out the Turnpike," a song that we had recently written.

"Why don't you join him?" Gene said to me, dangling a cigarette from the corner of his mouth. I stood by watching, unnerved that Tommy continued to ignore me.

"Go on," Gene insisted. "I want to hear you too." He gave me a vote of confidence, and I began harmonizing with Jim on the chorus. As I walked over to stand next to Jim, Gene added, "Nice ass—and she can sing too." Then a fifth person walked into the room.

Tommy interrupted our singing and said, "Jimmy, this is the producer I've been wanting you to meet."

"What's going on, boys?" Nik Venet asked in his booming voice.

"Here's the new talent I promised you," Tommy said. Jim stopped playing and stood up to shake Nik's hand. Over Tommy's praise, Nik reached out and shook my hand too. "Nice to meet you, too, Ingrid."

"Nik's producing some of the biggest acts around. He's worked with the Beach Boys, Bobby Darin, Linda Ronstadt and the Stone Ponies, and scads of others. He's the best."

"You flatter me, Picardo," Nik said.

"Play something for Nik, would ya, Jimmy?" Tommy coaxed him, still ignoring me.

"Sure," he replied, looking awkwardly at me. We had been performing as a duo for more than four years, but just as I had forewarned Jim, Tommy wouldn't acknowledge me.

After singing a few numbers alone, Jim turned to me.

"Come on, Ing. Sing with me."

I joined him on a few folk songs, including a couple we'd written together. We traded harmonies and leads. It was effortless and natural. Singing had become the most enjoyable and intimate aspect of our relationship.

"You're good, kids," Nik said warmly, when the impromptu audition was over.

"You remind me of Ian and Sylvia, and your writing style is a lot like Gordon Lightfoot. I think we can do something fun together."

Jim smiled sincerely and said, "That would be great."

"We need to get you into the studio, but in the meantime, get Gene to bring you down to my place at Gramercy Park. We'll hang out in the Village some night."

Tommy escorted Nik to the lobby and returned smiling. "He likes your music, Jimmy. Nik's going to help us coproduce a couple albums for Capitol. We got a three-album deal to produce two more acts after our current album is done. I think you could be next."

He handed Jim a promo picture that read, "Cashman, Pistilli and West."

"Who's this guy, West?" Jim laughed and pointed to Tommy's picture. "He sounds pretty white-bread to me." Tommy shrugged his shoulders but kept silent. "Your old man must be pissed as hell about you changing the family name," Jim said, looking up from the photograph.

"Yeah," Tommy said nonchalantly. "But Terry's real name is Dennis Minogue. He took two new names. We just didn't think Picardo, Pistilli, and Minogue worked. Shit, you know—you do what you've gotta do."

Jim was surprised that Tommy had given up his family name. Jim's own father had changed his name from Hermino Gildo Croce to James Croce, and Jim understood wanting to be more American. But he would never change his family name: it was his legacy.

Tommy and Jim's Italian-American families, college, and love of music had created a strong friendship between them. But now, things were changing. Jim was a Jew, and Picardo was West. Tommy was the music business, and Jim was the product. Tommy had the money, and Jim barely had enough to make the drive to New York and back.

Yet in spite of their differences, Jim still believed his friend when he said he could help him. He was counting on it.

When we brought our one suitcase up to Tommy's apartment to get ready to go out to dinner, Pat still wasn't dressed. It was 5 PM. She was cleaning the cabinets and didn't look at all like the Pat I remembered. She was warm but subdued and seemed really sad. After hugs, she disappeared into the bedroom.

Pat and Tommy had been childhood sweethearts in Neptune, New Jersey, and had married after he graduated from Villanova and Pat from Cabrini. Pat, a tall, attractive woman with an engaging personality, was a singer-songwriter who had performed with Jim and Tommy at college parties and events. What was she doing in her pajamas?

That evening Tommy took us to dinner in Little Italy, down in the Village, but Pat stayed home. He treated us to a visit at the Bitter End and afterward to an espresso at a nearby coffeehouse. It was a real treat for us, but I felt uncomfortable having Tommy pay for things we couldn't afford.

Pat was asleep when we returned to the East Side at Fifty-First Street and Second Avenue. The spacious, luxury apartment Tommy rented had contemporary Scandinavian furniture, oversized leather couches, and highly polished wooden floors, but only one bedroom. The three of us quietly entered the darkened living room, where Tommy pulled out a studio bed, and Jim and I spent our first night together in New York City.

After breakfast at the Stage Deli, Tommy's treat again, Jim and I drove back to Media.

"I'd love to get a record deal with Nik Venet," Jim said, "What did you think of him, Ing? Do you think he really liked us?"

"I think he did," I said. "I think the audition went really well. I want you to know, Jim, that if they just want to produce you and not me, I'm really okay with it. I have my art, and as long as we have each other, that's what really matters to me."

"Oh Ing, I can't do this without you. You're the reason for everything. I love you so much." He paused. "I'm so sorry that I can't talk to you the way you want me to. But I just can't."

I tried to understand the mixed messages I was getting but moved on to another uncomfortable subject.

"Jim, I have to admit, I'm uneasy around Tommy. What's going on with them? Are they still together? 'Cause it sure seems strange the way Pat is in pajamas all day long." He just shrugged. "Well, whatever their problem is, I can tell you that Tommy doesn't like me. He'd rather have you to himself. I just get in the way."

"That isn't true, Ing. You sing great, and I don't want to do an album without you."

"But you're the star, sweetie. I'm always happy to sing with you. But like I said, I have my art. And music is everything to you. It's what you have to do."

―――――

Once I was back at school, I was happy and busy with pottery and painting. When my father was dying of cancer, and Jim had been trying to get settled into civilian life, I'd dropped the one class I really wanted to take with the head of the painting department, Harold Jacobs. But this year I would be able to devote the time and energy that the class would demand, and I was determined to do well.

While music made me happier than almost anything, especially when I sang with Jim, I felt I had a gift for design.

Harold Jacobs was intense and not easily pleased. But he was attracted to my work and surprised by my confidence. He was especially taken with my mixed media.

Jim was proud of my art and complimented me often, always encouraging me with my studies. I excelled in this realm, and Jim was happy to be the supportive husband.

Once school was in full swing, things between Jim and me seemed to be getting back to normal. He still drove me to the Media train station every morning, and when I got home, a delicious dinner awaited me. Jim would prepare antipastos with roasted peppers and garlic, fresh tomatoes and mozzarella, prosciutto and crisp bruschetta. Our budget was limited, but pasta was cheap, and he varied his own homemade sauces. Though the meals were a wonderful gift, Jim had a knack for using every pot, pan, and plate in the kitchen, and it was left up to me to clean it all before we'd head out to our gig at the Paddock.

We played music together whenever we could, and things appeared to be getting better. But there were still times when the dissonance in the relationship would flare up out of the blue in full force. The trust that was once between us wasn't perfect anymore; it seemed conditional.

When Jim didn't hear back from Tommy the week after our trip to New York, he became discouraged. He wasn't happy at his teaching job and was increasingly insecure about whether he would ever be able to make music his career.

"I sure hope the guys in New York call you soon, Jim," I said one day.

"Well, they haven't yet. But maybe Gene Pistilli will call you. You sure seemed to enjoy your time at the office with him."

"What?"

"You know what I'm talking about. 'Nice ass!' I saw you leading him on. Shit, can't you go anywhere without flirting?"

"Flirting! What are you talking about? I didn't do anything to provoke him. Are you ever going to stop throwing the rape in my face? I can't stand this anymore!"

Twenty minutes passed before I broke the silence.

"Jim, I'm going to get counseling."

"Why?" he asked indifferently, and then added, "Well, maybe you could use it. Maybe they'll teach you how to avoid putting yourself in situations that lead to trouble."

"Maybe you're right. But I need your help. We both need to get counseling."

When he didn't respond, I pulled my sketchbook out of my bag, started looking through my work, and changed the subject.

"I really want to start planning for graduate school, maybe at Yale."

"You could probably get a scholarship. Shit! I can't believe I'm back at Palansky Junior High—going nowhere!"

"I'm so sorry you hate your job. I know something will come of our trip to New York, and you'll get that album deal. You'll see."

I was sad that he was postponing his career to put me through school, as he had promised my father he would. Though we were performing locally, Jim hadn't been pursuing his music career as aggressively as he could have. And there were no guarantees in the music business. It was always a crapshoot.

Nonetheless, we had become the Riddle Paddock's most popular performers. Jim learned to skillfully manage the unruly audiences even though they often tested the limits of his patience.

"I never wear a guitar strap in there," he once told Sal. "Too many times I have to put down the fucking instrument and move as fast as I can to get out of the way of a bar stool or a flying beer bottle.

"One time somebody kicked somebody else, and a bar stool flew over and busted two of my guitars. Two guitars in one fight! You never know when somebody is going to come up and turn their animal loose on you and go into their dance. I don't mind people expressing themselves and doing different things. But I don't want them doin' it all over me."

When he sensed the crowd getting unruly, Jim would try to quiet them by telling stories, often making up the raps as he went along:

"You know for my day gig I teach special education in Chester. The kids I have at school are what you would call serious discipline problems. You know those guys who go on safaris and shoot elephants with tranquilizer darts?" He paused. "Well, those guys have missed their calling. They don't know it, but they've got a future in the education system."

He waited for the audience to respond. "Of course, there are the other types of kids, too, the ones I call my beets and carrots. All I have to do with them is sit them by the window and rotate them every now and then, so they get enough sunlight." Then he'd play one of the songs by the Temptations, to teach his "beets and carrots" how to read.

The more popular Jim grew, the more the audience took part in his act. "It's time for a bawdy ballad, Jim!" someone would yell. "Sing 'The Chastity Belt.'" He'd sing a stanza, and the regulars would sing along. Or they'd ask, "Play us that new song," or "Get Ingrid up there!" Our repertoire had become so vast that the audiences rarely heard a song repeated throughout an entire week, unless it was requested.

Jim still played occasionally with Bill Reid, but they rarely saw one another outside the Paddock. Bill and Dee were now raising Arabian horses, Great Danes, and children on a farm in Sadesburyville, about an hour from Media.

Chris and Dave Sigafoos and a couple of other Riddle Paddock supporters, as well as my classmates and teachers, would invite Jim and me to their homes for social dinners. Jim graciously brought along his guitar and played for hours, often until the hosts were ready for bed.

Chris Sigafoos was one of our closest friends at the time. Her husband, Dave, was still in medical school and quite busy. Often she would come alone to the Paddock and sit with me while Jim performed.

Another good friend, Bob Knott, the banjo and guitar player from Jim's Middle East tour, and his wife, Ellen, moved to Philadelphia that year for graduate school at the University of Pennsylvania. Bob was getting his doctorate in early-twentieth-century art, and Ellen was a librarian.

Jim and I enjoyed the mental stimulation of Bob and Ellen's company and liked playing music in their highly academic home environment. In spite of everyone's busy schedules, we all found time to get together a couple of nights a month.

With the social unrest of 1968 amplified by the assassinations of Martin Luther King Jr. and Bobby Kennedy, the Tet Offensive in Vietnam, and race riots across the country, the counterculture was strongly influencing music.

Though Jim and Bob continued to play traditional bluegrass and folk tunes, Jim and I had started to write songs that reflected the growing dissatisfaction with the establishment, and we tested them out with Bob and Ellen. Our acoustic guitar and two voices distinguished us from the electric music that groups like Crosby, Stills and Nash; the Byrds; and the Beatles were playing. But our tunes carried similar messages.

Folk music had lost some of its luster and popularity when Dylan and the Band transformed the scene a few years earlier with electric folk-rock. Still, Jim and I kept the majority of our music tied to the traditional roots of American folk music. Jim enjoyed the immediacy of grabbing his guitar and playing whenever and wherever he was. He was a troubadour and a purist who didn't feel comfortable hassling with electric instruments onstage or with their artificially produced sound.

Other than the Paddock crowd, Bob and Ellen, and Chris and Dave, most of our social life was built around my school friends and professors. At their parties, we provided the entertainment, and no matter how tense things got between us, when we sang together, the problems went away or at least got put on hold.

———

A few weeks into my semester, Jim received a letter from the Chester Board of Education.

"I don't believe it, Ing," he exclaimed. "They've fired me!"

"What are you talking about?"

"The school board fired me. They said they warned me last year about playing music in the classroom, and they got word I was doing it again."

"Don't they know you do it to teach the kids to read?" Their bureaucratic reasoning pissed me off. "Are they so backward they can't see that your students are reading for the first time in their lives?" He tossed the letter aside.

"They're Nazi bureaucrats. I disobeyed orders, and that's all they know. What the hell—I'm not sure the Raisin would survive another year there anyway," he said, referring to the abuse the VW was taking at the hands of the students.

At this point, he had no choice but to return to the radio station full-time, selling airtime and writing commercials. But since the assassination of Martin Luther King Jr., racial tensions were running high in the predominately black ghettos of West Philly, and he was nervous about the rough neighborhoods in his territory.

Luckily, a client introduced him to FuFu Allenger, a flamboyant, black pool hall owner. FuFu wore an Afro so high he looked like a seven-foot giant, with silk suits and diamond rings on every finger. A "smoove" talker and a shrewd businessman, he took great pride in his advertising savvy. He had a giant picture of himself plastered across a billboard in the middle of his neighborhood. "Come on down and see FuFu," the text read.

On his first visit, Jim managed to sell FuFu air time and soon became a regular player at Allenger's Pool Hall. Jim talked jive with the black hustlers, knowing his safety in the ghetto depended on whether FuFu enjoyed his company. Two weeks after Jim had landed the Allenger account, he drove by the pool hall and noticed FuFu's face on the billboard had been blown away by a shotgun blast. He walked into the billiard hall and found a somber mood.

"FuFu's dead," said a big man, glaring from behind the bar, his arms folded across his chest. "They beat him with his own stick and laid him out on that table there and watched him bleed to death." The bartender nodded in the direction of the blood-stained table.

The afternoon Jim quit the radio station; he wasn't there to pick me up at the train station. Even though the station was only a few blocks from our street, he had insisted on picking me up every evening. I wasn't sure if he was trying to protect me or make sure I didn't lure anyone on the walk home.

When I got off the train, I waited a half hour and then called home. The phone was busy. So I decided to walk. When I arrived at the house, Jim was just hanging up the phone, an expression of exhilaration on his face.

"Hi, sweet thing," I said. He looked startled by my voice.

"It was Tommy, Ing. They want us to come up and make the album!"

"Oh Jim, I'm so happy for you. This is what you've been waiting for."

"I'm so sorry I didn't get to the train station on time. But Tommy called, and we were talking. How did you get home, Ing?"

"I walked. It's not far, and besides I didn't have much to carry."

"Well, sit down, sweet thing. I've made you a nice dinner of veal parmigiano, kohlrabi, and garlic bread, and I want to talk to you."

During the meal Jim seemed genuinely happy. He went out of his way to make me laugh, but when he stood up and started to clear the dishes, I felt something was wrong.

"Jim, what's the matter? Is there something bothering you?"

He looked at me for a long moment and sat down. "I quit the radio station today. FuFu's dead. He was murdered at the pool hall."

"Oh my God, Jim. Were you there?"

"No, it happened a couple of days ago. But I just found out."

"Jim, you know I was always scared about you working down there. I'm so glad you weren't hurt. What would I do without you?" I got up and went over to embrace my husband.

"Well, the good news is that Tommy said Nik Venet is interested in recording us on Capitol Records."

"That's great news, sweetie."

"But . . . Tommy wants us to move to New York City." His sad brown eyes were filled with anxiety. "So you'd have to leave school."

I quickly reviewed the move and its opportunities. The decision had to be made immediately, and I knew it was Jim's turn.

"When do we leave?" He crushed me with a hug.

"Ing, you'll be able to finish school sometime, I promise! It's just I don't know how many chances like this people get. I think we'd better grab it." I nodded as he ran into the kitchen to call Tommy.

"I agree," I called out. I prayed that this would help our marriage, which meant more to me than anything.

The next morning, I arranged for a one-year leave of absence from Moore and put our things in storage, and forty-eight hours later, we were packed and back on the New Jersey Turnpike, heading for New York City. Loaded with our belongings, the Raisin pushed against a brisk headwind at a top speed of forty-five miles per hour.

Tommy had invited us to stay at his apartment until we found a place of our own. This time, Pat greeted us at the door and seemed more like herself.

"I hope you don't mind sleeping on the hideaway bed again," she said.

"It's fine," Jim replied, squeezing my hand.

That night, we made love tenderly. For the first time in months I felt as if he might finally be getting over his resentment. The next morning, Tommy arranged for Jim to sing backup on some radio and television commercials. It wouldn't be steady or amount to much money, but it was a chance to get acclimated to working in the studio.

"It's just a beginning," Jim told me, his spirits clearly soaring. "I know it isn't going to be easy for us to live with Tommy and Pat. But we'll find our own place soon. This will work out, Ing. I promise."

Jim and Tommy left for the studio, and I stayed with Pat, who worked out of their apartment writing songs.

Pat and I had been friends since I'd met Jim and Tommy, but we hadn't seen each other since she and Tommy married. While catching up, she revealed what had been troubling her:

"Tommy and I used to love doing music together, but he's so serious about the business now; it's just no fun anymore." She spoke with grave finality.

"But—but you and Tommy still sing and play together, right?"

"Not anymore, and I don't know how much longer I can stay here."

I felt sad for her, but what she didn't tell me at the time was that she and Gene Pistilli were having an affair. They were also starting a new band with Tim Hauser and Erin Dickens called the Manhattan Transfer.

The day after we arrived in the city, Tommy took us to meet with Phil Kurnit.

With the same thin-lipped smile, Phil said, "To do the album, there are some papers you'll need to sign." He handed us each three contracts. Jim shrugged and reached for a pen. He trusted Tommy, but I hesitated.

"What are these for?" I asked.

"Read them," Phil said abruptly.

Jim scanned the words and shrugged again.

"What is this one-year option about?" I asked.

Kurnit read the legalese out loud. When he finished, I asked him to make sure I understood:

"So you're telling us, if things don't work out after one year, we're free to leave?" At the top of my mind was my $1,000 fellowship from Moore. I had to complete college the following year or pay the money back.

"That's the deal," Kurnit said.

"And what are these separate pages that give Cashman, Pistilli and West exclusive publishing, production, and management rights? I thought this was just a record deal."

Jim looked at Tommy and asked, "Are the contracts okay?"

Tommy responded by telling Jim, "We'll pay you $200 a week to write songs for the company. Plus, Capitol will give you an advance as soon as you sign."

"I thought you said you'd pay us as much as we were making back home, or at least enough to keep us going until the album comes out," I insisted.

"Well, the advance will help cover that," Tommy insisted.

Jim picked up the pen, ready to sign.

"Jim, I'm not sure," I said. "I don't understand these contracts." But Jim trusted Tommy and scribbled his name anyway, handing the pen to me. Reluctantly, I signed too.

———

Two months later, in December 1968, Jim returned from the office and told me the recording of our album was delayed until spring. "Capitol is going through some changes. Tommy says these things happen all the time, Ing. But he can get us a college concert tour so we can make some money. At the same time we can put together more songs for the album."

"Who's booking the tour?" I asked. I was beginning to worry that we might have made a mistake in moving to New York.

"Merv Frankel. He's their new partner. He's in charge of managing their acts through his company, Showcase Management. He wants to put us on Albert Grossman's college concert tour that'll start in Minneapolis and end in Tennessee. We'll perform five or six consecutive nights at each college, mostly at campus coffeehouses. We'll get $300 a week, minus 20 percent of the gross that goes to Showcase."

"What about travel expenses, food, and lodging?"

"I don't know," he said. "I guess the schools will put us up."

"Financially, Jim, I don't know how we can do it. You were making more money teaching, and we were living in Media, not New York City. This really concerns me. I know we don't need much to get by, sweetie, but we'll get in debt at this rate. We might have to borrow money. I don't mind not having things, but I don't want to owe anyone anything!"

"I know, but we can make it, Ing. Just think: we'll be traveling around the country and getting paid for playing music. Doesn't that sound romantic? It's like Woody Guthrie. We'll get a chance to really see the country. It's just too bad we won't have an album to promote." I began to soften. The money seemed scant, but getting out of New York and being alone with Jim sounded perfect.

Since leaving Pennsylvania, his anger had slowly melted. I knew Jim felt guilty for a lot of things: his response to the rape, taking me out of school, and breaking his promise to my dad about helping me graduate from college. To make it up to me, he had become tender again, caressing me when we lay in bed at night, bringing back foreplay, and telling me he loved me more and more often.

———

Two days later, as we drove northwest toward the University of Minnesota, Jim looked back at the New York skyline. "What a pretty sight," he said, "to see the armpit of America getting smaller and slipping away."

We had to drive the eighteen hours to Minnesota without stopping in order to make our first concert on time.

"Isn't it great how well Frankel is managing our schedule from the very start?" I asked cynically as Jim drove and I opened the cooler. "Who else does this guy manage?"

"I think he's managed a couple of baseball players. I really don't know much about him," Jim admitted.

"Baseball players? Jim, are you serious? Do you think he knows anything about the music business?"

"Who knows? What difference does it make? We're on the road, and that's a start at least."

"You're right, it's a good start, but we could get our own college concerts and pay a real manager. I don't understand the benefit here."

"Ing, could you grab me something to eat?" I pulled an Italian ham sandwich on a baguette with arugula from the cooler and poured coffee from the large thermos into its red lid-cup.

"Ing, you make the best food in the world," he said, changing the subject. "You've become such a good chef I may never cook again."

We drove through the night, stopping only to take turns at the wheel. It was almost evening when we finally pulled into the university's student union parking lot.

Otte Boersma, a handsome, blond Swede in charge of campus entertainment, was waiting for us. "There's only a few hours before the show," he said with a smile. "Let's go on over to the Hole and get something to eat." After dinner at the coffeehouse where we were playing, he showed us to our lodgings in a tiny room on the edge of campus. It was in an old brick building above another coffeehouse.

"There are a few other guests staying here tonight, too," he said, apologetically. "You'll have to share the bathroom at the end of the hall." The room was clean and neat, and after we'd spent so many cramped hours in the VW, it looked wonderful to us.

Later, we were disappointed to learn that our performance had not been advertised. Only twenty students showed up the first night. It was a casual gathering, and we enjoyed the intimacy of the friendly crowd anyway. When we finished, the small, enthusiastic audience begged us to stay. We were beat but sat down with the students. A few of them had guitars and banjos in hand and were ready for an impromptu jam session. Jim entertained them with a few bawdy ballads. Finally, Ottie politely interrupted, saying that the Hole was closing.

We performed nightly for a week. By the second night, all the seats were filled. And the crowd kept growing.

During the day, Ottie took us on tours of Minneapolis and St. Paul. We loved the excitement of being in a new city. We took in museums, historical sites, and even the local industries.

Jim was always interested in the local culture and history of the people we met, and I made sure to visit every art department at every college we went to.

In the Twin Cities, word about the Philadelphia folk singers spread. By the end of the week, we were playing two shows a night to packed houses.

"I can't believe there's such an interest in folk music here," I told Ottie. "I guess I just hadn't expected this kind of reception in the Midwest."

"Where do you think Dylan came from?" Ottie chided.

———

We drove south to Ohio. At one stop we performed at a Protestant college in a small country town.

"Golly gee, you'd never guess it was 1968," Jim joked in his Gomer Pyle imitation. "Most college students are burning their draft cards and growing long hair. These kids look straight off the set of *Ozzie and Harriet* or *Leave It to Beaver*."

Still, Jim was anxious to please them and even sang a few church hymns. "I guess I'll pass on the bawdy ballads," he whispered to me during the performance. "But wow, the temptation is great!"

Between shows in southern Ohio, students invited us to a church social. A potluck dinner was spread out across a huge table. Jim's eyes widened, and he nudged me. "Can you believe how many different uses these folks have found for mayonnaise and marshmallows?" He pointed to the ambrosia and Jell-O salads lining the table. "Look, even the tuna salad has marshmallows!"

Later, the students escorted us to the fanciest restaurant in town, the Bolo Inn. It was the former convention center and the pride of the community. The enormous restaurant was filled with naugahyde booths and large, round tables.

Hundreds of pictures of a dog and its master lined the walls. Jim thought it was some kind of joke until a student introduced him to the owner of the club, the same person in the pictures.

"I built this restaurant as a shrine to my dog, Bolo," he said sadly. "He was a black lab. He died last year."

Jim nodded in sympathy.

"You've done a good job of decorating. I especially like the repeating pattern of Bolo on the wall-to-wall carpet." He choked back laughter as I elbowed him.

"We just got this carpet," the man said proudly. "I had to send the first batch back because it didn't look at all like Bolo."

Later, when we drove south out of Ohio, Jim wondered aloud, "What do you suppose ever happened to that rejected carpet? My guess is somewhere out there in an Ohio trailer park are families eating crustless, white-bread sandwiches and marshmallow ambrosia salads, thrilled over the deal they made on their new Bolo carpet."

At dawn, Jim woke me up. I'd fallen asleep on his lap while we were driving. The sun had just climbed above the hills of eastern Kentucky and was glowing orange on the fields of bluegrass. He gently stroked my hair and whispered, "You've got to see this sunrise, babe." I looked up at him and smiled, then reached up and kissed him on the cheek. He was as relaxed as I had seen him in a long time. "I love this life on the road." We had been traveling for a month, logging thousands of miles in the VW.

We played music nearly every night. The students' overwhelming acceptance of our material encouraged us. We wrote whenever we could, in the car and motel rooms and college dormitories.

"Let's stop and have some breakfast," he suggested. He looked for a truck stop and pulled off the road. Jim and I thrived on the opportunity traveling gave us to meet ordinary people in every walk of life.

After we ate, we went back to the car, and he unpacked his guitar. "I want you to help me with this new song I've been thinking about all night," he said.

I took the cassette tape recorder from the dash and turned it on, as I always did when we began developing a new song.

"Listen to this," he said, strumming, and began to sing: "I like to think about her and the way she used to love me, but I just can't live without her, 'cause . . . dah-dah-dah-dah-dah-dah-dah," he went on, trying to come up with the end of the line. "And the season's getting later . . . dah-dah-dah-dah-dah-dah-dah-dah." I sang with him as we repeated the first verse a couple of times, and I helped him complete the words.

We moved on to the second verse and then the third. A half-hour later, we had a new song and named it "Vespers":

I like to think about her and the way she used to love me,
But I just can't live without her,
'Cause her arms are not around me,
And the season's getting later,
And my body's getting colder,
And the vespers ring and I'm all alone without my love beside me.

She'd call me in the evening
And ask me to come over,
She'd be standing by the window,
With her hair down around her shoulders,
We'd talk a while and then she'd smile.
And then she'd lock the door.
And she would sit beside me,
And we would talk no more.

The bells would ring at six o'clock,
And she'd be in my arms,
Her head upon my shoulder gently resting,
And then she'd wake and look at me
Not knowing I'd been watching,
Kiss me softly, then drift off to sleep.

As we packed up to get back on the road, I recited the song to myself. To me, Jim was not just writing a song when he put words to music, but communicating his deepest feelings to me in the best way he knew how.

———

To our delight, the colleges in the South often arranged to have us stay in private homes near the campuses. At the University of Tennessee, we were guests in a rundown plantation manor. Norma, who ran the house, was the epitome of Southern charm.

She was a housewife who needed the extra money she got from renting rooms through the university. She was comfortable with the lifestyle of entertainers and relished having them stay in her home. Norma had a lot of outrageous stories to tell and liked having an audience.

I caught a stomach flu a couple of days before we got to Kentucky, and Norma nursed me back to health with her special home remedies. "I've made you a treat," she said. "It's an old family prescription for youthful skin, good health, and a long life." She set a plate with an open-faced sandwich on it in front of me.

"What is it?"

"A bone-marrow sandwich. You see, the secret of youth is in the bone. I boil up some beef bones in a soup, extract the marrow, and spread it on white bread with salt and pepper. It's good for ya," she said. "Try it." I reluctantly took a few bites.

"It's delicious!" I was surprised. "It's definitely better than grits," I assured Jim.

While in line at the school cafeteria my first morning on campus, I had mistaken hominy for cream of wheat. Jim had watched but said nothing when I ordered a bowl of what I thought was cereal. The unusual flavor surprised me. Without hesitation, I brashly spit the mouthful back into the bowl.

"Yuck, this is disgusting," I complained so blaringly that everyone in the room turned to look. Jim pointed to my mouth and started laughing out loud. "Ing's instant reject," he called it. From past experience, he suspected I might react that strongly to grits, and his forethought made him giggle all the more. He loved setting me up to watch my spontaneous, uncensored reactions.

We both liked Norma's gutsy style, her generosity, and her sultry Southern accent. Jim listened to her tales and took the opportunity to ask her about her life story.

She said she'd come from a small, rural, Southern town, and when she was just sixteen, she fell in love with a tightrope walker and joined the circus. Her former husband taught her his trade, and she performed and traveled with him in the circus from town to town for several years.

"When I came to Louisville, I was ready to go back to school and get an education," she told us. "After I graduated from the University of Tennessee, I married a professor of mine, had three kids, and here we are, livin' happily ever after."

"Norma, before we leave tomorrow, let us give you a private concert. It will be our way of saying thanks," Jim offered.

Norma and her family invited a few of their friends to come over for the performance in her living room. Everyone was welcoming to us, and their home felt a lot like ours back in Pennsylvania. We played, ate, and shared in conversation all night. We promised that if we got back to Louisville, we'd come see them again. The following morning, we left, feeling full and happy.

But our carefree spirits sobered when we reached Harlan County, Kentucky, an impoverished coal-mining district. Jim had been sensitive to the miner's situation from his work on *The Miner's Story*, but this was the first time he had seen a mining community so close-up and personal. The hungry faces and worn clothing of the people affected him deeply. At Bellarmine College, the student representative, Jenny Hawkins, filled us in on the growing economic and political problems of the area.

"The United Mine Workers Union has just called a general strike. We're all on edge here. Every man in my family works in the mines, and none of them are being paid. Gunfights have broken out between the workers and the police. I'm scared," she admitted.

Consistent with what Jenny told us about their troubled times, the small town itself seemed to be dying. All that remained were a post office, two bars, and one movie theater, which played *Thunder Road* every night of the year. It starred Robert Mitchum as a Southern moonshiner and had been filmed on location nearby.

The next afternoon, Jenny took us to the mine where her family had worked before the strike. The entrance, an ugly black hole in the hillside, was boarded up and patrolled by armed guards. All signs to the mine had been blasted away by shotguns. Violence flared during the week Jim and I played at Bellarmine College. The police imposed a 9 PM curfew. Virtually locked in our tiny hotel room, we wrote a country song about the tedious part of traveling called "What Do People Do?"

Tell me, what do people do when there ain't nothin' to do?
When there's nobody else around to do nothin' with or to?
Have you ever been in that position in a small town hotel room
Where the diners all close at nine,
And the trucks keep rollin' by,
And you just can't get to sleep,
Even though there's nothin' on your mind?

Tell me, what do people say when there ain't nothin' to say?
When there's nobody else around to help you pass the time
of day?
Have you ever stared at the ceiling till you thought you'd lose
your mind?
Looked for a wall that you could climb? Still you just can't get
to sleep
Even though there's nothing on your mind?

Have you ever been stuck in a small town motel,
Lookin' all around but there ain't nothin' to see;
In a never endin' mind bendin' troublin' position
Sayin' why did it happen to me?
Doodle-ooh-doo-doo

NEW YORK'S NOT MY HOME

IN DECEMBER, AFTER NEARLY 100,000 miles on the road, we headed back to New York City. Our hopes were boosted by the enthusiastic reception the college students had given us. Jim's raps were more polished, and he and I were getting more comfortable writing songs together. The downside was we were broke and had no place to call home. Although Tommy had promised us an advance once the record deal was signed, we still hadn't received it.

"I wonder what's taking them so long to book the studio time?" Jim said, as we made our way northeast through Virginia.

"I don't know. But at least we got invited back to every college we played. That's a good sign."

"Yeah, and they liked the new songs. That felt really good. The problem is that we still need to get the album made."

"I know. Without a record we're just another unknown act." I paused, and decided this was as good a time as any to express my growing concerns about our finances.

"Jim, to be honest, I don't understand why Tommy had us move up to New York in the first place. They don't have any work for us. We could have stayed in Media and done what we're doing now. We're really down to our last few dollars, and I don't know what we're going to do when we get back to New York!"

"I'm sure Tommy will get us some studio work or something. The least we'll get is the $200 a week for our songwriting. We'll survive. Don't worry."

"Jim, that won't pay the bills, and even if they keep paying us as songwriters, is that an advance we'll need to pay back later? I just don't understand how this works. All I know is that it seems to me that the longer we stay in New York without making money, the further in debt we're going to get!"

"Tommy said we can stay with him at the apartment for a while."

"That scares me even more. I don't want to live off of Tommy or take another loan from him. If they'd just get us the work they promised, we could get along fine."

He ran his hand through his hair.

"Yeah," he said. "I guess their big talk is just bullshit."

"Tommy pays us as if it's a handout," I said. "As if we haven't earned it. What happened to the advance they promised us when we signed up? No one's even mentioned it since then, and, by the way, we haven't received our copy of the contracts either!"

"You're really starting to hate the music business, aren't you, Ing?"

"Well, I love the music, but I hate the business. This is the best time we've ever had doing music. I would honestly be happy just to stay out on the road, if that's what it takes to make our careers work. But we need to make a living, and I just don't see how we can do that unless we can earn more money." I took a deep breath. "I just don't know if Tommy and Dennis or Merv have enough experience to help us."

"I'm sorry we don't have a place of our own anymore, and I know it's been hard for you to leave school. But I couldn't do this without you."

"Yeah, maybe I just need to learn more about the business, but something just doesn't feel right."

———

Being together nearly twenty-four hours a day on the college tour was just the medicine we needed. Our music gave us a common enterprise, and in spite of the financial hardship, or perhaps because of it, our tenderness for each other grew.

Before we reached the office in Manhattan, Jim told me there was something else I ought to know:

"Tommy and Pat are getting a divorce."

"Wow, that was quick. They haven't even been married a year. But I guess I shouldn't be surprised. Pat seemed miserable the last time we spoke."

"And before we see Tommy, I'd better warn you that he has a new girlfriend. A flamenco dancer!"

"He's living with another woman already!"

"Yeah, Barbara Dodge. Jack Blake's sister-in-law. Tommy always had a thing for her. Remember Jack from the Coventry Lads?"

"Sure, I remember him. Well, I hope she's nice because it's going to feel really weird without Pat there."

As we rolled up West Forty-Fifth Street looking for a place to park the Raisin, I felt a sense of dread and wished that we were still in some little college town in the middle of nowhere.

———

Jim tagged along with Tommy to the studio each morning, hoping every day would be the day Capitol gave the green light to our album. I spent my days searching for a rent-controlled apartment. I walked from one end of Manhattan to the other, from the Village to the Upper West Side. Then back to Tommy's apartment on East Fifty-First Street.

Finally, Terry Cashman told us about a place in the Bronx, where he lived, near Harlem. It was a depressing one-bedroom apartment on the eighth floor of an enormous World War I–era housing complex. The long dim hallways were lit by a single, bare bulb. Over the years, the landlord had purchased excess paint from a nearby hospital and painted every hallway a different pastel color. Bars covered the windows. "Those bars are there so the tenants don't jump out," Jim joked as we moved in our belongings.

One day after Jim had been at the office, he came home to our new apartment and told me, "You know New York is like a Fellini film, and the subways are like rolling restrooms. People tell you that nobody will talk to you on the streets in New York, but it isn't true. On my way home today, a guy came right up to me and started talking. He said, 'Let me hold your dime sucka', or I'll cut you four kinds of bad. I'll cut you deep, long, wide, and often.'" Jim set down his guitar case and laughed to himself, then sighed. "I'll tell you, Ing, living here is making me lose a lot of my pacifist attitudes."

"Are you serious, Jim? Are you okay?"

"Oh yeah, I ran like hell. I'm fine."

———

The first Sunday in the new apartment in the Bronx, Jim was supposed to attend his first monthly National Guard meeting in Media. Just as we crossed the bridge into New Jersey on the way to the meeting, he begged me to stop at the next pay phone.

"Please call Sergeant Coyia for me and tell him that I broke my leg or something. Just . . . just tell him I can't make it."

"Jim, please, not again. I've been making excuses to the National Guard for you ever since we moved to New York. Besides, we already used that reason. Remember, first you broke your arm, then your leg; then there was a 'death in the family.' I'm afraid you've run out of bones and family members, and I'm not going to keep covering for you. I'm a terrible liar. Besides, Sergeant Coyia knows you're bullshitting."

"Oh, come on, sweet thing. You know I hate those meetings!"

"I'm sorry, Jim, but I'm not doing it. It was one thing when we were on tour, but now we're back, and there's no excuse not to go! You're just going to have to bite the bullet and do it."

About two hours later, we arrived at the armory, an unimpressive gray stone building in downtown Media. I dropped him off and left to hang out with my family.

Jim was early, and happy to see Ronnie Miller, a fellow National Guardsman, who was a tattooed good old boy and stock-car racing enthusiast.

Sergeant Coyia took Jim aside.

"Lots of hard luck, huh, Croce? Well, listen, I'll make you a deal. I'll forget all your excuses and give you a perfect attendance record—if you help me out."

"Okay, what do I have to do?"

"See, I'm in charge of catering a party for this big-shot general. And, between you and me, I figure us *paesans* could make a great Italian feast. But I need you to bring your guitar and perform."

"You got yourself a deal, man."

Three weeks later, we drove back down to Media from New York for the general's party and stayed at Jim's parents' house, as we always did on those rare occasions when Jim actually attended a Guard meeting.

"Let me do your wash," Jim's mother offered me, after we arrived late Friday afternoon. "I know going to the Laundromat in that neighborhood you live in must be awful."

"No, it's okay, Mom. I'll do it," I insisted. I appreciated Flora letting us use her washing machine but was intimidated by her perfectionism. Her laundry always came out whiter, brighter, and softer than I could ever get it.

I thought about it for a moment and then reconsidered.

"Well, okay, Mom—I'd like to learn how you get everything so clean!"

In the kitchen, Jim played his guitar softly, practicing for the general's party that evening. His father walked in the back door and set down his briefcase on the counter.

"So, son," he said, "you have nothing better to do than play the guitar?"

"That's what I do, Dad. That's my profession."

"That's the problem. What kind of a job is that?"

"It's what I love." His father leaned down toward him.

"Love and work are two different things. Why don't you get out and get a real job?"

I entered the kitchen, and Jim turned to kiss me as I passed through with an armful of clothes.

Jim Senior continued: "Then maybe you could afford to get Ingrid a washing machine of her own."

"Well, if Ing had a washing machine, what would Mom do when we came to visit?" Jim got up and followed me upstairs to put on his uniform for the party.

That night in the auditorium of the armory, the general and his wife thanked Jim for performing and told him how much they enjoyed his version of Fats Waller's "Oyster in the Stew." They asked him if he'd play again for them sometime.

Sergeant Coyia was commended for selecting the talent for the evening, and the dinner of veal parmesan and pasta was a smashing success, too. The sergeant wiped Jim's slate clean.

"You've earned yourself a perfect attendance record with this one, Croce," he said. "Just don't let me get any more of those phone calls from your wife with those pussy-ass excuses. *Capice*?"

"Listen, Pooch," Jim said, addressing Sergeant Coyia by his nickname. "How about for every concert I play for you from now on, I get a pass on a meeting?"

"We'll see, Croce, but don't push it."

The following afternoon on Sunday, Jim and I joined his parents at the wedding of Jim's longtime friend and fellow musician, Mike DiBenedetto. Mike had wanted Jim to be his best man, but in a traditional Italian Catholic ceremony, everyone in the wedding party had to belong to the Catholic Church. Because of Jim's conversion to Judaism he wasn't eligible to be Mike's best man, so Jim's brother, Rich, stood in. The wedding was held at the historic St. Mary Magdalen Church on Montrose Street in South Philadelphia, where Mario Lanza had performed and made the church's perfect acoustics famous.

Just before the ceremony started, Jim and I stood with the wedding party on the church steps talking with friends. Black kids were jumping double Dutch on the sidewalk, while at nearby vegetable stands Italian vendors fried up pepper-and-egg sandwiches. The aroma swept over the steps, making me hungry. Six black limousines, carrying the bride and her family, circled the block for the sixth time. Jim leaned over to me and said, "Jo Anne's family only lives about two blocks from the church. So either Jo Anne loves riding in limousines, or her father is making sure he gets his money's worth!"

Jim Senior and Flora came up the steps, and we all entered the chapel together, filing into a pew near the front. Jim's father went in first, and Jim sat between his mother and me. Flora knelt in prayer. Having never been in a church before, and unfamiliar with Catholic customs, I turned to Jim and asked in a hushed tone, "Is this where you're supposed to jockulate?" Jim threw his head back and laughed out loud. His mother turned and shot him a violent frown. The organ music began.

Still laughing, he whispered, "Ing, the word is 'genuflect.'"

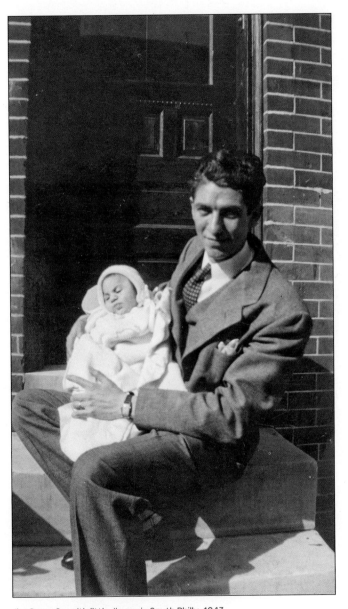

Jim Croce Sr., with little Jimmy in South Philly, 1943

SAVOIA THEATRE

The entire Croce family. *From left to right:* The twins—
Carmen and Patty, Paul, Evelyn, Philamina (Fanny), Santina
(Sadie), Florence, Angelina (Ginger), James Sr., Carmella,
and Pasquale.

Jim at his first communion

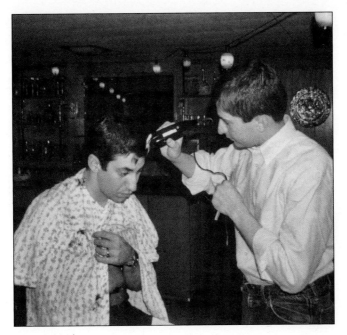

Jim and Rich, 1966

From left to right: Jim Croce, cousins Arlene Zungolo, Ronnie Zungolo, and Denise Catalano, and Rich Croce, 1962

Jim and Ingrid at The Riddle Paddock, 1967

Jim's passport photo, 1964

Bill and Greg Reid at their farm in Sadesburyville, Pennsylvania

Jim and Ingrid at Moore College of Art, 1968. Photo courtesy of Rita Bernstein.

From left to right: Jim's uncle from Rochester, New York, Massimo Babusci, Jim, and Pasquale Croce, 1963

Rich Croce and his "Pa," Massimo Babusci

Jim in his kitchen with a couple members of The Spires and friends, 1963

Ingrid's father, Dr. Sidney Jacobson

Jim Sr. and Flora Croce

Jim at Fort Jackson, South Carolina, 1966

Jim inside tub with Ronnie Miller

Jim at Ingrid's home, 1963

Jim and Ingrid on their wedding day, August 28, 1966

Jim at the Riddle Paddock, 1965

Jim and Ingrid celebrating their first Christmas as a married couple in the Croce family home in Drexel Hill, Pennsylvania, 1966

Jim, Ingrid, Flora, and Jim Sr. at Croce family home in Drexel Hill, Pennsylvania

Jim and Ingrid at their home in Media, Pennsylvania, in the late 1960s. Photo courtesy of the *Philadelphia Inquirer*.

Maury Muehleisen and Joe Salviulo playing
at Glassboro State College in New Jersey

Ingrid outside the house in Lyndell, Pennsylvania,
1971

Jim and Ingrid in Lyndell, Pennsylvania, 1971. Photo courtesy of Paul Wilson

Jim and Maury Muelheisen at Paul's Mall in Boston, Massachusetts. Photo courtesy of Paul Wilson.

Jim in Indianapolis, Indiana, June 13, 1972.
Al Parachini (photographer)

From left to right: Maurice Muehleisen Sr., Maury Muehleisen, and Judy Coffin at Meuhleisen home, 1971

Jim, George Spillane, Ingrid, and Adrian James in Lyndell, Pennsylvania, 1972

Jim and Adrian James in kitchen at their home in Coatsville, Pennsylvania, 1973

Ingrid, Adrian James, and Jim at Phil Petillo's guitar workshop. Photo courtesy Lucille Petillo

Jim, Ingrid, and Adrian James at the Croce family home, 1973

Jim getting his first Gold single (with Burt Sugarman), 1972

Jim backstage at The Troubadour in Los Angeles,
California, 1972

Jim shooting a gun in Lyndell, Pennsylvania, 1972

Jim and Maury Muelheisen in chartered plane, 1973

"Oh. I'm sorry." He stifled another laugh as his mother nudged him and said, "Behave!"

At the altar, the beautiful blonde bride and black-haired groom were a study in contrasts. Mike was as thin as his bride was round, and the sight of the two of them together made Jim giggle.

"I think I can hear Jo Anne's stomach growl," he whispered. "They aren't supposed to eat before they take communion. I think Jo Anne will need an extra helping of communion wafers." I gave him a "be kind" look as the priest began the invocation.

The parishioners knelt in unison. I didn't.

Caught between his Jewish wife and his Catholic mother, Jim wasn't sure what to do. His mother grabbed his right arm, pulling him down. He had his right knee on the kneeling bench and his left buttock firmly planted on the pew. He started losing his balance just as the bride began to reel.

She let out a cry that sounded like a seal's bark, echoing sharply through the church. As we watched wide-eyed, Jo Anne turned and threw up all over the groom, Rich, and the priest. She began to stagger forward, losing her headdress. A chorus welled up from the women in the congregation, "Oooh, the veil!"

"It's an omen!" cried Flora. Jim burst into laughter, lost balance in his contorted posture, doubled into a ball, and rolled past me into the aisle. At the altar, Rich worked on scraping the vomit off of the lapels of his jacket. Mike and the priest tried to steady the swooning bride, who was in danger of banging her head on the pulpit.

After a few moments, Jo Anne announced that she was feeling better. The ceremony was mercifully completed. In the reception line, Jim slipped the bride a breath mint before kissing her. He gave the rest of the roll of mints to Mike. "Be sure you feed her plenty of these tonight," he said. Mike frowned—then he and Jo Anne began to laugh.

———

There was little work for Jim and me that winter in New York. The album had been delayed again, with no spring release in sight. Holed up in our tiny apartment in the Bronx with no money, we grew more and more depressed. Jim tried getting jobs playing backup in the studios but had few offers. When he did get work, he didn't have enough money for gas or the subway, so he rode his bicycle through Harlem to get to Manhattan.

"How did it go?" I asked one afternoon when he returned exhausted.

"Absolutely nothing." He steered his bicycle into the living room and set the kickstand. "The album is no closer to being made now than last week. The story's the same: 'We're working on it, just a few scheduling problems.' Shit, to top it off, I've got a Guard meeting again this weekend." He flopped down on our old couch.

We stayed at his parents' house as usual that weekend. There was no concert to get Jim out of his National Guard commitment this time.

Just before we headed back to New York on Monday morning, Jim found a letter his father had left for him on the kitchen table before leaving for work. He opened it in his old bedroom as I packed our things, and Jim read the letter to himself:

> Jim, your seeming lack of initiative and interest to settle down has me somewhat concerned! How your mother feels is another story! It seems to me that you prefer to live a nomadic and gypsy sort of life, running from place to place. Possibly some visits to a psychiatrist will prove helpful. I don't know. But I would say that you are turning out to be an educated bum, if you will excuse the expression. There is no question that you know better. But why you choose to carry on in the manner you have elected is beyond my thinking.

Jim clenched his jaw and read on:

> Your desire to keep roaming may be what you call happiness, but I think you're unstable and may be off your rocker. I am getting to believe you wasted four years in college, and there's no question you've wasted four years since you've been out of school. Now that you have decided to be on your own, I attach:
>
> 1. Insurance bill for $85.10 for your insurance. Please pay it if you want to continue the policy, otherwise don't pay it and let insurance drop.
>
> 2. Please destroy all gas credit cards you have in my name. From here on out all my credit cards for gas are going to be charged to Associated Steam. My present cards are all being canceled.
>
> 3. I am seriously thinking about changing my will and mother's will that in the event of my demise, there shan't be a penny to you unless you're settled down working at a legitimate job or until you're 50 or 55 or even 60 years of

age, at which time probably you'll know better how I feel or felt about the situation

4. Please don't bring any more stray cats and shaggy dogs home, if you want to sneak them in during the day to see your mother, OK. But my command is that I don't want no S.O.B.'s who don't look 100% to me coming here. And as long as I've got something to say about who comes in my house, that's final!!!! And you had better believe it. And again I don't know how you ever got mixed up! At this point, my suggestion would be that you learn some trade, or go into some kind of business and let go of all that Ring around the Rosy you're doing now.

Pop

Tears filled Jim's eyes.

"What is it, Jim? What's the matter?"

"Take a look at this," he said solemnly, and held out the letter. "God, Ing, he's always been tough on me about my music, but never like this. Shit, doesn't he know how hard we're trying?" He threw up his hands. "Maybe he's right. Maybe I'll never make it in music. Do you think I should just give up?" I took hold of his shoulders.

"Absolutely not! You can't give up music, Jim!" I hugged him close and said, "Your dad has never wanted you to make music a career. But please don't worry, Jim. I know you can do this. I'll do whatever it takes to help you. I promise. I won't let you down."

Over the next few weeks, he became more determined than ever to show his father he was serious about succeeding. One night, in our Bronx apartment, we finished the words and melody to a new song we called "Hey Tomorrow."

> *Hey tomorrow, where are you going?*
> *Do you have some room for me?*
> *'Cause night is falling*
> *And the dawn is calling.*
> *I'll have a new day,*
> *If she'll have me*
>
> *Hey tomorrow, can't show you nothin'*
> *You've seen it all pass by your door,*

So many times now, I said I been changing,
Then slipped into patterns of what happened before,

'Cause I've been wasted and I've over-tasted,
All the things that life gave to me.
I've been trusted, abused and busted,
And I've been taken by those close to me.

Hey tomorrow, you've gotta believe that,
I'm through wastin' what's left of me,
Cause night is fallin'
And the dawn is callin'
I'll have a new day, if she'll have me.
I'll have a new day, if it'll have me.

In March, Tommy finally called to say that Nik Venet had booked studio time to do the record. We moved into high gear, polishing the songs being considered for the album. For two weeks we wrote and practiced eight to ten hours a day in our claustrophobic apartment. At last we made our selections, knowing the final decision belonged to the producers: Venet, and Cashman, Pistilli and West. Ten songs made the final cut, eight of them written by us: "Vespers," "What Do People Do," "Hey Tomorrow," "Age," "Big Wheel," "I Am Who I Am," "Just Another Day," "Spin Spin Spin," and "The Man That Is Me." Two others, "The Next Man That I Marry" and "What the Hell," were written by Cashman, Pistilli and West.

The selections were a mix of folk and country. We were asked to sing most songs as a duo, with Jim playing his twelve- and six-string acoustic guitars. We would sing two solos each, but both of us felt the strongest piece on the album would be "Age," a song about starting all over again, which we'd written in our Bronx apartment:

I've been up and down and round and round, and back again,
I've been so many places I can't remember where or when,
And my only boss was the clock on the wall,
And my only friend never really was a friend at all.

I've traded love for pennies,
Sold my soul for less,

Lost my ideals in that long tunnel of time.
I've turned inside out, and round about and back again,
Found myself right back where I started again.

Once I had myself a million, now I've only got a dime,
The difference don't seem quite so bad today,
With a nickel or a million,
I was searching all the time,
For something that I never lost or left behind.

I've traded love for pennies,
Sold my soul for less,
Lost my ideals in that long tunnel of time.
I've turned inside out, and round about and back again,
Found myself right back where I started again.

Now, I'm in my second circle and I'm headin' for the top,
I've learned a lot of things along the way,
I'll be careful while I'm climbing,
Because it hurts a lot to drop.
And when you're down, nobody gives a damn, anyway.

I've traded love for pennies,
Sold my soul for less,
Lost my ideals in that long tunnel of time.
I've turned inside out, and round about and back again,
Found myself right back where I started again.

We arrived at the Hit Factory early on the morning we were to begin recording. Our bodies fueled by nervous energy, we walked through the wood-paneled control booth and into the darkened studio. The engineer set up two floor microphones next to where we would sit. He handed each of us a headset and then gave one to Gary Chester, the drummer, and another to Joe Mack, the bassist.

"Okay," came the engineer's voice over the headset, "let's get a sound check." He sat behind double-paned glass, working the controls as Jim and I warmed up. Tommy, Nik, Dennis, and Phil sat watching from the control booth. "We'll go through a few of the songs so Gary and Joe can get a feel for the tempos," the engineer said. After a run through the tunes, the engineer called a break. "Okay!" he motioned. "I've got the levels set. Take five. Then we'll come back and do the first song. You pick it, Jim. We'll do a reference vocal. So don't worry about perfection. Let's just get down the basic tracks today, and we'll redo the voices later if we need to before we do the sweetening."

"That's when they'll add the strings, horns, and background vocals," Jim told me as we stretched and drank a cup of coffee.

Jim's freelance studio work had prepared him for the album, but I was new to the experience. I tried to conceal my own tense excitement. And Jim tried to help me. Facing the sound booth again, we began to sing and felt our voices embrace as they had from the first day we'd played together in my bedroom. "Let's try that one again," Jim said after completing a song.

"It's fine," Tommy commanded.

"Can we hear it back?" I asked.

"Yeah, I felt it was a little slow," Jim said back into the mic.

"Nah, it's OK. Don't worry, Jim."

"Your performance is meticulous," Phil chimed in, as he left the control room to return to his office.

For the next three days, we did nothing but sing, eat, and sleep. Every word we said to one another concerned the album.

On the second night, after we had recorded a few more songs, Nick Venet and the engineer stayed to listen to our takes.

When we came back to the studio the next night, Nick said, "Hey guys, instead of calling your album *Ingrid and Jim Croce*, we thought maybe we could call it *Bombs over Puerto Rico*," he joked.

Then Nick told us his story:

"We were sitting in the studio at four in the morning last night, and suddenly there was a huge explosion; the whole building shook, and we were covered in white plaster. When we all staggered into the street, the place was full of fire engines, policemen, the FBI, and everyone you could imagine. Apparently some radical Puerto Rican group figured they'd let off a bomb when nobody could get hurt, not figuring that two idiots would be listening to tapes in the basement at four in the morning. Well, maybe it's too much of an inside joke . . . but it just might sell!"

The third night, after the final take, I couldn't help worrying. "You know, Jim, I think you're right. We didn't get much direction or input on this album. We just did what we do at concerts. I really expected more interaction with the producers,

154

but all they did was tape us. Will we get a chance to work with the final mix after they sweeten it? I understand that's as important as recording the songs."

"I really don't know, Ing. This is our first album, so I guess we have to trust the producers. I just hope they know what they're doing! They all seem so distracted by their own problems."

Suddenly, the recording sessions were completed, and it was over.

Jim felt disappointed.

"It all seemed kind of rushed," he told Tommy. Tommy didn't respond. "We just have to decide which of the takes we like best and mix it, but we could have done it better, with a little more time," Jim continued. "Don't you think?"

"It's fine, Jim. Relax!" Tommy assured him.

Looking back, I remember thinking that if nothing else, we sure were dealing with some bad timing. Tommy was getting a divorce and had a new woman; Merv's wife was leaving him, and there was a child involved, making it really messy; and Nik had some serious problems at Capitol. It felt as if no one was really focusing seriously on our project.

Two weeks later, after sweetening, "the Boys" rushed the record out the door, under budget, calling it *Jim and Ingrid Croce*. I couldn't help wondering if we'd had a different producer, like John Simon, who had produced the Band and Joni Mitchell, we couldn't have made an album that brought us to a new level. But it was done now. And the best we could hope for was a good mix and strong PR.

That night, Tommy and Barbara took us to dinner at Paparazzi Restaurant across from Tommy's apartment and bought a bottle of champagne to celebrate. After months of delay, the album was finally complete.

"Nik wants you to go to his apartment in the Village tomorrow, so he can take pictures of you for the album cover," Tommy informed us. "I hear he's a pretty good photographer."

"Yeah, well, I hope so. If he can make me look good, he's great." Jim responded.

"Nik's also invited you to his mountain cabin in upstate New York for the weekend."

"I sure hope being a friend of the producer is a good omen for the album," Jim said.

After the photo shoot at Nik's apartment, Gene Pistilli cornered Jim and me. "Want a joint, man?" he asked Jim. "It's good shit!"

"I can use some good shit," Jim smiled.

"That makes two of us, man. I am fucked up. I figured we'd write, publish, produce, and make records together, but not share the stage," he said, referring to

Tommy and Dennis. "I can't believe I'm letting myself get on a stage with these putzes. I never expected to be part of a performing trio."

"Well, performing isn't their expertise," Jim admitted.

"Yeah, Dennis looks like fuckin' Nureyev with a hot foot. And Tommy is coma-tose. I have to check to make sure he's breathing. Christ, they're so embarrassing." He lowered his voice. "Shit, I wish I could get out of my contract!"

"But I thought you were a partner."

Gene took a deep breath. "Yeah, well, I am a partner, but when it comes to making business decisions, I don't count for shit. Part of it's my own fault. I'm not as driven as those bastards. Money isn't my bottom line, and they know it."

Jim didn't respond, and I didn't want to get into it while they were stoned.

———

By early summer the bills had piled high, and Jim's and my initial excitement about the album had waned. Little was going on for us with music. We called Merv regularly to ask about bookings, but there were none. And Tommy still had no word on when the album was to be released.

One afternoon in June, Jim went to the CP&W office to pick up our check.

"Hey, Joni," he said to the secretary. "How are you doin'?"

"I'm good, but did you hear about Gene?" she whispered.

"No, what's goin' on?"

"I think you better ask Tommy. Gene's in the hospital."

Tommy calmly told Jim that Gene had overdosed on sleeping pills and had to have his stomach pumped.

"What the fuck! And no one bothered to call me!" Jim yelled, storming out. We rushed to the hospital and found Gene alive but distraught.

"No one but you and Pat has even bothered to visit me," he said sadly. "I guess that tells you where 'the Boys' are at."

The day after Gene's release from the hospital, Phil Kurnit insisted that Gene sign papers, relinquishing his rights in their companies.

Jim phoned him and said, "I thought you guys were friends."

"Yeah, some kind of friends," Gene sighed. "But I guess it's best for everyone. They can keep their profits, and I can get the fuck out."

———

In July, Jim walked into the newly named Cashman & West offices just as John Stockfish, Gordon Lightfoot's former bass player, was leaving. Impressed by the musical iconoclast, Jim shook his hand and introduced himself. Then he went in to see Tommy.

"Are you doing business with John Stockfish?"

"We're thinking about finding him some gigs," Tommy replied. "He's talented as hell, but he alienates people. He just stopped working with Lightfoot. I guess John was trying to tell him how to write and arrange his songs, and Lightfoot didn't want to hear it." Tommy flipped a paperclip across his desk. "Stockfish is opinionated, never short on advice. But who knows?" With a dismissive shrug Tommy turned to a file cabinet. "Maybe we can do something for him."

The next week, Tommy introduced us to Stockfish, and Jim and I began playing with John, trying to overlook his idiosyncrasies.

"You're good, Croce," Stockfish told Jim with authority. "And you and Ingrid together have something unusual going on. I'd like to stay in New York for a few months so we can play together."

"You're welcome to stay with us for a while," Jim offered. Stockfish took him up on it, and within a week his girlfriend, Pat, flew in from Toronto and moved in with us, too.

"Are they planning to stay with us long?" I asked Jim, one night in our bedroom. "They're certainly welcome to share what we have," I offered. "But we don't have much. And it could get really tight."

"They shouldn't be staying with us that long," he said. "Anyway, it's worth it just to have the chance to play with John. I can learn a lot from him. His timing is fantastic, something I always just shrugged off, and he's a great bass player. Besides, maybe we can get better gigs with a backup musician of John's stature."

Within a week, Merv booked us as a trio at the Ship's Fare, a well-known restaurant and bar on Cape Cod. Stockfish turned down an opportunity to tour with Ian and Sylvia to play with us. The pay was slim, but we three musicians were compensated with all the lobster we could eat and a chance to get out of the city for the summer.

At each practice session, Stockfish would plant his metronome in front of Jim and me. "Come on, Jim, listen," he insisted. "Tick, tick, tick, tick."

"Yeah, I hear it," Jim told John.

"Just listen, man. Dah, dah, dah, dah. Hear it?"

"Hear what?" Jim asked.

"Don't you hear it, man?" John insisted.

"What kind of drugs are you taking, man?" Jim joked. "Give me some of them drugs, so I can hear what you do. You are out there, man."

"It isn't drugs!" he insisted. "I don't do drugs anymore, man."

"OK, John, calm down. I'll do drugs, and you can get high on the metronome." Jim laughed.

"Drugs are bad, man," Stockfish insisted. "Let's play." He pointed to the song "The Way We Used to Do."

"Now, Ingrid, you sing this part." Jim encouraged me by strumming the melody.

"No, Jim," John interrupted. "Stop playing. Let's really make this work. Just sing it in time to the metronome, Ingrid. No music yet. Jim, you sing with her and trade harmony parts on the chorus."

"Stockfish, you're about as much fun as a rubber crutch," Jim joked. "Let's smoke a joint."

"Man," Stockfish said with a straight face, "drugs can mess up your mind and your music real bad."

"Don't be so intense, John. There's nothing worse than a reformed alcoholic or druggie," Jim replied, grinning. "I say, 'If you dig it, do it. And if you dig it a lot, do it twice.'"

Not used to practicing a song more than a couple of times, Jim typically fought Stockfish's long rehearsals. I, on the other hand, thrived on them. I loved the discipline and attention John gave our music. Still, I had to agree with Jim; our Canadian friend was definitely "out there."

The serenity of Cape Cod was a stark contrast to New York's pressure cooker. The two-month hiatus gave us a chance to catch our breath before embarking on what we expected to be a grueling tour to promote the album. When we returned to the Bronx, on September 2, 1969, we were at last able to celebrate the release of the long-awaited Capitol album. Together, with Stockfish and Pat, we relaxed at our apartment and put on the LP for the very first time.

We listened in tense silence, without enthusiasm. Jim held back comment until the second cut.

"Ah, shit," he said. He leaned his head into his hands. "I should have been there for the final mix. I thought producers were supposed to make musicians sound better than they do live. This album doesn't come close to the way we sound in person. All the excitement is gone!"

"Don't be such a harsh critic," Stockfish admonished. "It's pretty damn good, man."

We listened until the album played all the way through, and Jim raked his hands through his thick, curly hair. "I just hope it's good enough to sell."

"It's good enough, man," John emphasized. "All they have to do now is put some energy and money behind it—promote it! Once we get out there, man, and play for the people, they're gonna love it. I promise you, it's as good as Ian and Sylvia—better!"

Later that month, as part of the record's promotion, we sang at Paul's Mall in Boston, a popular club that showcased new acts. We brought fresh energy to our performance, and the excitement and overwhelming response of the audience elated us.

"See, they love you," John told Jim after the gig. "This is the reaction you want from your audience. They're crazy about you, man."

"Yeah, they love us live, but the big question is: Will they buy the record?"

We got rave reviews in Boston, but our high was short-lived. In October, after we returned to New York, no work followed.

Then we received a registered letter on the new Cashman & West letterhead. I read the letter out loud to Jim.

It exercised the company's option under the original agreements binding us to another year under their publishing, production, recording, and management contracts.

"Isn't the option ours?" I asked.

"Yeah, they said it was, Ing. But I don't know about these things. What difference does it make anyway?" he shrugged. "If they can't get us work, I'm sure they won't expect us to stay."

"But the letter says they're renewing their option. It's our option!"

Later that week, Tommy called us into the office.

"Capitol is going through a major restructuring," he said without emotion.

"Yeah," Jim asked, bracing for bad news. "So how will that affect us?"

"They haven't budgeted any promotion money for the album," Tommy said. "That means the record distribution will be minimal, and there won't be much radio airplay either."

"I thought you guys were supposed to promote our album!" I said. "And what happened to our advance? Why haven't we gotten it yet?" Tommy didn't answer. "So what do you expect us to do now?" Tommy looked at Jim, beseeching him to control his wife. Trying to contain myself, I went on. "I'm confused about this whole thing, Tommy. It just doesn't make sense. Why did Phil send us this letter?" I held up the registered letter. "You said the option was ours, not yours, but Phil says it's the other way around. Why would we want to continue with you if there's no promotion, no jobs, and no money?"

159

Jim broke in.

"It's probably a misunderstanding, like I told you, Ing." I was furious. Jim was defending Tommy, trying to avoid the problem.

"We still want to continue with you, Jim," Tommy interjected with a forced smile. "We believe in you. I thought you'd be happy to have us handle all this business stuff for you."

Ever uncomfortable with confrontation, Jim tried to divert the tension and reassure Tommy. "Yeah, I'm about as nervous around business as a whore in church," Jim joked. "But I guess you guys know what's best for us."

"Jim, why are you doing this?" I couldn't listen to Tommy's patronizing us any longer. Angrily, I stormed out of the office.

Later that night, Jim told me that Tommy had said not to listen to me. Although Jim caved to Tommy, at home he expressed doubts to me about the true consequences of the contracts.

"Man, what did you sign with them?" Stockfish asked, overhearing our conversation.

"A contract for one year," Jim said defensively. "That's it."

"You'd better check into it. Here, let me see the contract."

"They never gave us one."

"You don't have a copy of your own contract?" Stockfish echoed incredulously. "You'd better get one, man!"

Within weeks it became evident that the album wasn't selling. Jim and I visited a dozen record stores, and not one had our album for sale. We called Merv, the manager to whom we'd been assigned, to find out about getting back on the road, but he couldn't get us a gig, not even a single small-college concert.

Then, in mid-October, we learned about an opening for a host position on a children's television show out of Boston. A television producer who'd heard us performing at Paul's Mall had become a fan, and enlisted us for the upcoming project. The show was to chronicle American history through music, and Jim and I were to audition by writing and recording sample songs for the program. With the opportunity to host our own children's show, we began writing immediately.

In the tiny apartment in the Bronx, we sat at our dining room table: Jim with guitar in hand, me with pen and paper, and the Wollensak. We liked the idea of being employed to write about the evolution of the country, and to do it for children made it really fun. The job seemed so appropriate to Jim's keen interest in history and his ability to teach kids.

160

Within three weeks, we wrote more than twenty original tunes and arranged them with Stockfish playing bass. Our publishers were pleased that their songwriters had been so prolific. Jim and I went into the studio to record the new songs. We were excited that we would be able to use these recordings as a demo for our audition with the television show.

Tommy and Dennis were in the control room with the engineer, while Jim, John, and I ran through every song in no more than two takes. Essentially, the producers turned on the tape recorder and let it roll.

Jim played the songs in a simple folk style. He felt nostalgic, almost patriotic, singing about the history of America. And because these songs were for children, it gave him a new direction from which to write. He and I told short stories in a plain, unpretentious manner, and Jim accompanied us with simple yet haunting melodies. Stories about the Native Americans were portrayed in "Iron Horse Lament." "Hard Times Be Over" was about the Great Depression. "Greenhill Mountain Lullaby" described the closing of the coal mines in upstate Pennsylvania and Virginia.

Jim and I considered "Railroads and Riverboats" and "The Migrant Worker" to be among the best songs we wrote for the show. We were optimistic that these songs strengthened our chances of being selected as the hosts for the program.

Railroads and Riverboats

The railroads and the riverboats
That bred the mighty men,
That we read about and we dreamed about
The men who built this land.
And the farmers and the lumbermen,
And the men who work the mills,
And the poor hard workin' miners
Who died inside the hill.
While the rivers that flow
Are the blood of our land,
And the trucks they keep rumblin'
On that great concrete band,
And the railroads keep pushin'
To be all they once were
And nature is callin'
No one's listenin' to her.

And the immigrants by the boatload
In a dozen different tongues,
Sang of freedom in the new land
Climbed the ladder rung by rung.
Some to Boston, some to Pittsburgh,
Philadelphia and St. Paul,
And the old way led to new days
They were welcome one and all.
With the railroads and the riverboats
And the bread lines far behind,
And the days we sang together
Long gone but still in mind,
And the men who came before us,
Men who brought us to today
And the story still unravels
From the dreams of yesterday.

Two weeks after we sent the demo tape to Boston, we learned that Hoagy Carmichael had been chosen to host the show.

"God, Ing, how much more disappointment can we take?" Jim asked when he hung up the phone and told me the bad news.

"I don't know, Jim."

"I feel like a yo-yo. First we're up; then we're down."

In the next room, Stockfish played a monotonous rendition of "Twinkle, Twinkle Little Star" to the methodical beat of the metronome. Pat had recently returned to Canada, but his strong presence was like having even more than two people in our tiny apartment.

"Stockfish is driving me crazy," Jim said. "I'd like to throw his fucking metronome out the window."

John glanced up at us but kept playing, concentrating on his timing. Finally, he spoke:

"It's hot in here," John said. "Is that freaking air conditioner working yet?"

"Are you kidding? It's almost winter, John. If the fucking manager hasn't fixed it all summer, what makes you think he's gonna do it now?" Jim punched the wall. "I'm getting out of here before I do some real damage."

A week later, Jim and I jumped at the opportunity to leave New York and get back on the college concert circuit as a duo. We were relieved to perform on our

NEW YORK'S NOT MY HOME

own again and hoped that by the time we returned to New York, John would have arranged to move back to Canada.

But the tour was short, and when we returned to our apartment, Stockfish was still there, keeping in sync with his metronome.

"I can't find any studio work, man, and I don't have enough cash to get out of New York," he complained.

"Well, we can't offer you anything more, John. You know we don't have any money," I told him.

When there was no reply, Jim added, "Stockfish, you're gonna have to do something. We can't put you up any longer, man. It's murder in this apartment with the three of us here."

The following morning Stockfish went to Tommy and begged plane fare. When he came back, he told Jim, "I'll be going home to Canada in early December."

Just before Christmas, Jim and I went on another college tour through upstate New York. It seemed a futile attempt to promote an album no one could buy or hear. And on top of everything else, several universities where we were scheduled to play had been plagued by campus strikes and riots. At others, only a handful of students showed up for our poorly publicized performances. After a few weeks we reached our final stop, Alfred University in Alfred, New York.

I was excited to get to the university, as I'd heard that the ceramics department was among the best in the country. But the campus had been overtaken by a flu epidemic, and the ceramics department was closed. We were given a room next to the infirmary, which was packed with sick and complaining students. We had a whole day to spend before our first show.

"What's there to do around Alfred?" Jim asked Lee Schumacher, the student representative assigned to us.

"Well," the animal husbandry major said, "you can either go to the livestock barns or participate in the race riots." His expression indicated he was not at all excited about his host-playing role.

"That's no contest, Lee," Jim said, trying to implore him. "Let's go to the barns."

The student gave him a slow smile, warming up to Jim. "The horses, goats, and sheep are in heat right now," he said, "so you can watch them mate."

"That sounds like fun," Jim grinned.

Only two students showed up for the first concert. The rest were either sick, gone for Christmas vacation, or taking part in student protests. The next night the audience doubled in size to four. Afterwards, backstage, I blew up. "Jim, this is ridiculous. I don't understand why we have to stay here if no one is coming to hear us. Please call Merv and tell him we want to come home for Christmas. I'm going to go soak in a hot bath."

Sitting in the tiny bathtub, I found myself swatting at the black flies I was convinced were breeding in the heating ducts of the infirmary. In the adjacent room Jim very reluctantly phoned Merv.

"No one is showing up to the concerts, man. A crowd of exactly two the first night, then four the second. The campus is just about shut down with a flu epidemic, and the rest of the students are already gone for the holidays. What do you say we go home for Christmas?"

"You've got to stay—you're booked through the end of the week," Merv reminded him. "If you don't stay, no one gets paid!"

Jim was silent a moment.

"I guess you're right." He paused. Then he added, "Say hello to Tommy and Dennis for me. Tell them I'm spending my spare time at Alfred University at the School of Animal Husbandry. Tell them, if they're interested, that the sheep are in heat."

"Jesus, Jim," I screamed from the bathroom. "Tell him there are fucking flies in the bathtub, and everyone here has the flu!"

But by then Jim had already said good-bye and hung up the phone.

"Ing," he said in a defeated tone, "they won't pay us if we don't finish here, and we don't have enough money to get home! We're stuck." The next morning, the college closed the entire campus because of the flu epidemic. The university cancelled the remainder of our shows and paid us through the end of the week.

Depressed, but also relieved, Jim and I decided to begin vacation early. We were packed and on our way back to the gloomy Bronx apartment before breakfast time. On the way back, Jim came down with the flu. I drove on, while Jim vomited through the open window of the VW. He spent the next week in bed.

———

The new year, 1970, found us once again with no money and no plans. Dreariness settled around us. We tried to avoid quarreling but couldn't.

"You need to talk to Tommy," I fumed. "If they're not going to get us work, then why would we sign and agree to an option? You and I both know that's not what Tommy promised us."

"Yeah, you're right. Why don't we just leave?" he said sarcastically.

"Please talk to Tommy and tell him how you feel. If he's really your friend, he'll do the right thing."

"Oh Ing, you certainly are an ornery one."

"Well, we can't stay holed up in this apartment forever!"

"Come over here and give me a kiss right here," he said, pointing to his cheek.

"Goddamn it, Jim, can't you discuss this with me for just a minute?" I pleaded. "I don't want to be so serious. But one of us has to be concerned about our future. You say you'll talk to Tommy, but you never do. You know he won't listen to me. He won't even acknowledge me. Please, Jim, could you please just find out what's going on?"

"Okay. I promise I'll go in on Monday and get some answers."

"We need to get a copy of the contract," I reminded him.

"Come over here and give me a kiss." He moved over, leaving room for me to join him on the couch. In spite of our quarrels about the business, I usually softened and accepted his overtures. It was hard for me to say no to him. I sat down next to him. "Lay down on your belly, Ing, and I'll give you a back rub." He lifted my sweater and began kissing the small of my back.

"Just a backrub," I cautioned, though I knew he wouldn't stop there. He had a way of persuading me to give in to his amorous appetite no matter how angry I was. And I loved making love to him, especially when he was tender.

We met with Tommy on Monday afternoon, but once again Jim skirted the business issues.

"Tommy, you should have come to Alfred with us," he joked. "I don't know what was more fun: watching the people vomit all over themselves or catching the goats reveling in fornication."

I sat seething. "Jim, please ask him!" He ignored me and went on with the small talk before singing for Tommy the chorus to his favorite song about animal husbandry.

> *Cats on the rooftop,*
> *Cats on the tiles,*
> *Cats with the clap, and the crabs and the piles,*
> *Cats with their bums all wreathed in smiles*
> *As they revel in the throes of fornication*

———

Life in New York was intolerable, and the friction between us increased.

"Jim, we just got a bill from Moore for my scholarship. We owe them $1,000 by the end of January. Since I didn't go back to school this year, I have to pay it back."

He didn't respond. I wanted to be supportive but felt angry and trapped. Why was he so afraid to talk honestly with his friend?

Finally, in late February, Tommy got Jim a commercial for Big Sur Cigars. Jim had no gas money. So he rode his bike through Harlem, in spite of the ongoing race riots, and then through Central Park to a studio on the West Side. After the session, he went out to unlock his bike from the pipe at the front of the building.

As Jim bent over the lock, a panhandler came up behind him.

"You got a dime for a cup of coffee?" he asked.

Startled, Jim jumped back. Before he could reply, the transient said, "Man, I'm sorry. It looks like you need it more than I do."

"Let me buy you a cup." Jim said, leading him into the coffee shop.

"How did you get so fucked up, man?" Jim asked the guy. The homeless man told his story about living on the streets of New York City. As they left, Jim paid the check with the last dollar he had. Inspired by his conversation with the man, he wrote a new song that night called "Box #10."

> *Well, out of southern Illinois come a down home country boy,*
> *He gonna make it in the city playin' guitar in the studio.*
> *Well, he hadn't been there an hour,*
> *When he met a Broadway flow'r;*
> *You know she took him for his money*
> *And she left him in a cheap hotel.*
> *Well, it's easy for you to see*
> *That that country boy is me,*
> *I'm sayin' how'm I gonna ever break the news*
> *to the folks back home*
> *Well, I was gonna be a great success,*
> *Things sure ended up a mess,*
> *And in the process I got messed up too.*
>
> *Hello, Momma and Dad, I had to call collect,*
> *'Cause I ain't got a cent to my name;*
> *Well, I'm sleepin' in the hotel doorway*
> *And tonight they say it's gonna rain.*
> *And if you'd only send me some money,*

I'd be back on my feet again;
Send it in care of the Sunday Mission, Box #10.

Back in Southern Illinois,
They're still worry'n 'bout their boy,
But this boy's comin' home just as soon as he gets the fare;
'Cause as soon as I got my bread,
I got a pipe upside my head;
You know they left me in the alley
took my money and my guitar too.

Hello, Momma and Dad, I had to call collect,
'Cause I ain't got a cent to my name;
Well, I'm sleepin' in the hotel doorway
And tonight they say it's gonna rain.
And if you'd only send me some money,
I'd be back on my feet again;
Send it in care of the Sunday Mission, Box #10.

A few weeks later, Jim walked up to me while I was toasting a bagel in the kitchen. "Let's get out of here. Let's go home."

I put down the butter knife and turned to him.

"Where's home?"

"Anywhere you want, Ing."

"Let's move to the country, away from this insanity."

I called my painting professor, and now good friend, Harold Jacobs. Some of the best times we'd shared together were out at his farmhouse. Though I was Harold's student, Jim and I had become good friends with him and his French wife, Berenice, while I was at Moore. We'd stayed overnight at their country home while I was studying and Jim was teaching. And we enjoyed the quiet morning walks along the country roads and the delicious French gourmet meals that Berenice had prepared for us.

With the thought of moving away from New York, I felt my anger dissipate. Jim said, "I feel better already," as I dialed Harold's number to ask if he knew of a place near them that we could rent.

Harold was happy to hear that Jim and I were moving back to Pennsylvania. He told me he did know of a place that their friends, the Kaltenbachs, were renting.

It was in Lyndell, a small town fifty miles west of Philadelphia on the Brandywine River, not too far from their home.

"That sounds perfect! Thank you so much, Harold. Can you give me the phone number?" I knew our checking account had the last of our savings, less than $300, and I hoped that would be enough to make a new start.

After I hung up the phone with Harold, I immediately called John Kaltenbach, introduced myself, and told him I wanted to rent the apartment, sight unseen. John was kind and told me he would hold it as a favor to the Jacobs until we got there. Then we could take a look at the place and discuss the rent and all the details.

When I hung up, I was thrilled. "I can't believe it, Jim. We're actually leaving New York!"

"It sounds like just the kind of place we need, Ing. A place in the country away from all this shit! I'll rent a trailer in the morning. I'm sure Pistilli will help us to load up. I'll give him a call. . . . Thanks for taking care of this. "

"See, sometimes being serious isn't so bad."

"Come over here, sweet thing."

This was the first time since the attack in Mexico that things felt really right again between us. We were both ready to start over again.

Together with Gene, Jim and I maneuvered our belongings into the elevator and down to a U-Haul trailer in the parking lot. Before we could finish, the elevator broke down. While Jim and Gene made trips up and down eight flights of steps, I stayed at the door to guard our things. A young woman, arms filled with groceries, hiked up the stairs and asked me excitedly, "Are you going to be our new neighbors?"

"No," I said, apologetically. "We're moving out today! I'm sorry, but it would have been nice. I've been in this apartment house for over a year, and I haven't made a single friend."

"Well, good luck," the young woman told me.

"You too," I said.

Jim's bike was the last thing to be loaded. He flung it up on top of the trailer to rope it down, but it fell back with a crash, catching his ear in the spokes. He winced, gritted his teeth against the pain, and heaved it back again. Blood streaked down his cheek, and his head began to throb. All at once everything hopeless and mean-spirited he had experienced in the building seemed to collapse on top of him. In a fit of rage, he sprinted back up eight flights to the old apartment. Adrenalin pumping, he yanked the heavy, broken air conditioner from the window, and, gaining momentum as he descended, he lumbered to the landlord's office on the ground floor. In a final farewell gesture, he hurled the air conditioner at the manager's office door.

Gene and I stood back, watching the spectacle.

"Man," Gene told Jim, "you are a strong motherfucker!"

Jim grabbed his bloody ear. "Yeah, well, this place upsets me!"

"Yeah, I can tell, man." Gene shook his head. "I bet your landlord's gonna know it, too." He glanced at the wrecked door and then threw an arm around Jim. "Good luck, you guys," he offered.

"I couldn't have done it without you, man," Jim told him. He gave him a quick embrace. "You've gotta come see us when we get settled in the country."

I hugged Gene. "Thanks for your help," I said, and gave him a big kiss on the cheek.

Exhausted, we got into the VW with the U-Haul in tow and headed south. As we approached the tollbooth on the New Jersey Turnpike, I looked at Jim in despair. I dug deep into the bottom of my purse and came up with 34 cents. "We don't even have enough to pay the toll." We slowed down, threw the change into the basket, and kept on driving. Mercifully, we weren't stopped.

As we crossed the bridge, I saw terrible disappointment in Jim's eyes. I hugged him and kissed his injured ear. That night, too tired to drive further and too broke to afford a motel, we snuggled together and slept in the VW in the parking lot of a Howard Johnson's. Embracing, we looked back at the New York skyline. It was the end of a very bad time. But we'd survived it. And out of our sad and desperate departure came the song "New York's Not My Home."

> *Well, things were spinnin' 'round me,*
> *And all my thoughts were cloudy,*
> *And I had begun to doubt all the things that were me.*
> *Been in so many places,*
> *You know I've run so many races.*
> *And looked into the empty faces of the people of the night,*
> *And something is just not right.*
>
> *Cause I know that I gotta get out of here,*
> *I'm so alone;*
> *Don't you know that I gotta get out of here,*
> *'Cause New York's not my home.*

Though all the streets are crowded,
There's something strange about it;
I lived there 'bout a year and I never once felt at home.
I thought I'd make the big time,
I learned a lot of lessons awful quick and now I'm
Tellin' you that they were not the nice kind;
And it's been so long since I have felt fine.

That's the reason that I gotta get out of here,
I'm so alone;
Don't you know that I gotta get out of here,
'Cause New York's not my home.

TIME IN A BOTTLE

WITH JIM AT THE WHEEL, and U-Haul trailer in tow, the dented Raisin bumped along a winding rural road toward our new apartment in a converted Pennsylvania farmhouse fifty miles southwest of Philadelphia. A cold, early morning mist surrounded the tall pine trees and carpeted the fields of clover. I was relieved to be away from the mind-mugging metropolis. Lyndell, Pennsylvania, population 138, looked like the perfect place for weary musicians to purge themselves of the insanities of the business and start all over again.

"I hope Bill Reid can flex some muscle and land a construction job for me," Jim said, rubbing his swollen, bloodstained ear. "We'll need something to live on, and I'm ready for some hard physical labor. I'm sure you'll be able to sell your paintings and pottery, sweet thing. That is, if the Boys don't find out and decide your art is under contract too."

"I don't think that's a problem Jim. They don't want my art any more than they wanted my music. They only want you, sweetie."

As we neared Lyndell, I read him the directions: "Make a left at Eagle Tavern, and go one-tenth of a mile to Lyndell Road. Then turn left, and go a ways until you cross Marsh Creek Bridge. Turn right, and follow the Brandywine River down toward Frank's Folly."

Finally, in the distance a huge old stone farmhouse came into view. Adjacent to it was a large two-story home. On the other side of the gravel road was another old, plantation-style mansion and, beyond that, a greenhouse surrounded by fields of flowers.

Harold and Berenice Jacobs told us that the landlords were good people, that John Kaltenbach used to be a professor at Harvard and a colleague of Richard Alpert, who had since transformed himself into Guru Baba Ram Dass. Harold said John's wife, Ruth, was a Quaker and that a decade ago John became a Quaker too. They had left Boston and bought the place, and they'd been making a living renting out the apartments and raising flowers and kids.

"This is great!" Jim said, slowing down as we approached the peaceful series of buildings. He stopped the car in front of the old stone barn.

John Kaltenbach, a giant of a man in overalls and a red flannel shirt, walked over with a trowel in one hand and a cup of coffee in the other.

"You must be the Croces," he said, lifting the muddy garden tool. "We've been expecting you. Here, hold on to these flowers, Ingrid, and I'll get the key so you can unload. By the way, we require all of our tenants to help with the plants and picking the flowers on the property, so I hope one of you has a green thumb." He took long slow strides toward the house.

As a city girl with no prior experience working the land, I was excited by the possibility of learning about gardening. I never imagined I'd have the opportunity to pick flowers as part of my rent payment, and I was hoping I might be able to grow our own vegetable garden too.

John came back, key in hand, and led us to the vacant apartment in the two-hundred-year-old farmhouse.

"When we bought these thirty-three acres, this big old empty house came with it," John explained. "We spruced it up a bit, made three apartments out of it, and have rented them out ever since. Yours is the smallest. It used to be the smoke house." He unlocked the door and extended his arm, ushering us inside. As we entered the small living room, we noticed an enormous fireplace. "That's where they used to smoke meat," John said. "Here's the kitchen, and upstairs you'll find the bedroom and bath."

I ran up the winding wooden stairs, and Jim followed. A double bed with a metal headboard stood in the middle of the bedroom, flanked by two boxy chests of drawers. There were two large windows; the one above the bed looked out over the barn. The north window opened to the Brandywine River. Though the entire apartment was less than eight hundred square feet, it seemed spacious and romantic after our cramped rental in the Bronx.

"It's perfect," I told Jim as I returned to the living room. Jim hesitated.

"I'll be starting work in a week or so. Can we give you the rent then?" he asked our new landlord.

John gave him an affable smile.

"That's fine with me. The Jacobs already informed me that you wouldn't be able to pay until the fifteenth. Why don't you two get comfortable, and come up to the big house for dinner around six o'clock? I know Ruth and the kids will want to meet you both."

———

During our first few days in the farmhouse, Jim relaxed. He took peaceful walks by the river and played his guitar endlessly at the kitchen table. I unpacked everything, cleaned and painted the walls, and scrubbed the kitchen and bath. Two days later, our new home was in perfect order.

"Today, I start decorating," I said, kissing Jim happily as I handed him a plate with a big breakfast of eggs, sausage, and homemade blueberry muffins.

After he finished breakfast and I was cleaning up, he told me he was going out to the old stone outhouse. He thought he might be able to convert it into an office. I set up the table so I could do batik. The apartment's aging cotton curtains were dingy and boring, and since we didn't have money for new ones, I decided to use some brightly colored dyes I had and melt some wax in my old battered saucepan. I laid newspapers in thick layers on our prized dining room table, which my parents had given us for a wedding gift, and opened the windows for ventilation. After I completed my batik window dressings, I cut up old white sheets into rectangles for placemats, to match the curtains. In the distance I heard Jim call me.

"Ing, come on out here!" I set down the placemat I was dyeing and ran quickly to the outhouse to see what Jim wanted.

"I think this will make a perfect office," he said. "All we'd have to do is lay a new floor, slap on some paint, and it'll work fine. Look, you can see the Brandywine through the window." We peered through the arched window and saw smoke billowing overhead.

I was heartbroken when I saw the clouds of smoke pouring out the door and windows of our newly painted apartment. As I went inside to turn off the stove, I saw streaks of black waxy vapor running from the pan on the stove. I extinguished the flames quickly, but the freshly painted walls were coated with wax and smudged black and grey.

"So much for the white walls," Jim joked. "This time, I bet you paint them even better. In fact, if you keep it up, we can rent you out as a house painter, Ing."

When Jim went out to survey the neighborhood, I felt like crying for the dumb mistake I'd made and for all the extra work I'd caused myself. I started cleaning up my mess, and after feeling sorry for myself, and blaming the world out loud, I started to laugh. There was a freedom in the peacefulness of the country, and I felt there was room to make mistakes and time to make changes.

Once I finished cleaning, I walked outside through the kitchen door and took a good look at the backyard, deciding on the perfect place to plant my garden. I'd never grown anything in the ground before, so I wasn't quite sure what I should be looking for, but I was hoping it would come as naturally to me as art did and that, as John said, I'd have a green thumb.

When Jim returned home from his walk, I asked him if he'd help me start our garden. Immediately he went up to John's to borrow a pick and shovel. I drew out a line in the dirt by the back kitchen door to show him where I wanted to do the planting. I was going to grow zucchini, tomatoes, Swiss chard, green beans, melons, and herbs. According to the farmer's almanac, the timing was perfect.

I'd been athletic at school, but neither Jim nor I had been exercising in New York. Jim began to loosen the soil with the pick, and I worked the shovel. We must have looked comical to our new neighbors. Preparing the land for our first home garden was really difficult. It took us all day to ready the hard dirt. I felt a great satisfaction when we were finished, and while I planted the seeds, Jim cleaned up and then went to get some cold beer.

At the bottom of the hill, along the Brandywine River, stood the large, weather-beaten building with a sign that read, "Frank's Folly." It served as a combination trailer park, country store, bait shop, post office, and gas station. Frank was a dour, tight-lipped man, and he and his wife took great pride in their family business. Although Frank complained about the abundance of "hippies" moving into the area, his prejudice didn't stop Jim from trying to get to know the man behind the scowl. Each morning when Jim walked down to get the newspaper and mail, he prodded Frank for local gossip. The more Jim egged him on, the more Frank opened up, and the more fodder Jim had for new lyrics and raps.

"Those damn dope-smokin' commie fags are ruining this whole damn country," Frank told Jim. "I hope they don't try growin' that weed around here. I'll shoot those sons of bitches. You don't smoke that stuff, do ya? I heard you're a folk singer."

"Unh uh, not me," Jim said shaking his head. "I don't be hardly messin' around with no dope. I just came down to buy some beer, man."

In contrast with our dreary social life in New York City, we made friends quickly in the new surroundings. When our landlord told the neighbors, Carole and George Spillane, that a folk singer and an artist had moved in next door to them, they came over to introduce themselves. George was a warm and robust middle-aged Irishman with a ruddy complexion and a quick smile. Carole, his unlikely new bride several years his junior, was an attractive blond Italian from South Jersey with a sharp tongue. Both were professors at Delaware County Community College.

Eager to make friends, I invited Carole and George over to try my freshly baked bread, Jim's favorite. I served it warm with churned butter and local honey. After Jim poured them coffee, he picked up his guitar, and they joined us at our kitchen table.

"Mind if I play for you?" he asked.

"No, no, not at all," George quickly answered. "We'd love it."

175

Jim played a few songs without stopping.

"Hey, honey"—George reached over and stroked Carole's hair—"this guy's good. He's really very good." Then he turned to Jim: "You'll have to play at the Kaltenbachs' get-togethers."

"What are those like?" I asked.

"Well, living way out here with only two of their eight kids still at home, John and Ruth are starved for company. So a couple of times a month, they invite friends and neighbors in to feast on Ruth's home cooking and share thoughts."

"It's a trip," Carole said. "You might enjoy it, and we could definitely use some good music to liven things up."

We soon became regulars at what turned out to be bimonthly dinners filled with talk about art, culture, religion, and politics. Our new extended family included farmers, teachers, poets, philosophers, fellow musicians, and artists. John was a stoic and an intensely driven convert. He ran the evening parties like a Quaker meeting and loomed over the gatherings, starting each meal with a theatrical invocation while everyone held hands around the table in prayer. After dinner we retired into the living room, where John gave a dramatic reading, and then he'd ask Jim to respond with a song. With no preparation, Jim always managed to play something that related directly—or sometimes inappropriately—to the subject. Afterward, the august leader asked others to respond with their thoughts or feelings. The ritual lasted several hours until friction, boredom, or fatigue overtook the crowd.

In no time, I joined other local artists and showed my work at the Kaltenbachs' old stone barn, which had been converted into a gallery shortly before we arrived. I was happy to have such a convenient outlet to sell my work, and I began painting furiously and throwing a new line of sensual pottery. It was great to have vessels for the bunches of wildflowers I picked regularly from the nearby fields, and it was easier to sell the pots with the flowers in them.

The week we first settled in, Jim invited Bill Reid over to play some music and have a few beers. Jim lit a joint, took a toke, passed it to Bill, and, as he exhaled, asked, "Do you think you can get me a job, man?"

"Shit," Bill replied with a grin as he inhaled, "you've got a union card, don't you?" then paused to hold in the smoke.

Jim went to work the next day as a part-time truck driver for Sweeney Construction Company, hauling rock from a local quarry. Several days a week, he headed out by 4 AM to load and unload rocks or concrete pipe at the quarry near Chester. He always stashed a notebook to jot down ideas and phrases he picked up around the site. He also put a small cassette recorder in the backseat in case he came up with a tune. Jim liked handling the big rigs and, of course, being around blue-collar workers. And getting a paycheck revived his confidence. Still, he never imagined he'd be driving a truck for a living. He still hoped music was his future, despite the New York fiasco.

After work, I would greet him with a big hug and a home-cooked meal. I really enjoyed creating a warm, inviting home for us, tending our garden, and usurping Jim's position as head cook.

Though Jim was in many ways an intellectual who devoured books, studying philosophy, history, anthropology, haiku, and art, he fit in easily at the construction company.

"It feels good to be back with Emil and Crazy Frank," Jim told me one evening. "These guys are rugged sons of bitches. If I ever need anything, I know I can count on them. Not like those pussies up in New York."

On mornings when Jim didn't have to work, he'd sometimes go into the local bar about 7 AM to watch the "breakfast club" and pick up on the local color. Later he would tell me about the clientele.

"They sit around drinking shots and beers all day, Ing, and they look like they're riveted into their seats and into the bar with little screws in their elbows. All they need now are brass plates on their backs. Like the ones they have under those old taxidermy, funky animal heads hangin' on the walls. But I guess it's not all that different from the folks down on Race Street in Philadelphia. I remember my father would take me down there, near where he worked, and tell me about those bums that were down on their luck. I wish he could understand that's where I am. I'm just down on my luck, trying to find a way to make my music work for us."

Nights at our home in Lyndell soon began to look like John's Quaker dinners, but with more fun-loving and irreverent guests. Jim couldn't resist inviting all kinds of folks from our new community. There were musicians, young girls and earth mothers, the chaste and the horny, sinners and saints. And because I always had a pot of soup on the stove and a loaf of bread in the oven, Jim knew that between the music and the food, there would be a good time for all.

Although our lives had been transformed, and we were happier, in the back of my mind I still wondered if we could ever completely resolve what happened in Mexico.

Jim's rugged, chauvinistic friends at work joked about women and their wanton ways. These truckers were caricatures of the kind of men that myths are made of. And Jim taped hours of his talks with Reds, Emil, and mostly Crazy Frank. He knew how to listen and when to speak to add fuel to the fire. I understood, on the one hand, that Jim enjoyed hearing about the truckers' escapades. As a songwriter, he gathered material from his pals at work that helped him understand and portray their lives, but I thought Jim was different from these guys who wanted "all the women." I truly believed he valued monogamy.

Jim had been so supportive in helping me get through college. He'd encouraged my artwork and studies, helped me with harmonies, and complimented me when we sang together. Yet sometimes I noticed a moody distance or unwarranted jealousy on his part. I knew he was processing a lot of anger, and I hoped that somehow he could work it out through the music.

———

In Lyndell, Jim's old, loyal Volkswagen began to break down. Often he was left stranded on dark country roads on his way to or from work. With more than 200,000 miles on the odometer, the car was too far gone to repair. The Raisin had become part of the family, and Jim decided it deserved a proper funeral. When he covered it with a coat of black spray paint, he and I were surprised at how much better it looked. We were even tempted to postpone the burial and see if we could make any money by selling it. Jim cracked a bottle of Budweiser and poured some over the hood, blessing the worn-out old friend. Then we drove the car to a lot by our old home in Media and parked it, leaving a sign in the window that read, "For Sale. Runs. Best Offer." Two days later it sold for $50. My stepmom took pity on us and donated the Oldsmobile that had been sitting in her driveway since my dad had died three years earlier. Jim and I graciously accepted the handout, tinkered with it, and got it running. It sparked and sputtered up the road to the farmhouse, then died in the driveway. It never ran again.

Over the next few months, we went through a couple of $50 junkyard specials. In late spring, Bill Reid loaned Jim $100 for a down payment on a gunmetal-grey 1956 Ford sedan in great condition. But the thrill of driving the beautiful $500 four-door lasted only two days; someone played a dirty trick and poured sugar in the gas tank. The Ford never ran again.

By summer, the word of the Croces' car jinx spread. Jim's friend Ronnie Miller offered to let us trade in his old jeep for a more reliable one. Jim took Ron up on the offer, and we drove to New Jersey, where Jim bargained with a used-car dealer and traded the old jeep for a newer one, agreeing to take it "as is." He thought the jeep looked perfect. We cleaned the sticker price off the windshield and headed for the Jersey Turnpike. A few miles down the road, the transmission dropped out. Two hours later, Ronnie towed the just-purchased jeep to our home, where it sat and never ran again.

A neighbor's brother leaving for Vietnam also wanted to help us out and lent us his beautiful 1968 Peugeot station wagon. We scored a perfect three days on the new wheels. In the middle of the night the emergency brake mysteriously released. Early the next morning, when Jim went down to Frank's Folly to get the paper, he discovered the car had crashed into a cement bridge abutment right in front of the store. The wrecked Peugeot never ran again.

Mercifully, because Jim was working, even though it was a blue-collar job, Jim's father bought us a navy-blue Opal station wagon. Embarrassed by his need, Jim didn't dare tell his father the car was a lemon. He had to park it on hills to jumpstart it. And the second day we got it, the passenger-side door fell off the hinges. Then the front seat came loose, and the outside mirror fell off.

"I swear they delivered this car to the wrong address," Jim told me. "This one was intended for the clowns at Ringling Brothers!" He laughed outwardly at our "car curse," but perpetually penniless, he grew angry and frustrated at his inability to get ahead.

One day after seeing Jim jumpstarting the Opal, Bill told him about the time he had towed his brother's car at seventy-five miles per hour. The next time our car broke down, Jim persuaded Bill to go one better and tow him at eighty. They roared down the winding highway, Jim shouting encouragement the entire way.

That was the childlike way Jim and Bill always acted together. Bill brought out a playful, competitive streak in Jim. One afternoon, they started on a wild hot chili pepper challenge. Jim ate one, then Bill ate two, then Jim ate three—until both men had grueling stomachaches. Another time it was raw eggs. Then it was home-made dandelion wine. Like two misbehaving kids, they drank themselves under the table and laughed until tears came rolling down their faces.

The two men also bartered their "prized" possessions with one another, each trying to get the better end of the deal. They traded mandolins, banjos, gadgets, guns, and knives. Each tried to outdo the other. The monetary rewards were negligible; initially they did it for sentimentality. But when work was slow, and with multiple car payments and basic expenses, Jim swallowed his pride and sold his guitars to Bill or anyone he could.

"I'm like an old widow selling off her jewels one at a time to pay the rent," a dejected Jim told me one fall night. "I need to do more than just play for my dinner and my 25 bucks at the Riddle Paddock."

One day in late September, after driving his truck to Chester and back, he came home to change clothes.

"Look what came in the mail today," I said. I hesitantly handed him a letter from Phil Kurnit in New York. As Jim read, he began biting his lower lip. He bit harder, until he drew blood.

"Kurnit says they're exercising their second option on our contracts." Exploding in anger he slammed the letter on the table. "He can go fuck himself!" Escaping from New York and working at the quarry had toughened him. I watched him march to the phone. "I have no intention of ever playing again for Cashman & West," he shouted into the receiver.

The lawyer was not intimidated.

"No matter where you or Ingrid play or what you write," Kurnit told Jim coldly, "even if it's written on toilet paper, it's ours. That's the way this business works." The two shouted back and forth until Jim slammed down the phone in a fit of anger I had never seen before. He brooded for hours after the call.

"I can't understand how they can renew the contract. The renewal option is ours. That's what Tommy told us, and Phil too. Why the fuck don't they leave us alone? This is just fucking bullshit!"

———

On the advice of Jim's parents' friends, we hired Robert Cushman, a Philadelphia lawyer, to help us resolve the contract dispute. The lawyer's $500 retainer fee was five months' rent and seemed like a fortune, but seeing it as a necessity, I borrowed the money from my stepmom.

"Do you have copies of the contracts you signed?" the attorney asked.

"No," Jim told him.

"Was there an attorney present when you signed them?"

"Only Kurnit."

"The same Kurnit who represented the company you were signing the contract with?" our attorney asked.

"Yes," Jim answered sullenly.

"What about Gene Pistilli, the other partner?" Cushman asked.

"Somehow they got him out of the partnership," I said. "But he told us that he always felt the partners had taken advantage of us and of him too."

"Ask him to put his position in writing and send us a letter," the attorney advised.

Armed with Gene's letter, Cushman suggested meeting with Cashman, West, and Kurnit in their office in New York. In the days prior to the meeting Jim became nervous and upset and began to fear the confrontation. His earlier bravado evaporated by the time we reached the intimidating atmosphere of Kurnit's New York office. Jim kept his anger bottled up and sat biting his lower lip.

Cushman stated that he wanted Jim and me to reason with the partners and reach an amicable dissolution of the contracts.

Jim didn't reply, but I pleaded with Kurnit: "Jim and I understood, based on what you told us, that we would be able to cancel the contracts after a year. Won't you please just let us do what we all agreed to and let us move on?"

"You signed the contracts," Kurnit replied, "and we intend to hold you to them." He pointed an accusing finger at me and then threw down an invoice for several hundred dollars. "This is for promotional photos. You can expect to receive other bills for management fees and commissions," Kurnit said, and walked out coolly.

Jim and I sat there stunned. No one had ever mentioned we would be responsible for photo sessions or that there were unpaid management fees. Kurnit not only flatly denied our request to break off the relationship but handed us bills we didn't know existed.

We left the meeting in horror, and over lunch our attorney told us, "Unless you can afford to pay thousands, maybe even tens of thousands of dollars, and are willing to endure a few years embroiled in litigation, well, you're going to be bound by their contracts."

The train ride home to Lyndell was dreary. Jim sat in silence most of the way, staring off into the distance. I felt betrayed by everyone: the partners who didn't keep their promises, Jim for not standing up to Tommy, and myself for signing the contract in the first place.

The train passed through city after city, and a half hour went by before I said, "We don't have the money to fight them in court, Jim."

"We'll just have to wait them out," Jim responded. "Maybe if we fade into the woodwork and don't sing or write music for a year or two, they'll lose interest and forget about us." He vowed to play exclusively at small clubs and parties, and write music only in the privacy of our kitchen. Not able to share his music the way he had always dreamed, he felt his parents were being proven right, and that hurt even more.

———

When we returned to Lyndell, Jim immersed himself deeply in the blue-collar world. Although he enjoyed the Kaltenbachs' intellectual circle, he associated more and more with the tough guys he worked with. He enjoyed visiting with Ronnie and his hardcore biker and stock-car racing buddies like Roy Harris, who had grown up in Jim's neighborhood. The stock-car drivers had tattoos and kept cigarettes rolled up in their T-shirt sleeves. Jim was attracted to the men's macho attitudes and appreciated the chance to dive into the world of stock-car racing. The "pits" were a far more subversive world than anything he had ever encountered before, and the challenge of being accepted in it was irresistible.

As much as watching the races, Jim liked talking and mingling with the motor-heads at the track. Most of the drivers were hardworking, tough-talking, outspoken individuals. He loved their colorful personalities and the uncertain dynamics of the racetrack, where a fight could break out any minute.

He began to hang out at the track for longer periods of time.

"You always know where you stand with these guys," he told me. "If you don't, you'll find out pretty quick, because somebody will knock you flat on your ass." The drivers became his inspiration for his song "Rapid Roy."

> *Rapid Roy that stock car boy,*
> *He too much to believe*
> *You know he always got an extra pack of cigarettes*
> *Rolled up in his T-shirt sleeve.*
> *He got a tattoo on his arm that say, "Baby"*
> *He got another one that just say, "Hey"*
> *But every Sunday afternoon he is a dirt track demon*
> *In a '57 Chevrolet.*
>
> *Oh Rapid Roy that stock car boy*
> *He's the best driver in the land.*
> *He say that he learned to race a stock car*
> *by runnin' shine outta Alabam'*
> *Oh the Demolition Derby and the Figure Eight*
> *Is easy money in the bank,*
> *Compared to runnin' from the man*
> *In Oklahoma City with a 500 gallon tank.*

Yeah Roy so cool, that racin' fool,
He don't know what fear's about.
He do a hundred thirty mile an hour
Smilin' at the camera
With a toothpick in his mouth.
He got a girl back home name of Dixie Dawn,
But he got honeys all along the way.
And you oughta hear 'em screamin'
For that dirt track demon
In a '57 Chevrolet.

———

Despite Jim's sporadic work at Sweeney's construction site and the loose change he earned from local gigs, he continued to open our home to an excessive number of friends and acquaintances. After speaking to a stranger for five minutes, it wasn't unusual for Jim to invite them home. These impromptu gatherings of twenty to thirty people would congregate at the farmhouse on weekends.

I would feed them all, and Jim would play music late into the night, often until folks left or ended up sleeping on the floor of our tiny apartment, creating wall-to-wall bodies and an enormous mess for me to clean in the morning.

Jim seemed oblivious to how much time and energy I was putting into taking care of his guests. I was working at breakneck speed to get everything done so I could find time to make art, but it was difficult with all the company he invited into our home. I continued to cook, bake, and clean up after everyone, trying to make things the best I could, but I was losing my patience and my self-esteem.

For some reason my compulsive behavior was humorous to Jim. He complimented me on what I could accomplish on such a meager budget.

"Our table is like the parable of Christ with the loaves and the fishes," he told me one day. "I don't know how you do it." I was pleased that Jim was proud of my ability to be a good wife, but I had my own dreams of becoming a professional artist, and he seemed to have forgotten them.

One day I told him that I really wanted time to do my art and that I was happy to have his guests over, but I needed just a couple of nights alone.

He apologized immediately: "I'm so sorry for not realizing how hard it's been on you, Ing. I want you to do your art. And if you want, I'll help you."

During one of our now solitary mornings together, Jim sat on the front steps, figuring out a song and watching me working at my potter's wheel. He liked to be near me while I worked in the sun, so we could write and sing together. When I paused in my work, he stopped playing, and we sang a cappella.

George, our neighbor, looked up from where he was grading papers on his porch.

"When I hear you two sing," he called out, "a shiver runs down my spine."

"Glad we could provide the entertainment," Jim called back.

"Yeah," George replied, "It sounds X-rated to me. There's so much electricity between you two, I feel like a voyeur peering in while you're making love."

George's actual voyeurism was more innocent. The Spillanes' kitchen window looked directly across a small courtyard into our kitchen. Jim often stayed up all night singing into the tape recorder and writing new songs. Before shutting out the lights and going to bed, George could see Jim, guitar in hand, singing into a cassette tape recorder. In the morning, Jim was often still sitting there playing.

One morning, a few minutes after seeing George's lights come on, Jim tapped on the kitchen window.

"You wanna hear the new song I wrote last night?" he asked, holding up an empty coffee mug. George motioned for him to come in, and filled the cup with fresh brew as Jim started picking. From the dark hall, Carole, who worked as a drama coach, appeared in the kitchen doorway. As he finished, she said, "That's really good, Jim. You know, I was thinking. How would you like to do a concert series at the college?"

"Sounds great."

"It only pays $100."

"It's the rent. Would I be teaching or just performing?"

"I'd like to see you do both," Carole told him. "Give the kids some history about the music, about the business, and tell them how you write your songs."

Jim was excited about the opportunity to teach others about the musicians who had influenced him. And he wanted to impart his experience of the music business to the students, so they didn't run into the same fate he did.

Even with his limited experience, he started to write a book called *The Pitfalls of the Music Business*. He was so serious about it that he had my stepmom type it up for him; he'd use it to teach the class and also hoped to sell it.

In addition to Jim's interest in playing at the local college and writing a book, and in spite of Kurnit's warning, Jim and I had continued to perform at local clubs. The Main Point, our favorite, featured acoustic musicians. The roster had included such luminaries as Simon and Garfunkel, Gordon Lightfoot, James Taylor, John

Hartford, Dave Von Ronk, John Hammond, Linda Ronstadt, Bruce Springsteen, Don McLean, Taj Mahal, the Manhattan Transfer, and Arlo Guthrie. Jim and I were the opening act for many performers, who often crashed overnight at our home. Because we lived nearby, when the featured talent cancelled or a performer showed up late, Jeanette, one of the Main Point's owners, called us to substitute.

One night, out of the blue, during the drive home from the Main Point, Jim blew up: "It fucking pisses me off that we have to wait out Cashman & West! This stalemate is keeping us from getting another record deal, and there's not a goddamn thing we can do about it!"

I held my tongue. I knew he was right. Without an attorney or money to buy our way out, we were prisoners, and all I could say was, "I'm so sorry."

———

One evening in late August, Sal showed up at the farmhouse with a skinny young musician named Maury Muehleisen.

"Glad to see you again," Jim said, remembering that he and I had met Maury briefly in Tommy's office, and that Maury had come to see us at our apartment in the Bronx once with Sal. I really liked Maury's music, especially, "A Song I Heard," one of Maury's early tunes he'd pitched when he came to New York City.

"Remember I told you I'd only leave my teaching position at Glassboro State to do something great?" said Sal. "Well, this is it: I'm Maury's full-time manager."

Jim and I shared a surprised glance.

"Really?" I asked.

"We just left New York," Sal went on with a grin, "where my young protégé cut his first album with Cashman & West on Capitol."

"Uh-huh," said Jim. He didn't want to spoil Sal and Maury's excitement. He said, "I sure hope it works for you." He looked cautiously at me; I was already staring at him.

"We're just waiting for Tommy to start the promotion."

"Sounds familiar," Jim said, half under his breath.

"I'll go get something together for us to eat," I suggested, hoping to ease the tension.

After dinner, Jim moved to the living room, picked up his guitar, and started to play. Maury took his own instrument out of the case, and he and Sal joined in.

When I'd finished doing the dishes, I joined them, and for the next few hours the four of us played and traded songs and harmonies.

"You've got quite a repertoire," Maury said to Jim just after midnight.

"And you play that guitar like a piano," Jim told him sincerely, as he passed around a joint. Sal grinned in pride. He had long believed Jim and Maury would complement each other musically, and his intuition had been proven right.

"How did a nice Catholic boy like you get mixed up with marijuana?" Jim laughed, as he took another toke and passed the joint along. Maury took a drag and held in the smoke.

"When I was packing meat in the Hamilton Township," he answered, "I learned a lot of bad habits." He smiled impishly.

"What kind of meat did you pack down there, Maury?" Jim joked. Maury didn't pick up on the suggestive remark.

"Scrapple," he answered seriously. "Scrapple is made of what's left over after sausage is manufactured."

"Yeah, well, they should make more shit out of that stuff. It would be good for the ecology," Jim laughed. "When did you start playing music?" he asked warmly and with increasing interest in this talented young musician.

"Well, I studied piano for ten years with the organist from St. Mary's Cathedral. And I went through some real changes when I taught myself guitar."

"Maury's the second eldest of eight kids and was born with a veil over his face," Sal chimed in.

"What?" Jim asked.

"Oh," Maury said, embarrassed that Sal would repeat a story Maury's mother had told him.

"It's a rare phenomenon, when a membrane cloaks a baby's face," Sal explained. "According to folklore the veil signifies the arrival of a gifted child. When the Muehleisens recognized Maury's talent for music, they got him piano lessons."

"How long have you been playing the guitar, Maury?" Jim asked.

"About two years," Maury said shyly.

"Can you imagine playing a guitar like that after only two years?" Sal boasted. "That's why I decided to give up teaching to be his manager. That's how much I believe in him."

Maury became a fixture at our cozy country retreat. He found our home a welcome escape from Trenton.

A month later he had scheduled some coffeehouse gigs and asked Jim to play backup guitar. Jim agreed, sensing that he'd enjoy the change of pace—and we needed the money. He and Maury rehearsed Maury's music and a number of songs they played just for fun.

"Man," Jim said after the first show, "I'm not sure I can continue." He paused and Maury gave him a quizzical look. "Unless you can burn that green velvet Lord Fauntleroy outfit Sal dressed you in," Maury laughed.

"We can torch it tonight," he said, pulling at his blazer. "Besides, I couldn't let Lindsay see me this way."

"Lindsay who?"

"Ah, this eighteen-year-old long-legged beauty I met by the Brandywine." He smiled dreamily. "I don't have to pray for inspiration to write music anymore. All I have to do is look at her."

Lindsay spent a couple evenings with Maury at the farmhouse, but after a month or so it became apparent that she was equally, if not more, attracted to Jim. Soon, it didn't matter to Lindsay if Maury was at our place or not. She showed up whenever she pleased.

One morning, after singing with Jim at a friend's party the night before, I was making breakfast and slamming pots and pans in the kitchen.

"Ing, can't you be quiet in there?" Jim looked over at Sal, who had passed out in our living room after the party and was still snoring lightly.

"Shit, Jim, do you have to be so obvious?"

"What are you talking about?"

"Those pubescent groupies at the party last night threw themselves at you. And you act like nothing is happening!"

"Give me a break, Ing."

"You know what I'm talking about, Jim. Lindsay was all over you."

"I don't need this guilt crap from you! Who the hell do you think you—"

"Good morning! Take two," Sal shouted from the sofa bed in the living room.

Jim stopped mid-sentence. Like an actor in a bad movie, he suddenly transformed.

"I'm sorry, sweet thing," he said to me. "Here, give me a kiss."

I turned away.

After breakfast, when Jim was showering, I went over to Sal and thanked him.

"Hey, we all have our problems, but no one deserves to be treated badly, Ingrid. I sure don't want to see it," Sal explained. "You're the only one Jim doesn't perform for. With everyone else he's on his best behavior."

"Thanks, Sal. Sometimes I feel like I must deserve it for what happened in Mexico."

Sal said, "That's between you and Jim. I'm just an innocent bystander."

"Not innocent, Sal. Definitely not innocent!"

Only Sal knew the difficult details underlying our problems. He loved us both

187

very much and felt certain that time would heal the wounds. He just hoped we could hang in there and not hurt each other too much in the process.

"I don't know why Jim can't just say what he feels and get it all out and over with," I lamented.

"Because he hurts a lot, Ing. He's not like you. And Italian men are different. He's afraid to express his real feelings. His emotions are all bottled up, and he hurts you because he's hurting. It's almost like, to him, the two of you are one."

———

Several weeks later, when Jim purchased a pair of running shoes and announced that he was taking up jogging, I knew something was up. He had never done anything athletic in his life, yet he insisted he had discovered running and loved it.

Maury's girlfriend lived only a mile down the Brandywine, in the direction Jim was jogging every day. One afternoon I arrived home from a friend's house unexpectedly to find him lying face down on the floor of the living room. Lindsay sat on his back, massaging him.

At the sight of me, she cried, "Oh shit!" and stood up quickly. "My sister is a nurse, and she taught me how to give back rubs!"

"Did she teach you to give hard-ons, too?" I asked icily.

Jim roared with laughter. Ignoring both of us, he got up and went into the kitchen to get something to eat.

I marched into the kitchen, leaving the young woman behind.

"Get her out of here now," I yelled at Jim. I picked up his running shoes and threw them in the back of the closet.

After Lindsay left, I spoke my mind: "Is this your way of getting even with me for being raped? Well, maybe you'll never believe me, but it wasn't my fault!"

A few days after Thanksgiving, I couldn't hide my pain any longer.

"I love you, Jim, and I'm so sorry I've hurt you so deeply. It's the last thing I ever wanted to do. But more than anything, I want our marriage to work. Haven't I been punished long enough? Isn't it time to put the past behind us?" Tears poured down my cheeks.

"Please stop crying, Ing. Please just stop." He was silent for a while.

"Jim, I can't do this anymore. I can't walk around feeling guilty while you take your anger out on me. If you want to be with other women, then please leave."

"Ing, please don't. I love you, and I promise you: I'll try harder. Please believe me," he pleaded. "Don't make me leave."

"Jim, just tell me honestly: Do you really want to be with me? Can you accept that it wasn't my fault?"

"I swear, Ing. I want you more than anything. Please don't leave me. I need you. . . . I really do."

Jim embraced me tenderly. We went upstairs to our bedroom, and he made passionate love to me. I wanted to believe the tide had turned and things would get better between us.

————

Maury's friendship with Jim cooled a bit over Lindsay. But once Maury's album, *Gingerbread*, was released, they left on tour together. Jim and I wondered if Maury's album would fare better than ours. We certainly wished him and Sal the best, and Jim worked hard to help Maury in every way he could.

As Christmas neared, Jim wanted to try and repair his relationship with his parents. We began to visit his family every other week, and slowly their attitude softened.

"It's a good thing you left New York, and gave up that idea about playing music for a living," his father said one evening. "It's time for you to get a good job for you and Ingi." Jim had concealed from his father that he still dreamed of making music his life. He was just satisfied he and his parents were getting along. Yet it was a nervous truce. If he didn't make some kind of white-collar career move soon, his father would come down on him again.

"I still don't understand why you have to drive a truck," his father said, shaking his head. "You wasted four years in college just to become a truck driver! That's a sin!"

We spent Christmas Eve at Jim's parents' house, making love under the crucifix in his tiny childhood bed. Jim seemed full of love and passion again.

"Let's make a baby, Ing," he told me. "Can you imagine the combination of the two of us in one little boy? A Roman Catholic Jew—what a dynamic mixture he'll be." When we were first together, we had often talked about what our child would be like, how he would look and sing.

————

Jim's part-time hours at the quarry had been cut back for the winter, and he began to work even harder to make ends meet. He tried to find more gigs, and filled the extra time writing another book for musicians, called *How to Buy a Guitar*. Again, he asked my stepmother to type it, but once the manuscript was ready, he never sent it out for publication. Instead, he turned his attention to a mail-order business for a telephone antibugging device.

"There's a lot of paranoid people out there growing weed, and they're all worried about having their phones tapped," Jim explained to me. "Maybe I could make this antibugging device look real nice. Then I could add $10 to the price and make some money." He ordered a few of the devices and painted them "basket brown." Then he took ads out in music magazines and tried to peddle them at his gigs. Only one sold before he gave up on the scheme.

In January 1971, Maury returned to Lyndell with no place to stay. Jim and I put him up at our house, and the friendship between us all deepened. The two Capricorns celebrated their birthdays together: Jim turned twenty-eight on January 10, and Maury, twenty-two on the fourteenth. While Jim worked construction, Maury slept through the days, plagued by the chronic allergies and asthma that left him exhausted. When he'd finally wake up in the afternoon, he'd nibble on Nestlé Crunch bars and down flat, stale Coke, which he'd opened the night before, and then he'd reach for his pack of Marlboros. He'd play his guitar until Jim got home around 2 or 3 in the afternoon, and the three of us would play until dinner.

My new best friend, Judy Coffin, a recently divorced, thirty-one-year-old woman with three young sons, often came to visit in the afternoons. She was earthy, attractive, intelligent, and beaming with vitality. Judy enjoyed listening to Maury's music and was attracted to his kind and gentle qualities. She invited him to her house, and soon he moved in with Judy and the boys.

By the end of January, Maury learned that his album wasn't selling. His thin, ethereal voice and ultra-romantic subject matter had eluded a commercial audience, so he and Jim set out to find work at local hangouts. Maury's music was too delicate for the tough atmosphere of country bars, so Jim became the focus of their performance onstage, and Maury began to back up Jim wherever they played. As Jim's lyrics and presence became dominant, Maury found comfort on the edge of the spotlight. There he was free to play his guitar without distraction. Together they presented a masculine image that was both strong and subtle.

In February, I went to a fertility specialist to find out why after five years of marriage I had never conceived. As the doctor examined me, he discovered I was about two months pregnant. Thrilled, I thought back to Christmas Eve and Jim's tiny bed under the crucifix. I left the doctor's office excited to tell Jim the good news.

When I told him, he feigned excitement but stared off into the distance, his eyes glazed with terror as the weight of the responsibility of fatherhood descended upon him.

That night, when George Spillane went to bed, he saw the light on in the Croces' kitchen and heard Jim singing the lyrics to his haunting melody:

If I could save time in a bottle
The first thing that I'd like to do
Is to save every day 'til eternity passes away
Just to spend them with you.

If I could make days last forever,
If words could make wishes come true,
I'd save every day like a treasure and then, again,
I would spend them with you

But there never seems to be enough time
To do the things you want to do once you find them.
I've looked around enough to know that,
You're the one I want to go through time with.

If I had a box just for wishes
And dreams that had never come true,
The box would be empty except for the mem'ry
Of how they were answered by you.

But there never seems to be enough time
To do the things you want to do once you find them.
I've looked around enough to know that,
You're the one I want to go through time with.

TOMORROW'S GONNA BE
A BRIGHTER DAY

ONE DAY IN EARLY MARCH 1971, Tommy received a package from Jim. He probably hadn't expected to hear from him, not after the hostile meeting over the contract dispute at Kurnit's office several months earlier. Inside the package was a cassette and this short note:

> *Tommy,*
> *I just wrote these songs and I'd really appreciate just anything you could do with them. Get them recorded by somebody else. Things are kinda tough.*
> *Jim*

Tommy listened to the tape and called Jim.

"Jimmy, these are your best tunes yet! You must have been working on them for months."

"Thanks," Jim said. He was pleased Tommy responded so quickly. In reality, he had written all the songs in only one week. With a child on the way, it was now or never if music was ever going to be his career. The songs on the tape included "You Don't Mess Around with Jim," "Time in a Bottle," and "Operator."

"Listen, Jimmy," Tommy said, "I'd like you to make a demo of the new material and send it out to all the big labels. I really think we can get some interest in these songs."

––––

While awaiting further news from Tommy, Jim continued working at Sweeney's Construction Company, leaving home at 4 AM and not returning before 2 or 3 in the afternoon. He spent the rest of the day focusing on our soon-to-be-born baby. Although he didn't let on, the physical aspects of childbirth frightened him. He checked out scores of books from the library on natural childbirth and child care, and within weeks he considered himself an expert on the subject.

Hovering over me like a Jewish mother, he made me adhere to a special diet that included vitamins, health foods, lots of milk, and dark bock beer, something he had read was good for mother's milk. Returning from work, he would say, "It's time for our medicine." He'd pull his church key out of his pocket and pop open the beers. I choked on the dark, thick brew.

"Are you sure this is necessary for the baby's milk?"

"It's the best thing I know." Enjoying another swig of beer, he added, "Don't worry, Ing. I'll do it with you."

———

One snowy afternoon, Jim arrived home from a half-day's work and suggested we take a walk to Carole and Roger's house. They were some new friends he'd met at the food co-op he wanted me to meet. And he was insistent that I get some exercise.

"But it's snowing outside. How about we wait until the snow stops?" I told him.

"Walking in the snow will be fun," he said. "And besides, I really want you to meet Carole." Jim had befriended Roger at a local Lyndell bar a few months earlier. I knew of Roger's reputation for maintaining a healthy supply of excellent weed, and I suspected the real motive for the visit was to replenish Jim's stash. "Remember, I've told you about Carole: she's eight months pregnant with their second child. She can tell you firsthand about natural childbirth. Come on, Ing, you'll like them," he said persuasively. "They're cosmic. Roger used to be the Marlboro man on those gigantic billboards. Then he worked in the family business sewing sequins on costumes for country and western stars. He's a real character. Wait 'till you see him, Ing—he looks just like Rumpelstiltskin now, with a long skuzzy beard down to his belly button."

"Oh, that sounds so inviting."

"He's got a degree in business, and I think Carol has her master's in math or accounting, but they're hippies. And they rent this gigantic, dilapidated mansion. It's Gothic. It looks like the place where the Munsters hung out. They're great!"

When we arrived at the ominous mansion, Carole and Geena, their five-year-old daughter, were deep in snow, gathering wood.

"Carole, this is Ingrid," Jim said, rubbing his hands together in the cold. A small woman wearing brown hiking boots and purple tights, and wrapped in a heavy army parka that barely covered her big stomach, welcomed me with a warm smile. She loaded a large pile of wood into a wheelbarrow.

"Jim, help her," I insisted, concerned to see a very pregnant woman lifting such a big load.

"Ah, don't worry about it," Carole said, waving him off. "I'm used to this. Just go inside and get warm. I'll be right up. Geena, you go with them and show them where your dad is." Turning back to us she continued, "During the winter, the whole house is closed off except for the two central rooms. That sure makes it easier to heat, but you can get lost in this place if you're not careful. I'll be up in a minute to make some hot tea."

Jim and I followed Geena up the stairs and through a long, dark hallway.

"Hey, Rog," he called out as we entered a small, shadowy room, "it's Jim and Ingrid."

"Croce, far out!" came a voice from an antique velvet couch. Roger lay flat on his back in bib overalls. His long beard and shoulder-length dishwater blond hair looked as if it covered one end of the couch. He clutched a pink fluorescent yo-yo to his chest. In front of the sofa was a coffee table strewn with weed, hash, and smoking paraphernalia. "What'll it be?" he asked, giving me a nice-to-meet-you nod. "Daytime or nighttime hash?" He leaned up on an elbow, ready to weigh our choice on the brass scale. "Actually, the nighttime batch is a little potent; I suggest the daytime stuff if you are going to try to get home before dark." He looked to me for my preference.

"Oh, no thanks," I said. I began fidgeting with my jacket zipper.

"I'll take her share," Jim joked.

Carole carried the wood up the two flights, entered the dark room, and rekindled the fire.

"Would you like some hot tea and biscuits?" she asked, standing by the fireplace, which doubled as their makeshift kitchen.

"Sure, let me help," I said, grateful for something to distract me from the weed.

"Man," Roger drawled, "I had a mystical experience this morning while Geena and I were on our walk in the woods." He lit a pipe filled with the strong stuff. "A tree gave me the name for my new kid."

"Oh yeah?" Jim replied, interested. "What did the tree say?"

"Far out, man. The tree said to call my new daughter Licorice Theresa."

"Nice name!" Jim said. After a couple tokes on a pipe, Jim asked if he could play Roger's guitar, which was propped against the end of the couch.

While Jim strummed and sang a ballad in Scottish brogue, Roger lay in a horizontal position, dropping his yo-yo. The string was only about a foot long, and the yo-yo never hit the floor before it returned perfectly to his hand. I turned from the fireplace and burst out laughing when I noticed the abbreviated string.

"It's a custom-made couch yo-yo,'" Roger explained.

"You ought to package them with this nighttime hash," Jim said as he passed the guitar to Roger. "Why don't you play something?"

Roger sat up and began strumming a new tune he had dreamed up called "Tweeter Babe." The entire song consisted of the same line repeated over and over:

> I take care of my tweeter babe,
> And she takes care of me.

I take care of my tweeter babe,
And she takes care of me . . .

"That's great, Roger," Jim giggled. "Do you have any others?"

He responded seriously: "Yeah, man, I've got loads of them. Here, let me play you some." We sat in the living room, laughing hysterically at Roger's simple, quirky songs.

"It's Roger the Amazing," Jim said, bestowing the new name on his friend. And for the rest of the afternoon Roger put on a magical performance.

———

By spring of 1971, Jim had decided I should eat only organically grown fruits and vegetables. He visited the local food co-op in Birchrunville every week, near where Maury, Judy, and her boys had recently moved. Judy had quickly become involved in the community and introduced us to her new neighbors; among them were Hy Mayerson, a local attorney and patron of the arts, and Melvin Goldfield, a long-haired, street-smart graphic artist, painter, and sculptor from South Philly. Melvin had also recently moved to the area and was in the process of building a geodesic dome on Hy's property for himself and his pregnant girlfriend, Cara Lee. Jim and Melvin began making fruit and vegetable runs to the open-air food market in South Philly. They were in charge of purchasing in bulk for the Kimberton Co-op to help everyone save money. The two had a lot in common: they were both dedicated artists, expectant fathers, and flat broke.

One week, Jim suggested they set out for Philadelphia late on a Friday evening so they could visit a few bars and pool halls before the docks opened at 5 AM the next morning. Melvin didn't particularly feel like venturing out on the streets that night but consented to show Jim his old neighborhood.

Into the early morning hours the two drank and shot endless games in a dingy pool hall on South Street. Jim became fascinated by Jim Walker, a big, flamboyant black man who seemed to be a fixture at the tables. A crowd of rowdy men and a few lonely women watched in awe as he sank ball after ball with his two-piece, custom-made pool cue. By 3 AM, Jim and Melvin were so tired, and had consumed so many beers, they decided to go to a diner and drink coffee until dawn. Finally they headed out past the Tinikim Swamp to the docks.

"Damn," said Melvin, "that guy was good!"

"Yeah, man. And he was big!" Jim said. "I'd hate to be on his wrong side."

"There were plenty of guys like him where I grew up," Melvin added. "You always had to watch your step 'cause you never knew who was out to get you."

Melvin Goldfield was a Jew, raised poor in a tough, racially mixed neighborhood. He was the youngest in a family of five boys, and he remembered his mother telling him how she had to fight off the rats from the junkyard while he nursed. His mother had scraped together what she could for the family, but it was always a difficult existence. Initially, Jim was surprised to hear about Melvin's raw past. But it was his past that attracted Jim, and he wondered how such a gentle artist had emerged from such rough beginnings.

"Jeez, Melvin, you sure got your lessons in character development early. While we were asking questions like 'How did you do in shop class?' you were fighting for survival."

"Yeah, it was violent."

"Well, violence is right under the skin," Jim said. "It's more natural for man to fight than to levitate."

"I never saw it that way," Melvin said.

"Well," Jim continued as they walked passed a fenced junkyard, "I guess I was pretty mellow until the army. Before that I never even hit anyone. But those sergeants, those eggheads with teeth, they forced me to fight. I remember one officer dropping a guy and kicking him in the head with his helmet on. The soldier was pinned, and the sarge kept yellin' at him, 'Fight fair, motherfucker!' Those kinds of things drove me crazy. I wanted to let my animal loose on him. Shit, even nature isn't a pacifist." Suddenly, a predatory, snarling Doberman jumped against the chain-link fence, barking ferociously. Jim was startled and seemed to leap two feet straight up. "Christ, man, that dog scared the shit out of me."

"Yeah, man," said Melvin with a straight face, "there's nothin' meaner than a junkyard dog!"

"Except Big Jim Walker with a knife at your throat on payday."

A couple of hours later, he and Melvin had a dozen wooden crates of fruits and vegetables loaded in the co-op's truck and were headed back to the country.

"When is Cara Lee expecting?" Jim asked Melvin.

"In September sometime," Melvin replied. "I'm really happy about becoming a dad."

Jim sat back, admiring Melvin's ability to express his feelings. "Yeah, me too, but it makes me nervous. I don't really know what to expect, and all the responsibility and shit. Does it scare you?"

"Yeah, but I think becoming a father changes you," Melvin said. "It definitely brings out my sensitive side. You've got to be able to show your feelings, especially with a baby."

"I'm not very good at that," Jim admitted. His voice had grown serious.

"But what about all those sweet lyrics you write?"

"Oh, that's easy. I can write and sing what I feel, but trying to say the words is hard for me."

"You're serious, aren't you?"

"Yeah," Jim stared ahead. "Maybe it's because anytime I tried saying what I really felt, I got slapped for it."

"I guess parents can be like that if they're not careful," Melvin agreed.

"Yeah, and the church does a number on you, too. I remember those vicious nuns beating their rulers across my knuckles just 'cause they didn't like my answers. I don't want it to be like that with my kid. I'm going to love my kid no matter what he wants to do. I'm going to let him express who he really is . . . or she is."

"You sure learned how to express yourself on your guitar," Melvin said. "Man, I wish I could play like that."

Jim smiled then shrugged. "It just takes practice, Melvin. In fact, to be a really good musician, that's about all you can do—practice. Just play all the time. Maybe that's why I love music so much. It's a great excuse not to get a real job."

"Well, I'm not thinking about becoming a professional or anything, man, but do you think I could learn to play?" Melvin gave him a sidelong glance.

"Sure, I'll teach you."

After dinner on Tuesday, Jim drove to Melvin's to give him his first guitar lesson. "Tonight, you learn," he said in an exaggerated Italian manner, reminiscent of his grandfather. Jim was an excellent teacher, and he enjoyed helping others conquer what came so easily to him. He unpacked his guitar and began the lesson.

The admiration was mutual. Jim respected Melvin's art as much as Melvin enjoyed Jim's music.

I called Melvin's at about 2 AM. Jim came to the phone, just sober enough to say, "I'll be right home, sweet thing. I'm sorry."

I was waiting up in the living room when Jim pulled up, driving the truck across the front yard.

"I'm sorry I got so fucked up, Ing," he said, apologizing like a bad little boy as he walked into the house. "I was just having some fun."

"I'm glad, Jim—I want you to have fun." I hugged him. "Just remember to call me next time when you're going to be late, so I don't have to worry. I don't know what I'd do if anything happened to you."

He swept me into his arms.

"I promise I'll call you next time. You're so beautiful, Ing. I think you're even prettier when you're pregnant. You're softer and rounder and . . . Let's go up-stairs and make love." I started up the steps to the bedroom as Jim lingered be-hind to watch me.

———

Although Jim worked with truck drivers and construction workers all day, living in Lyndell's creative surroundings gave him the opportunity to express himself. He liked the fact that we were putting down roots in a community. He began to ap-preciate his friendships and made a concerted effort to strengthen bonds with those he held dear. One of those was Maury, whom he had begun to regard not only for his fine qualities as a musician but for his intelligent sensitivity. After prac-tice sessions at the house every day, they talked about life and relationships. Al-though much younger, Maury seemed impressively mature.

"What happened to your parental guilt?" Jim asked Maury one afternoon. "You were raised Catholic. How come it didn't affect you like the rest of us?"

Maury sat back in his armchair. "I guess having all those nuns around me at school made me feel loved." Maury smiled, brushed back his hair, and began playing his guitar.

Jim sat still, listening to the new tune. Maury wrote most of his songs from be-ginning to end without interruption. He'd write the words down in ink in a compo-sition book, hardly ever crossing out or changing a single word. Slowly Jim began playing along, setting his capo on the third fret and trying out harmonies.

When they finished playing Maury's tune, Jim took the lead with his new song, "Time in a Bottle." Maury accentuated Jim's tender words with classical flourishes. "Hey, Maury, let's practice that again. I like what you're doing."

Jim was energized by Maury's skillful playing. It took the pressure off, and Jim could concentrate on the melody and lyrics. They played until dinnertime, only taking a break for my vegetable lasagna. Then, back in the living room after dinner, Maury picked up his guitar and started tuning it. There was a hard knock at the door, but Maury ignored it, concentrating on his strings. Another knock prompted Jim to yell, "Come on in!"

Bill Reid opened the door and walked through the living room, disregarding Maury sitting on the overstuffed couch. He joined Jim and me in the kitchen, and Jim offered him a beer.

"God, he looks awful," Bill said. "What a spaced-out, pimple-faced creep he is."

"Bill, don't be an asshole. You're so rude. Do you want some lasagna?" I asked him.

"Sure," he said, before adding, "Is he a faggot? What the fuck's the matter with that guy? He's so puny."

"He may look that way to you, but the girls follow him in droves," Jim said, enthusiastically. "And I guarantee you that Maury gets more ass than you do."

I was offended by Bill's comments but happy that Jim defended Maury. While Bill brought out the rowdy, prejudiced, and angry side of Jim, Maury encouraged Jim's sensitivity. With Maury around, Jim wouldn't step out of line for fear of offending his friend, and seemed genuinely softer and more caring. On the other hand, Jim saw it as his duty to introduce Maury to life's harsher realities. Like a big brother, he began taking him along on the vegetable runs to Philadelphia and introduced him to Melvin's colorful friends. He also recruited Maury to help solve a raccoon problem.

The three apartments of the Kaltenbachs' farmhouse shared a common area where trash cans were kept. Every morning our garbage was strewn all over the yard.

"I hate picking up this shit," Jim yelled one day. "I swear someone is trying to play a practical joke on us."

The next evening, Jim's neighbor George was sitting on the toilet in his second-story bathroom when he heard a loud scratching outside. From the window he could see a raccoon sitting on the fence, feasting on our garbage. The next morning he told Jim about it.

"That critter sat there just like a person, trying to pry the lid off of your trash can. It was the biggest son of a bitch I ever saw."

Night after night the raccoon raided the garbage can. Jim took the varmint on as a personal vendetta. "I swear I'll catch that goddamned son of a bitch," he said, placing a heavy rock on top of the trash-can lid. When that didn't work, he tried to trap it with bait. But still he had no luck.

One afternoon when Jim railed on about the trash-can dilemma, John Kaltenbach joked, "You know, raccoons can be dangerous. They can get as big as Ingrid and twice as mean!" Jim stayed up several nights sitting at the kitchen table, looking out the window with his rifle and his guitar, but as long as he watched, the damn raccoon never appeared. In exasperation, he asked Maury and another friend, Jimmy Wright, to stay up with him one night.

"Guys, I've got a treat to help us stay up tonight." Jim held out a handful of little white pills.

"What is it?" Maury asked hesitantly.

"They're 'white crosses.' To help us stay awake. Don't worry, they're prescription." Jim was becoming an expert on pharmacology. His pharmacist friend had given him a *Physicians' Desk Reference*, and Jim was experimenting with whatever his friend offered. That night's agenda definitely called for uppers.

In the middle of the night, while the boys were sitting around the kitchen table, Maury heard what he thought was the raccoon. Jim handed Maury the rifle. When he saw the reflection of the animal's eyes, Maury proudly took aim out the kitchen door and fired. "I think I got him," he yelled, "right in the eye!" He triumphantly held the rifle up over his head. "He's over by the outhouse, I think!" Cautiously Jim went out the kitchen door to the garbage can, Maury and Jimmy following close behind. A great stench exploded on them. "Jesus Christ, Maury!" Jim shouted. "It's a fucking skunk! You didn't hit him in the eye; you shot him in the ass."

Awakened by the gunfire and the stench, George came down. When he found out what had happened, he laughed, ran upstairs, and grabbed his bottle of brandy to share with the boys. Early the next morning in the clear light of day, while Maury was fast asleep, the raccoon brazenly appeared. Jim finished it off with a single shot. With great satisfaction, he and George toasted the victory over coffee.

———

Every few weeks, Jim called Tommy to see if he had made any headway in getting an album deal or other artists to record his songs. One afternoon, while I was cutting out a pattern for a baby sleeper, the phone rang, and both Jim and I picked it up at the same time. I didn't hang up.

"Hey, Tommy, what's happening, man?" Jim asked.

"Well, not much. But the songs are really good, Jim, your best ever."

"Thanks."

"So just keep writing. We need a whole album's worth."

"Yeah," Jim said sullenly. "I'll keep writing. In fact, I've got a couple new ones I'll play for ya soon. Maury put some great licks to them, too."

"I've got a good feeling about these songs, Jim," Tommy reiterated.

"Yeah, but good feelings don't pay the bills. Give me a call when you get me something, okay?"

I had followed the conversation and was surprised and grateful that Jim had expressed himself so directly to Tommy. He came into the kitchen with his guitar and headed for a chair.

"I don't know what I'll do if these songs don't get me a deal, Ing. I'd be a terrible salesman, and I'm not ready to go out in the job market again. Villanova prepared me for life in the twelfth century."

"Jim, it's gonna happen. Please don't worry so much. The baby won't take much money, and I'm going to breast feed and wash diapers. We'll be fine."

"What about our health insurance? Remember we didn't send a check in last month."

"I already spoke to Maury. He said he hadn't cashed the last couple of checks you gave him for $100 each. So I sent a check in for the insurance, and we're reinstated." After a short silence, I added, "It's gonna be okay, Jim. Your music is terrific, and it's gonna work."

"Well, if any of my songs could make it, 'You Don't Mess Around with Jim,' should," he said and began to play.

Uptown got its hustlers,
The Bowery got its bums.
Forty-Second Street got big Jim Walker,
He's a pool shootin' son of a gun.
Yeah, he big and dumb as a man can come
But he stronger than a country hoss.
And when the bad folks all get together at night,
You know they all call big Jim "Boss," just because . . .

And they say, "You don't tug on Superman's cape,
You don't piss into the wind,
You don't pull the mask off the old Lone Ranger,
And you don't mess around with Jim."

Well, outta south Alabama came a country boy.
He said, "I'm looking for a man named Jim.
I am a pool shootin' boy, my name is Willie McCoy,
But down home they call me Slim.
Yeah, I'm lookin' for the king of Forty-Second Street,
He drivin' a drop-top Cadillac.

Last week he took all my money and it may sound funny
But I come to get my money back."
And everybody say, "Jack, whoa, don't you know that:

You don't tug on Superman's cape,
You don't piss into the wind,
You don't pull the mask off the old Lone Ranger,
And you don't mess around with Jim."

Well, a hush fell over the poolroom,
Jimmy come boppin' in off the street.
And when the cuttin' were done
The only part that wasn't bloody,
Were the soles of the big man's feet.

Yeah, he were cut in 'bout a hundred places,
And he were shot in a couple more.
And you better believe they sung a different kind of story,
When Big Jim hit the floor.

"And you don't tug on Superman's cape,
You don't piss into the wind,
You don't pull the mask off the old Lone Ranger,
And you don't mess around with Slim."

Yeah, big Jim got his hat,
Find out where it's at,
Not hustling people strange to you.
Even if you do got a two-piece custom-made pool cue. Shit. . . .

And you don't tug on Superman's cape,
You don't piss into the wind,
You don't pull the mask off the old Lone Ranger,
And you don't mess around with Slim.

———

During the spring of 1971, Sal brought an astrologer to the farmhouse, a slight man with sandy blond hair.

"Dan's a psychic," Sal announced. "He can tell the future."

"Oh, so he's been looking at your crystal balls, has he?" Jim smiled at Maury, who had been over all day playing music. "You know, Ingrid's psychic, too. She's convinced we're having a son, so tell us what else we need to know about our baby."

Dan Wexler sat everyone down on the floor of the living room and spread out the astrological charts that matched their zodiac signs.

"How did you know when we were born?" I asked.

"Oh, Sal filled me in on you," Dan said. He spoke with an effeminate lilt and gave Sal, his cohort, a glance. "I know more about you than you'll ever want to hear." He smiled mysteriously. First he said, "You will have a son," with his eyes transfixed on the chart of constellations. We listened closely. "And he'll be born with a strange birthmark."

"Far out!" Jim said, imitating "Roger the Amazing."

"There's more," Dan continued with a studied expression. He moved his hand across the charts. "Your son will be very rich one day."

"Is he going to be a bank robber?" Jim asked with a laugh. "Or maybe Ing's bought a big insurance policy." Dan's expression grew even more serious.

"It seems that he's only going to have one parent by the age of two."

"Hey!" Jim forced a laugh but looked at me and bit his lip. "Are you going to leave me for someone else?" I smiled and rubbed his thigh, but Dan's words had jolted me like lightning.

I never told Jim, but I had often had premonitions about something happening to him. Maybe it was because both my parents had died young and most of my family was gone by the time I was nineteen.

"I'm yours forever, Jim," I told him. "Maybe it's the other way around," I whispered.

All at once the apartment was strangely quiet. Dan excused himself to go to the kitchen.

"Does the chart say anything about my career?" Jim yelled out. "Or a murder I might commit if something doesn't happen soon in New York?" He grabbed his guitar.

Jim changed the subject and played a new song he was working on, called "Photographs and Memories."

"Try this in G Maury."

Photographs and memories,
Christmas cards you sent to me;
All that I have are these
To remember you.
Memories that come at night,
Take me to another time;
Back to a happier day,
When I called you mine.

But we sure had a good time
When we started way back when,
Morning walks and bedroom talks,
Oh, how I loved you then.

Summer skies and lullabies,
Nights we couldn't say goodbye;
All of the things that we knew
And not a dream survived.

But we sure had a good time
When we started way back when,
Morning walks and bedroom talks,
Oh, how I loved you then.

Photographs and memories,
All the love you gave to me;
Somehow it just can't be true
That's all I've left of you.

But we sure had a good time
When we started way back when,
Morning walks and bedroom talks,
Oh, how I loved you then.

Jim began to work feverishly on music, often sleeping only a few hours a night before getting up to head to the quarry. He also began making regular visits to see the pharmacist. On one occasion when he was depressed that he hadn't heard from Tommy, he took me with him to the pharmacy in Media.

"I'll be just a couple of minutes," he said, as he got out of the driver's seat and went into the store.

I waited in the car while he was gone, and when he reappeared, he looked revived and walked happily to the car holding a bag of what he called "candy."

"What do you have in there?" I asked.

"Just a little medicine to cure what ails me," he joked.

"They aren't drugs, are they, Jim?"

"Think of them as vitamins that keep my spirit healthy."

It worried me greatly that Jim was turning to pills. Although grass was as commonplace as wine within our circle of friends, acid and prescription drugs frightened me. I had grown up wanting to be as healthy as I could be. I was petrified from what I had seen my mother go through with her addictions to drugs and alcohol. And I was scared that Jim was getting too comfortable with his pharmaceutical "candy."

With the baby on the way, Jim professed to have a renewed commitment to me. He wanted things to be right for our family. One of the songs that came from that prolific period was "Tomorrow's Gonna Be a Brighter Day," an apology for the hard times we'd been through.

> *Well, I'm sorry for the things that I told you,*
> *But words only go so far;*
> *And if I had my way I would reach into heaven*
> *And I'd pull you down a star, for a present,*
> *And I'd make you a chain out of diamonds,*
> *And pearls from a summer sea;*
> *But all I can give you is a kiss in the mornin'*
> *And a sweet apology.*
>
> *Well, I know that it hasn't been easy*
> *And I haven't always been around*
> *To say the right words, or to hold you in the mornin',*
> *Or to help you when you are down.*
> *I know I never showed you much of a good time,*

But baby, things are gonna change;
I'm gonna make up for all of the hurt that I brought you,
I'm gonna love away all your pain.

And tomorrow's gonna be a brighter day,
There's gonna be some changes;
Tomorrow's gonna be a brighter day,
This time you can believe me,
No more cryin' in your lonely room, no more empty nights,
'Cause tomorrow mornin' everything'll turn out right.

Well, there's somethin' that I gotta tell you,
Yes, I got somethin' on my mind;
But words come hard when you're lyin' in my arms,
And when I'm lookin' deep into your eyes.
But there's truth and consolation
In what I'm tryin' to say
Is that nobody ever had a rainbow, baby,
Until he had the rain.

The baby was due on August 16, what would have been my father's fifty-third birthday. Jim convinced me that we didn't need to go for Lamaze instructions and that we could do it by ourselves. I guessed that Jim was avoiding classes for his own reasons, yet as the due date got closer, I was becoming increasingly nervous.

"Are you sure you know what to do, Jim?" I asked. "My mom always told me that childbirth was the most painful experience she ever had, and I'm really scared."

"I know just what to do," he assured me.

"Great, but you're not having the baby!"

"Carole says that breathing is essential."

"Yeah, I know, but we don't have any of those techniques down. Come on, practice with me, Jim."

"I read that singing is better than breathing during childbirth. But the book said it had to be a simple song. How about 'Yankee Doodle'? Come on, let's practice." With concentration he started singing, "Yankee Doodle went to town. . . ." He kept time like John Stockfish, and his mood was just as serious.

I breathed in and exhaled, "Riding on a pony."

Jim said, "Now inhale." He had me lie down and watched my chest rise.

"Come on, sing, 'Stuck a feather in his cap.'"

I tried again, choked on the words, and began to giggle. "I'm hyperventilating, Jim."

"Try again: 'He stuck a feather in his cap'! Sing it, Ing!"

"I don't think this is going to work," I said, lying on my back laughing hysterically.

"Don't worry," Jim shrugged. "When it happens, you'll know what to do."

"I don't think so. That's why they have classes, so we can learn."

———

Money grew even tighter over the summer. Jim operated a jackhammer at the quarries, joking with the guys that it was teaching him rhythm, but inside he was wearying of construction work and had grown impatient for Tommy to cut a record deal. Tirelessly, he wrote new songs and refined ones he had already written, often singing them into his tape recorder as he drove the big trucks.

I continued to develop creative ways to save money. With my old pedal sewing machine, I made all my maternity clothes, as well as shirts and jackets for Jim. I knitted him sweaters, embroidered over the holes in his work shirts, and put trim on the hems of his worn-out jeans. Wanting to help relieve the financial pressure, I even entered my blintzes in the Pillsbury Bake-Off contest. "I think I've got a good chance," I told Judy. "And just think of the house we could buy with the $10,000 prize money."

Tommy finally called in August.

"I've got some good news," he said, "not quite the response on the songs I had hoped for. But Phillips, a record company out of Holland, wants to record an album."

"Great!" Jim said. "What's that mean in dollars?"

"Well, we don't have a distribution deal in the States yet, but they did put up some 'good faith' money. I'm sending you an advance that should tide you over until you can get here to record. Then you can get on the road and earn more."

"Okay," Jim said. "But I can't go anywhere until Ingrid has the baby. It's due the sixteenth."

"All right, Jimmy. Let's plan for the end of the month."

When Jim received the check for $500, he quit his job at Sweeney Construction. Carefully, he listed monthly expenses in his notebook.

"The way I figure it," he told me, "we can live off this money for a little more than two months if we have to. By then, I'll be on the road."

"How much did Tommy get for the advance?" I asked.

Jim shrugged. "I have no idea. He didn't say."

————

August 16 came and went, and the baby showed no sign of appearing. The recording session was postponed to early September. Everyone grew impatient. The pressure was on.

"The baby's never coming out," I told Judy. "I guess he just wants to keep his dad at home."

"Come on," Judy replied. "I'm going to take you on a long jeep ride over some bumpy back roads. Maybe that will move the process along."

Finally in late September, on a rainy Sunday night, I was lying in bed wondering if the baby would ever arrive, when my water broke.

"Sweet thing, it's time," I whispered to Jim. He leaped out of bed.

"Start breathing! Start singing!" he coached. Stark naked he ran to the bathroom, stepped into the tub, and turned on the water. While it filled, he stood motionless and in a state of shock. "Ingrid," he shouted in panic, "run next door and ask George what to do!"

"Don't you think you should go?" I told him.

"Oh, yeah. Yeah, of course I should," he said, and dashed toward the stairs.

"But you're naked!" I laughed, holding my stomach. "Take your time, and put your clothes on." He ran back into the bathroom, wrapped a towel around his waist, and hurried outside to knock on the neighbor's door.

"How far apart are the contractions?" George asked calmly.

"The water just broke," Jim gasped.

"Well, relax. The blessed event probably won't take place for a few hours. Call the doctor." Jim raced back.

"Call Dr. Carpenter, Ing," he said breathlessly. I dialed while he sat on the couch, his eyes wide as saucers. I put down the phone.

"The doctor said to leave for the hospital when the contractions are five minutes apart." Two hours later, at 5 AM, Jim helped me into the car. By then he had calmed down enough to grab his guitar and drive me to the emergency room.

Inside Bryn Mawr Hospital, he turned pale.

"I hope this isn't one of those hospitals that believes in human sacrifice," he nervously joked. A nurse led me to my room, leaving him behind to fill out the hospital forms. He was sweating through his clothes. With his guitar, ragged jeans, and long curly hair, he looked like the disheveled folk singer he was.

"How do you intend to pay for the delivery?" the hospital admissions clerk asked.

"We have insurance!" he said defensively.

"What religion will the child be?" Jim threw both hands into the air.

"A Roman Catholic Russian Jew. Or maybe he'll be a Hindu. I have no idea. It's his choice," he blurted out.

Jim took his guitar into my room and began to play for me. Soon several nurses were at my bedside listening to Jim's beautiful voice. Between songs, he rubbed oil on my back and my belly. We spent the whole day and night in the hospital, but the baby still didn't come.

By the next morning, when I still hadn't dilated, the doctor decided to induce labor. I readily agreed. Jim looked concerned. One hour later labor began.

"Start the breathing exercises," the doctor ordered. Jim looked sheepishly at me, and his expression said he was not about to start singing "Yankee Doodle." "We haven't really practiced any Lamaze methods," he admitted. The doctor looked at him disapprovingly and started giving me a crash course.

Less than an hour later, the baby arrived. Jim saw a shock of black hair appear and leaped up shouting, "It's a girl! It's a girl!" But when the rest of the baby emerged into the doctor's hands, it was evident Jim's judgment had been too quick. He looked down, leaped up again, and shouted, "It's a boy! It's a boy!"

On September 28, 1971, at 8:45 AM Adrian James Croce was born with a bright blue birthmark on his buttocks. Jim ran into the hall to call my stepmom and his parents.

"Ingrid's fine," he shouted. "We have a healthy, seven-pound baby boy, born with a blue ass!" He returned to the room, held the baby awkwardly, and took a good, long look. "He's so handsome, Ing," he said, his voice breaking with emotion. "We sure made a beautiful baby." He kissed us both and hurried out of the hospital.

It was past ten in the morning, and he had a concert and lecture to do at Delaware Community College in just an hour. It was the last of four small gigs our neighbors Carole and George had arranged. Jim's nerves were jangled, and he sped to the college, tired and disoriented. "I'm a father," he thought. "A father!" He was exhausted from sharing in the birthing experience for the last two days and didn't feel up to performing, but he couldn't let a friend down. More importantly, he needed the money. Afterwards he called Tommy in New York and said proudly, "We can start the album now. Adrian James Croce has finally arrived."

YOU DON'T MESS AROUND WITH JIM

AFTER TWO DAYS IN THE HOSPITAL, Adrian James and I were ready to go home. Jim picked up his new family, bringing Bill Reid along for the ride. On the way, we stopped on the Main Line to celebrate at the Beef and Ale House. Over a roast beef sandwich and a cold brew, we toasted our son.

"Here's to the best-looking, smartest kid in town," Jim said, holding his beer in the air.

Adrian James was born a Libra and was named with the guidance of numerology and the Kabala.

"Well, he may be smart," Bill allowed, "but no kid's tougher than my Greg."

Not to be outdone, Jim put a tiny bit of horseradish on the tip of Adrian's little pink tongue.

"What are you doing? He's only two days old!" I yelled. Adrian's eyes grew as big as saucers, his face scrunched together, and he turned bright red. It took him a moment to catch his breath before he let out an enormous squeal.

"Now he's officially baptized," Jim proclaimed over the shrieking. Pissed off, I tried to wash the horseradish off Adrian James's tiny tongue. "Don't worry, Ing, my little old man loves it."

Bill laughed and bought another round of beers.

———

The week Adrian James was born, Paul Wilson, a Philadelphia photographer and friend, was scheduled to come to the farmhouse to take promo shots of Jim and his family for the forthcoming album. Jim had already played a tape of the songs for Paul.

"What am I going to wear in the pictures?" Jim asked me the morning of the shoot. "I have a choice between the three-piece suit I wore for our wedding or work clothes."

"Wear your work shirt and jeans, of course," I shot back quickly.

He pulled on his jeans, a dark blue T-shirt, and his Levi jacket with a CAT patch on the pocket.

"Yeah, that works great," I said, kissing him and ruffling up his dark, thick, curly hair. "You look very handsome, sweetie. The girls are gonna love you."

"Oh, Ing, I'm so ugly. I hate having my picture taken. It makes me so self-conscious."

"I wish you could stop thinking of yourself that way, Jim. You're rugged looking and sensitive at the same time. You look like your songs sound: sexy and terrific!"

"You're just saying that because you love me," he said in a sad voice.

"Of course I love you. And your fans will too!"

"Thanks. I don't know what I'd do without you."

"And I don't want you to find out," I joked.

Paul Wilson arrived at 10 AM, and Jim offered him a toke of his joint before he started work. I made eggs, bacon, and popovers for breakfast and after a cup of Jim's strong Italian espresso with lemon zest, Paul took a walk around the property and decided to start the shoot outside the house.

"Let's use that antique wooden chair you're sitting in for one of the props," he said. "We'll take some pictures of you with Ing and the baby first. Then we'll go out back to the old outhouse. We'll get some out by the road too. Sit right there," Paul directed, "and we'll get started."

"What do you want me to do?" Jim asked uncomfortably.

"Just relax and play your guitar. And here, hold this cigar in your teeth while you strum. Give me a mean look, like "You Don't *Dare* Mess Around with Jim." Paul stepped back to get a sense of the picture, and started shooting. He took hundreds of photos and finished in the late afternoon. "I'd like you to come down to my place in West Philly on Thursday to finish the session," he requested. "We need some isolated shots of you, Jim, with a solid background. It will be better to do that at my studio, where I have the right lighting."

———

On October 5, 1971, one week after Adrian James was born, Jim and Maury drove to New York to meet Tommy at the Hit Factory, the studio Cashman & West had booked to record Jim's album. Jim and Maury were well rehearsed, and together with Tommy they sat in the control booth and went over the final list of songs Jim wanted to record. Joining them in the studio were two renowned studio musicians who had recorded previously with Jim and me and with Maury on his *Gingerbread* album: Joe Macho on bass and Gary Chester on drums. Gary and his wife were good friends of ours. Tommy told Jim that Gary was writing the quintessential book on drumming.

"That's nice," Jim nodded. But what was really important to Jim was that he and Gary had a great rapport, and they had built a close friendship that went beyond music. Tommy played keyboards on several tracks and did some background vocals with our good friend Ellie Greenwich, the successful singer-songwriter with hits in the '60s like "Da Do Ron Ron," "Then He Kissed Me," "Leader of the Pack," and "Doo

215

Wah Diddy Diddy." Tasha Thomas, a rhythm and blues artist who did commercial work on the side, added some backup vocals. Maury sang the parts he always sang when they performed live, and Bruce Tergersen was the recording and mixing engineer.

During the twenty-day recording process, Jim made it home only once, but he called every day.

"The album's going great, Ing," he told me during one phone conversation. "So much better than last time. The boys have it down now, and the songs really feel good. They've decided to put 'Hey Tomorrow' on the record, so your name will be on it too," Jim said, feeling bad that I was left out of the new album. "We should be finished in another week or so, and then I'll be home to spend some time with you and my little man."

Tommy and Terry produced the album for Interrobang Productions Inc., one of their new companies. Their publishing, producing, and recording empire was growing larger and more sophisticated, but Jim never understood why they needed so many corporations. Besides Cashman & West Productions Inc., they published Jim's and my songs under Blendingwell Music Inc. and Wingate Music Inc., both with ASCAP. When the album was mixed, the Dutch record company Phillips applauded the final production. Sadly, however, they admitted that as much as they liked it, their budget for the release was slim, and they could only offer limited PR and foreign distribution.

The Boys started shopping the record to major US labels to get national distribution, but everyone they approached turned them down, some saying Jim sounded too much like James Taylor or Ricky Nelson. Columbia Records rejected the album three times: once at the demo stage, another time after three tracks were mixed, and finally when the album was completed.

Before Jim left New York, Tommy gave Jim a cassette of the final mix, and when he came home to Lyndell, he proudly handed it to me.

"I think you'll like this, Ing," he told me with a confidence he'd never shown before. While I nursed Adrian James, I listened to the songs over and over again, and I was thrilled with what they had achieved.

To me, the album was more than just songs strung together to sound good. It told Jim's personal story and our story. "You Don't Mess Around with Jim," the title song, evoked the characters Jim encountered in high school listening to R&B; it was about Frankie and Johnny and Stagger Lee, the "bad dudes" he'd met selling airtime in West Philadelphia, and the guys he ran into with Melvyn Goldfield in the streets of South Philly while they were out doing their early produce runs for the Kimberton Co-op.

"Operator" was born out of the "Dear John" experiences Jim had witnessed in basic training at Fort Jackson, South Carolina, listening to the soldiers in line at the pay phones, as well as some of the cowboy conversations he overheard near the stage at the Riddle Paddock.

"Rapid Roy (the Stock Car Boy)" came from Jim's association with Ronnie Miller; his friend the tattoo artist, Billy Blue, from Southwest Philly; and Roy Harris from Drexel Hill and Upper Darby. "New York's Not My Home" was about our less-than-idyllic experience in New York. "Hard Time Losin' Man" gave a glimpse of Jim's street wisdom and alluded to the notorious Croce car curse. "Photographs and Memories" came after the rape, the end of our innocence. And "Time in a Bottle," the most prophetic song of all, was written when Jim found out that I was pregnant with Adrian James. Others included "Tomorrow's Gonna Be a Brighter Day," "Walkin' Back to Georgia," and "Hey Tomorrow," a song we had cowritten in the Bronx, a celebration of our partnership and the love that kept us going.

"I love this album," I called out to Jim. "Finally, there's a record that sounds like you." Now all they have to do is get you out there and promote it like crazy!" Before I'd finished my sentence, it hit me that Jim was going to have to leave really soon. He had to get out and perform everywhere he could if he wanted to make the record successful. My best friend was leaving me and our new son, and the music that had once brought us together was going to take us apart.

Suddenly, I felt incredibly sad and frightened about being left behind. I didn't want to raise Adrian by myself. I had no experience around infants or even small children.

"This album can do it, Jim," I said with tears in my eyes. "But I'm not sure I know how to be without you or how to take care of our little guy all by myself. I've never done this before."

Jim put his arms around me, and I buried my head in his chest.

"I know you're gonna be a great mom. I just hope this time around I can make this work. I want my dad to know I can earn a living making music."

Through the fall and winter of 1971–1972, Jim waited at home in Lyndell for Tommy and the Boys to interest a major label in the album. He played at colleges and coffeehouses, and Sal booked some gigs for Jim and Maury together too.

"These clubs and colleges don't pay much," Sal acknowledged, "but at least it's something."

"I appreciate your helping us out, Sal. Man, the bread's been tight. I just put an ad in the local paper for the Martin D28-S with the hard-shell case for $400. I hate to sell it, but what choice do I have? Ya gotta do what you gotta do."

217

Though the small gigs paid little, Jim loved the opportunity to be in front of an audience. With the album completed, he was anxious to try out the new material and practice his raps. From West Virginia to Niagara Falls, Jim went out to test the new songs. At Glassboro State, Bonnie Raitt opened the show for Jim. She was a friend and fellow troubadour who had played the Main Point, the Second Fret, and the Philadelphia Folk Festival with us. That night she played a half-hour set of blues to an excited crowd, and over the applause she introduced her friend, Jim Croce. Adrian, Bonnie, and I watched from the wings of the stage as Jim and "his one-man band," Maury, entertained the audience with songs from the new album. The crowd sat in rapt attention while Jim told anecdotes before each song. Maury, a former student at Glassboro, played a couple of his songs and got enthusiastic applause and cheers from his fellow students and fans. When Jim closed the concert with "You Don't Mess Around with Jim," the crowd cheered and insisted on an encore.

The next day, Bonnie, Maury, Jim, and I, with Adrian in tow, decided to give an impromptu concert on a knoll near the student union. Many of the students, who had appreciated the concert the evening before, sat around between classes to enjoy the free concert on the grass.

———

In early November 1971, Gene Pistilli surprised Jim and me with a phone call.

"Jim, it's Gene. I'm here with the Manhattan Transfer and Pat. We're opening for James Taylor at the Main Point next weekend. Do you think you guys can come to the show?"

"What day will you be there?" Jim asked.

"Friday and Saturday night. Can you make it?"

"Yeah, I think we can. We've got no gigs this weekend," Jim admitted. "So, yeah, we'll be there."

Gene paused.

"And I was wondering . . . could we all stay at your place?"

"Of course, man, we wouldn't have it any other way."

Pat, Tommy's ex-wife, had started the Manhattan Transfer with Tim Hauser, who was Jim and Tommy's old buddy from Villanova. After Pat and Tommy split up, Pat and Gene had found an apartment together on Prince Street in Greenwich Village.

"Thanks. Appreciate it. So ya know Pat and I are together now."

"Yeah," Jim answered, "I heard."

218

"How did you hear?"

"Tommy told me," Jim said. "He also told me that you made an album together. That's great."

"I bet Tommy had some other nice things to say about us too," Gene joked. "Come on, Jim, 'fess up."

"Well, you know Tommy. He did say that you were living like gypsies." Jim laughed. "I guess he's not that thrilled about the two of you being together or about your act."

Gene didn't understand why Jim and I had stayed with Tommy and the Boys, but he didn't ask any questions. He wondered why, after we had hired an attorney and received his letter explaining the details of their contractual negotiations, we were still involved with those guys.

Before the show, Jim, Adrian James, and I went down to the Main Point. Tim Hauser interrupted the Manhattan Transfer sound check and came to greet us. He was eager to talk about old times at Villanova and catch up with Jim and me. He introduced us to Marty, his horn player, and Erin Dickens, his lead vocalist and girlfriend.

"Hi, guys!" Gene warmly embraced Jim and me.

"What's that you've got there, man?" Jim teased. Gene held up his hand to show off his new rose tattoo. "Nice!" Jim said. "I'd like to get a couple of those myself someday." I tried not to hurt Gene's feelings, but Jim knew I hated tattoos. I gave him a look as if to say, "Don't even think about it!" Pat came into the dressing room to give us both a hug and to kiss the baby.

"You guys look terrific!" I said.

"Thanks, Ing. There's so much to catch up on. I can't wait to come over and see your new home."

Back at our house after the show, James Taylor showed up first. He sat down on the couch. He was shy and a bit withdrawn. I offered him something to eat or drink, and he took a glass of our homemade dandelion wine. Soon after, Gene showed up in his brand-new, shiny red VW convertible.

"Screw the Boys! I bought this with my own record advance. I wish you could see it better," he said, opening the doors under the starlit sky.

Inside the house I filled the kitchen table with an antipasto and linguini with an arrabbiata sauce and fresh parmesan.

"There's warm toasted garlic bread too," I offered.

"What would a meal be without Ing's homemade bread?" Jim called out, handing a joint to Gene. "I saw your new album in *Billboard* with a bullet," Jim told them. "Good for you."

"Thanks, Jim," said Pat. "We're excited. But enough about us—I want to hear your new record."

"The record's not pressed yet. I only have a cassette of the final mix," Jim said, "but that works out alright 'cause our record player's broken anyway." Jim got up and started for the living room. "Even better, come on in here, and I'll play you some of the new songs." Jim picked up his guitar and began the intro for "New York's Not My Home." He followed the ballad with "You Don't Mess Around with Jim."

"That's a great song, Jim. Sounds like something I should have written," Gene joked.

James Taylor picked up his guitar and played "Sweet Baby James," the song I sang to Adrian James every night when I put him to bed. It was reassuring having someone in our home who had already topped the charts.

Music was fun again, the way it used to be before we moved to New York. After Jim played them the tape of some of the tracks from the new album, we jammed together for a couple of hours. After 1 AM, Taylor packed up his guitar and asked if he could come by again the next day. Tim was tired, too, and headed off to bed with Erin. Marty took his sleeping bag and found a place to camp out. Back at the kitchen table, Jim and Gene continued to take turns playing songs for each other, while Pat and I chatted nonstop. Adrian James caught some z's in his portable crib. By 5:30 AM, we were all ready to go to bed just as the baby woke up.

"Come on," Gene said. "The sun's coming up, and I can't wait anymore. As long as the kid's awake, let's go for a ride in my new wheels." He went outside to put the top down. Pat and our little family piled into the car, and a weary Pistilli took the driver's seat. We headed to the all-night diner twenty miles away.

Halfway there, Gene took a wrong turn and barreled onto the interstate going the wrong way, doing sixty miles an hour against traffic.

"Oh my God, turn around, Gene," I screamed. "The baby's in the car!" Gene tried to turn but did a 360-degree spin onto the meridian. When he stopped, he pulled into the opposite lane, once again heading in the wrong direction.

All of us started yelling directions and advice. Fortunately, it was so early that traffic was light. Gene maneuvered a quick U-turn, finally joining the flow of traffic. I was scared out of my mind.

"Jim, maybe you better drive," I begged, still shaking. "You know your way around here. Please, take the wheel away from this madman!"

Then, noticing a freeway sign, Jim yelled, "Hey Gino, you dumb fuck, you just passed the exit sign!"

Gene jammed on the brakes, and everyone reeled forward. He did another violent U-turn, throwing all of us sideways, and then drove along the shoulder to the exit. When we finally got to the diner, I sat clutching Adrian James. I couldn't find anything funny about our near-death experience. Then again, I was the only one, except the baby, who wasn't stoned.

———

In mid-December, with only a few hundred dollars left from a second advance Tommy sent Jim, we paid the rent and used the rest to buy Christmas presents for friends and family. We gave $100 to Sal, who came over to tell us that he was sorry that he had quit his job as a professor at Glassboro and lost his tenure. Tommy and the Boys were now managing Maury on their own. They had convinced Sal that with their connections they could do far better for him than he could. Not wanting to stand in his protégé's way, he encouraged Maury to take their help. Before Sal knew it, he was totally out of the picture.

"Take the money and go to New York," Jim told Sal. "Or better yet, take a trip to your brother's in Southbridge."

———

A week before Christmas, while Adrian James was taking his midday nap, Jim surprised me.

"I've got an S for you," he told me, hiding the package behind his back.

"A surprise, really?" I said. Inside the box was a new suede winter coat. I had admired it one weekend while we were window-shopping in Philadelphia.

"Oh, Jim, I love this so much I can't stand it!" I tried it on and stood on a chair to look into the antique mirror that hung above the couch. I snapped the buttons closed. "Look, it fits me perfectly. But we can't afford this."

"Don't worry, sweet thing," he said. "I wish I could get you nice things all the time. Last year I could only afford to buy you a pomegranate," he remembered.

"Yes, but it was a beautiful one. I couldn't buy anything for you this year Jim," I apologized as I handed him his Christmas present wrapped in my homemade wrapping paper. "But I hope you like what I made for you." Jim opened it and found a hand-knitted, light blue wool sweater and a colorfully embroidered work shirt. "These are beautiful, Ing. When did you find the time to make them? I love them," he said, giving me a big hug.

Two days before Christmas, Jim returned home from Frank's Folly with milk and cigarettes, which was all he could afford. Though he'd been writing great songs in Lyndell, he was still playing the Paddock for only $25 a night plus tips. And he was embarrassed to go to his parents' house for Christmas Day, for fear they'd remind him that he was a bum.

"You know, Ing, I wonder if I'm doing the right thing, waiting around for Tommy until something happens. Look at us." He threw up his hands. "You have hardly anything to wear. I have holes in my boots. And there's not even 50 bucks left in the goddamn checking account!"

"Let's just enjoy the holidays. Mom and Dad will be focused on Adrian James. It's going to work out."

On his first Christmas, three-month-old Adrian was dressed in Santa pajamas with a matching stocking cap that Jim's parents had given us. Adrian James heightened everyone's holiday spirits. Because of Christmas and the baby, Jim and his dad got along better than usual. Jim cautiously decided to play the title cut from his album, which he'd just received from Tommy. He put the record on the stereo as his father listened intently. He tried to read his dad's face but couldn't, and he fidgeted in the armchair waiting for a response.

"Jim, this is really good," his father said before the song was over. "I think you've got something here."

Jim nodded, taking in the praise. Later, when we left for Lyndell, our arms full of Christmas presents and dinner leftovers, Jim's father put his arm around his son and said, "I just hope it works this time, Jimmy. I think *You Don't Mess Around with Jim* could be a hit. I really do."

"Me too, Dad. Thanks."

———

Finally, in February 1972, Tommy called Jim with news.

"Kurnit went to Switzerland last week for a music conference," he explained. "He met Sherwin Bash of BNB Management, just after Bash gave his speech saying that his company would listen to any new artist. Bash is a heavyweight manager in the music industry. And Phil jammed your tape of *You Don't Mess Around with Jim* into his hand and made him promise to listen to it."

"Did he like it?" Jim asked into the receiver.

"Well, he played it while he was driving through the mountains of Switzerland

and got so excited he stopped at the first payphone he could find and called Phil. He told him, 'Croce's a star.' And he'd be interested in talking with us about signing you when he got back to LA. With a guy like Sherwin Bash and BNB, you could get some major distribution. I think this is it, Jimmy."

Jim hung up the phone.

Ing!" he shouted. "I've got some great news!"

———

When Sherwin returned to Los Angeles, he and Kurnit put contracts together. Sherwin flew to New York to meet Jim, and Adrian and I came with him. As soon as we arrived at the office, Phil asked Jim to put his signature on the bottom of some blank publishing forms, saying, "It's merely a formality." At the same time, Phil tried to smooth over the fact that my name was being removed from our cowritten song, "Hey Tomorrow." He explained that the record company only wanted songs that Jim had written exclusively and asked me to sign off on it and remove my name as coauthor, just for this album.

When Sherwin Bash showed up, he seemed like a movie star himself. He was well-dressed, composed, tan, and handsome, with a close-cropped beard. We all shook hands, and Jim told Sherwin, "I know you handle some big stars like Randy Newman. I sure hope I can do as well for you."

"No doubt about it," Sherwin replied confidently, his light blue eyes sparkling. Kurnit held out a pen and told Jim where to sign the new management contract, and Jim did what he was told, as usual without reading it. BNB Management had already secured a booking agent, a public relations firm, a travel agent, and an accounting firm for Jim, and gave him an itinerary of the gigs he would be playing for a six-week tour, starting almost immediately.

In March, BNB assisted Cashman & West in signing Jim to an ABC/Dunhill contract for three albums in two years. ABC would distribute domestically; Kurnit was securing contracts throughout the world for further distribution. Everything was in place and poised for Jim's career to take off.

On another trip to New York, Jim had to do some overdubs for the album. At the office, we found there were more contracts ready for Jim's signature. Once again, I cautioned him, but he refused my advice and signed.

I waited in Tommy's office with the baby while Jim went to the studio with the Boys. Around noon, I offered to answer the phones while I nursed Adrian, so

Tommy's secretary, Joni, could take her lunch break. When the phone rang, I picked it up and heard Tommy's father introduce himself. "Hi, Mr. Picardo, this is Ingrid Croce. I'm just helping out in the office for a few minutes."

"Jim Croce is dead. Have you heard the news?" he said nervously.

"What? What are you talking about?" I asked. Mr. Picardo talked with a gruff New Jersey accent, and he repeated what he had said, but just a bit louder.

"Jim Croce is dead." I then realized he was talking about Jim's father. He told me Jim Senior had suffered a heart attack in the shower at home alone.

I was heartbroken. I loved Jim's dad, and I was shocked. I knew Jim's mother was with her sister-in-law in Hawaii, vacationing, and this was the first time that his parents had ever been apart. I felt awful for her. I wanted to tell Jim immediately and tried calling him at the studio but couldn't reach him. I waited for him to return to the office and thought about how sad he would be and how his father would miss the release of Jim's album. When the boys arrived back at the office, an hour or so after the dreadful call, I hugged Jim and took him to the back office to tell him the terrible news.

He broke down and cried. He wanted to leave immediately for Drexel Hill so he could be there for Flora when she returned from Hawaii. We also needed to help notify the rest of the family. Jim's brother, Rich, and his wife, Diane, flew up from Florida, and Flora's family drove down from Rochester, New York. All the Croces and Babuscis and their families and friends gathered for the Catholic funeral, a solemn requiem Mass.

Jim took his father's death hard. He moped around the house, not once picking up his guitar. The afternoon after the funeral his mother called.

"Oh, Mom," Jim said, "I feel so bad."

"His death," she screamed over the telephone, "it's all your fault! He had a heart attack because of you. It's your fault he died. You and your music killed him!"

"But, Mom . . ." Jim tried to defend himself, but he was so broken up by what she was saying, he couldn't go on. She hung up on him. He cursed and then dropped to the couch, with his head in his hands.

Then he told me what his mother said.

"She's just not thinking rationally, Jim. She's grieving and striking out."

He ran his fingers through his hair.

"I didn't kill my father, Ing. We may not have seen eye-to-eye on my music, but I never wanted to hurt him."

"Please, don't take her words to heart, Jim. I know they're not true and she doesn't mean them."

———

In spring 1972, ABC/Dunhill released *You Don't Mess Around with Jim*, nine months after it had been recorded. Matty Singer, an ABC/Dunhill sales representative, fell in love with Jim's music. Determined to get the album on the air, he personally visited every radio station in Philadelphia and the rest of his region.

"You've got to play Jim Croce," he would tell them. "The guy's the best, and he's just as nice as he is talented. Play Croce! You have to play Croce!" And they did. Within four weeks, "You Don't Mess Around with Jim" became a hit single, and the album began receiving positive reviews in newspapers and magazines across the country.

"Jesus!" said Maury, as they packed for their tour. "Years of work, and in one short month you're an overnight success!"

Jim read the reviews that began pouring in, stunned and not quite able to believe what was happening. In June, they debuted in New York City to promote the new LP with shows at the Bitter End and the Persian Room. The leading national music magazine, *Cashbox*, reviewed Jim's show. The following week, he excitedly read the article to me over the phone:

> *Jim Croce didn't mess around. Combining a Bill Cosbyesque patter with a firm hand on his acoustic guitar and sweet/mean voice, he is certainly sure of where he wants to go and gets there. The album's title tune (and also his new single) is an example of a song in which characters are introduced, described and fully developed and all in under three minutes. Jim really gives you what you can't get in too many other places. Croce is ably assisted by guitarist Maury Muehleisen, whose licks flow like spring water, making Jim's tunes all the more refreshing and welcome.*

"And, Ing," he continued in a rush, "the June 10 *Billboard* chose the album as a 'special merit pick.' God, Ing! It's just what we've been waiting for. I guess it just takes one!"

After his debut in New York, he opened at the Main Point for Randy Newman. On Friday, June 16, the *Evening Bulletin* announced:

> *If Croce's guitar strings ever break, he can ride on his mouth. While Croce's songs are witty, telling and, above all, intelligent, his between song patter is as funny, make that funnier than most stand-up comics.*

225

Back home, I clipped out the review.

"I hope you remember your dad," he said quietly, looking over at Adrian James in his playpen. "I have a feeling he'll be on the road a long time."

———

Jim started on a whirlwind coast-to-coast tour as the opening act for Randy Newman, whose dry humor, songwriting, and musicianship impressed Jim.

At the end of June they played the Bitter End a second time, and Jim and Maury were an even bigger hit. A few days afterward, Maury came to Jim's room with a new copy of *Cashbox* magazine.

"Hey, did you read this, Jim?" Maury read out loud:

> *Although ABC/Dunhill's Jim Croce and wonder back-up guitarist Maury Muehleisen had gotten a hold of some bad yogurt at a "health" food store a few hours before their performance, they looked and sounded anything but pained on stage. Croce is continually polishing and tightening up his raps without leaving them over-rigid, and the combination of his musical styles continues to improve from good to great. Although his debut LP and single are both proving the points we made a few weeks back about his mass appeal, we won't say we told you so (even though we did!).*

"That's really nice," Jim said, and took the magazine out of Maury's hands so he could look at the charts. Jim pointed to a list of the top LPs in the nation. Maury looked over his shoulder. "You Don't Mess Around With Jim" had elbowed out "Saturday in the Park" by Chicago, "Long Cool Woman in a Black Dress" by the Hollies, and "Lean on Me" by Bill Withers.

"Jesus!" Maury responded. "Look at the singles. 'Time in a Bottle' is on the charts too, with a bullet!"

Jim took every interview that was offered, thanking every DJ with a handwritten, personal note for playing his songs. He was raised to show his appreciation for the smallest of good deeds done on his behalf and didn't let a single opportunity pass without thanking the people who had helped him. He wasn't just being polite: he was genuinely grateful and never wanted to let anyone down.

In July, Jim and Maury went to California and performed in San Diego at the Funky Quarters to an enthusiastic audience. Afterward, they decided to celebrate. A tall, blonde cocktail waitress with big blue eyes caught Jim's attention.

"What will it be, guys?" she asked.

"Well," Jim smiled, "how about a Coors . . . for starters?"

"Hey, you're Jim Croce," she gushed. "I love your music. My favorite song is 'You Don't Mess Around with Jim.'"

"Can I see you after the show?"

"Yeah, well. I guess I'm free after work. My name is Gracie. I'll give you a tour of San Diego when you're done." Maury eyed Jim accusingly.

"Don't say anything, man," Jim whispered. "After all, I am separated. She's back there, and I'm here." Maury sipped his beer and didn't say a word when Jim later slipped away.

In Los Angeles, they opened for Randy Newman at the Santa Monica Civic Center. The crowd was the biggest yet. There were loud cheers of familiarity for the songs on the charts.

"Californians love us!" Jim said after their second show.

"Yeah," Maury replied with sly disapproval, "we saw that in San Diego. And, by the way, Patty Dahlstrom is waiting for you backstage with Elliott."

The next morning a reporter from the *Los Angeles Times* called, wanting to write a feature on Jim. Jim readily agreed, and when the reporter arrived, he asked Jim to reflect on his music.

"Your subject matter seems to be the blue-collar worker," the reporter said.

"Yeah, I tell stories of men who have experienced life in a physical way, because they often have a knack for creating pattern images about what they did, and the images come back to me in flashes. Many of my songs reflect the mood of a moment. It's an emotional thing. The lyrics are intellectual creations, but the music and the songs are very much in the emotions."

The interviewer asked about his background, and the new star began to tell stories about his life.

"After college, I got a whole different kind of wisdom," Jim said. "I began listening to people, people who probably never read a book and don't give a damn about the symbolism in F. Scott Fitzgerald. I write songs about the hundreds of conversations I've listened to. Like the time I stayed up all night on a Pennsylvania passenger train and heard a black Pullman porter talk about his thirty-five years on the trains."

227

"What else?"

"Well, once I got a job painting the hospital ward in Upper Darby, with a man named George Blair. He told me he had anthrax from an ill-spent youth. George wasn't an educated man, but he had street wisdom. He told me stories about how he'd gone over to fight the French. He said, 'They forgot more than we ever knew.' And at work, while we'd brush thick, white paint on the emergency room walls, George would recite the poem about 'Dangerous Dan McGrew'":

> A bunch of the boys were whooping it up
> in the Malamute saloon;
> The kid that handles the music-box
> was hitting a jag-time tune;
> Back of the bar, in a solo game,
> sat Dangerous Dan McGrew,
> And watching his luck was his light-o'-love,
> the lady that's known as Lou.

The following week, the *LA Times* article was published and entitled "Jim Croce—A Laborer in Lotus Land":

> *Jim Croce is perhaps the only popular singer who has a license to drive a caterpillar tractor. He flew to Los Angeles a few weeks ago but he was here as a foreigner, an alien in an unnatural environment. He quickly returned to his home in Lyndell, Pa, a crossroads stop, which features a gas station with a red metal ten-cent coke machine and about five other weather-beaten homes. 'It has a random plank floor put down with pegs and hand forged nails,' Croce said. 'And you can see that the beams overhead have been cut with an adz.' He lives a simple life with his wife, Ingrid, and their new son, Adrian, in a rough hewn home dating back before the American Revolution.*

Back in New York another reporter interviewed Jim.

"You're the new poet laureate of rock 'n' roll," he declared.

Jim modestly refused the honor. "No," he said, "the great poets like Robert Frost and Dylan Thomas had melody in the words themselves. My lyrics don't contain that melody. It's the music," he insisted, "the guitar and piano that provide the rhythm and flow. The work of those poets is far superior to mine."

After the interview, he called me.

"The music's going pretty good, Ing. A lot of people seem to like it, but everything is starting to look the same—the hotel rooms, the rented cars, the fans. The boredom is the worst! I really miss you. And I can't wait to see how my little old man is growing."

I tried to imagine what it must have been like for Jim without the intimacy we used to share. As hard as it was for us on the road, we had each other. I wondered if he was succumbing to the pressure of his female fans, who I suspected were throwing themselves at him after the shows. But I tried not to dwell on it.

Jim would joke about his misfortunes with others, but with me he could say what he really felt about his work and the road. I listened to his complaints and sympathized with him.

"Your fans would never believe you were bored," I laughed. "But I do." I paused. "I know a way to take it away," I whispered seductively. "Let me come up and make love to you."

"That would be great. But I'll be home soon."

Sometimes during those days of endless touring, Jim would tell me he wished I could be on the road with him and we could sing together again. But we both knew it was different now. He was expected to live up to the image he had created. And on the road, it was definitely a man's world.

"This is tough for us both, but I've got to work, and it's better for you and Adrian James to be safe at home," he added with sudden tenderness, avoiding my solution to his boredom. "Tell me what Adrian's up to today?" he asked.

"Well, he's a serious little guy. And he's learning new things every day," I bragged. "He's saying more words and points at the cows and goes, 'Moo, cow.' He can't say 'duck' yet, but his new thing is to run out on the porch and get the ducks to chase him. Then he screams at the top of his lungs and comes running back inside before they can catch him. They can be vicious . . . and they go for his hands." I paused. Jim seemed so far away. "Sweetie, it's our anniversary next week. I know you're busy and you probably forgot, but it's been six years. Do you think you could make it home, just for a day or so, or maybe I can come out and we can celebrate wherever you are?"

He had forgotten. "We'll see. Let me talk to Adrian!" he interrupted. "We'll talk about it later. I don't want him to forget me."

———

On August 26, on his way home for our anniversary, Jim stopped by the rock quarries near Lyndell, and the truck drivers and construction workers crowded around him.

"Way to go, Croce!" they said, slapping him on the back. "Congratulations, man. The chicks must be eatin' you up!" Jim talked with them for more than an hour and played a few new songs.

"You haven't changed a bit, Croce," Emil Sanfranni told him.

"Shit, Emil," Jim replied. "I've done too many things in my life to let a little fame change me. Some people get to the top too fast. They forget they have a god-damn belly button."

Though Jim was hounded by fans and media, he was always happy and willing to take the time to talk with folks. Jim didn't believe fame had affected him, but I knew it had. On the road he was treated like a celebrity. No one said no. He always got what he wanted, when he wanted it. And there wasn't anyone out there who would interfere in his relationship with prescription drugs. He took them to sleep, to wake up, and just for the hell of it. Those around him also began to recognize his drastic and unpredictable mood swings but did nothing about it.

One afternoon when Jim was home, he was playing with Adrian and singing to him. It was naptime, and Adrian began to cry. Out of the blue Jim yelled:

"Make this kid stop crying, and do it now!" His voice had a sudden brutality that shocked me. I came running into the living room and could see that Adrian looked frightened, and I assumed it was Jim's raised voice that had scared him. Jim yelled at me again, "Goddamn it, Ingrid! Shut this fucking kid up, or I'm leaving right now! I can't even come home and relax for a minute without a fucking baby screaming his head off. Shut him up! Do you hear me?" He scolded, raising his hand as if threatening to slap me.

I scooped Adrian up off the floor and took him to his room. A half-hour later, Jim came and stood in the doorway. It was as if the violent incident had never occurred.

"Would you guys like to come with me to visit Ronnie Miller? I'd really enjoy the company." Once we were in the car, he apologized. "I'm sorry, Ing. I'm so sorry. I know I get crazy sometimes. I'm just exhausted and uptight from being on the road so much."

What he couldn't admit was that he was also weighed down by the "vitamins" that his druggist friend had given him and by the guilt of his double life. He was becoming addicted to the lifestyle, and being at home on the farm was a reminder of how much he had really changed.

As we approached Ronnie's house, Jim suddenly pulled over to the curb in front of a tattoo parlor.

"Come with me, baby," he said, and he jumped out of the car. I followed behind him, with Adrian in my arms. We walked into the tattoo parlor, where dozens of designs were displayed on the wall. "I want you to pick one out for me."

"You've got to be kidding. You know I hate tattoos!"

"Come on," he insisted. "I want you to watch while I get one." He stared at me with his big, brown, sad eyes.

"Please, Jim, don't do this."

Just then, the owner of the shop came out from the back room. Tattoos covered his face, arms, and hands. I smiled weakly. Jim laughed, knowing I wouldn't protest further. Reluctantly, I picked the smallest and least offensive design I could find, a rose tattoo. He asked me to sit with him and watch as the tattoo was etched into his chest. The needle pierced his skin, raising large drops of blood, and he winced in pain as the artist drew the petals over his breastbone. When it was done, we returned to the car.

"That's my penance, Ing," he joked. "I'm sorry I've been so mean. I'll try to be better, I promise."

———

In early fall, Jim waited in a bar in Mason City, Iowa, to meet Jonathan Moore. The talkative, stand-up comedian from Bristol, England, had been booked to join him on the tour. He was a slight, fair-skinned man, and he came in holding several suitcases, including one that seemed to have odd-looking horns sticking out the top.

"What are those?" Jim asked after they introduced themselves.

"Me bagpipes," Jonathan replied. Jim pulled a penny whistle out of his pocket.

"Take them out," he said. "Let's play the folks a tune." Jonathan warmed up with a series of screeches that almost got them thrown out of the bar, but then people gathered around in fascination. The two entertained customers for a half-hour with Scottish marching tunes.

"Where," Jonathan asked, obviously impressed, "did you learn all those English and Scottish folk songs?"

"Ah," Jim said with a grin, "I'll tell you later. Let me buy you a drink first." Jim ordered them both a shot and a beer. "I started drinking boilermakers when I drove trucks," he told Jonathan. "The little one builds the fire, and the big one puts it out," he continued, as he toasted his new companion. Jonathan was a nonstop conversationalist and proved to be just what Jim needed.

"Where's your mate?" Jonathan asked Jim. "I've seen you guys onstage, and he's one hell of a guitar player."

"He's gone back to the room to lay down. Getting some rest is his main occupation," Jim told him.

"You mean he's like a human red?"

Jim laughed. Jonathan talked his language.

"Hey, while we're on the subject, I've got this pharmacist friend. Let me know if you need anything. As I always say, what's good for the sick is better for the well!"

"Couldn't agree more." Jonathan smiled and sipped his cognac, a gift from an appreciative fan.

Jonathan prided himself in performing practical jokes, which helped ease much of the boredom and tension of the tour. Outside a concert hall in Minnesota about an hour before their performance, he showed Jim how to make hot air balloons from plastic laundry bags provided in the hotel rooms.

"Always take these with you," he said as he twisted the ends of the bags around two twigs, taped candles to them, and lit the wicks. Smoke and hot air filled the bags and quickly lifted them hundreds of feet high, so they began to look like flying saucers. "You can't imagine how many UFO sightings I've been responsible for. Tomorrow we'll check the morning paper," Jonathan said gleefully. He let another glowing bag soar into the dark midwestern sky.

On September 20, 1972, Jim made his first television appearance on the *Dick Cavett Show.*

"I don't like working," Jim told Cavett. "I used to have a job selling air time and driving around town for this radio station. I went through ten cars that year. None of them worked. I had to abandon one of them at a traffic light. I'll tell you I didn't make any friends that day."

"How do you like New York?" Cavett asked, not very familiar with Jim's songs.

"Ya know, I have a song I wrote about New York on my new album. I don't know if I can say this on TV, but have you been on the subways lately?"

Cavett laughed, "No, not lately."

"Well, they're rolling restrooms. There are mutants in the subways now. I saw one subway dweller yesterday who had a face like an old pizza. He said, 'Give me your money or I'll kill you!'"

"What did you do?"

"I didn't know whether to take out my black jack or my jar of Vaseline. Ya know the people in New York—they've lost their pacifist attitudes."

A week later, on September 28, Jim surprised me and Adrian James by coming home for Adrian's first birthday. Jim was saddened that Adrian didn't run to him when he first saw him. When Jim had called from the road, Adrian would point to his daddy's poster on the wall by the phone, but he was confused that the person in the room and the picture were one and the same.

Arrangements had been made for Jim to do another photo shoot with Paul Wilson. Adrian and I went with him to Paul's Philadelphia studio. Jim was more comfortable now posing for the camera, and he was even relaxed enough to take his shirt off and expose his rose tattoo.

Paul was pleased with Jim's expressive postures and captured him expertly. The pictures were used for his new album, his two songbooks, and the majority of his promotions. Paul also took a couple of rolls of film of Adrian James, some wearing his daddy's big straw hat and a tiny Jim Croce T-shirt. One of these photos of Adrian James covered the inner sleeve of Jim's album *Life and Times*.

———

Back on the road, Jim told a reporter from the *Montreal Gazette*, "I was raised on Fats Waller. Most of the stuff I do is good-time music. Like, when I sing my experience songs. I like 'em because they don't make people feel introverted. I like to make an audience feel close and together." He knew he was building a following.

In late September, he was finally interviewed by *Rolling Stone*.

"Let's see what the godfather of rock rags has to say about us," he told Maury, after picking up the issue from a newsstand.

The magazine reporter had bypassed Jim's recent accomplishments and dwelled on his background.

"What happened to the first album you made with your wife in '68?" he asked. Jim felt it no longer seemed like such a tragedy.

"They ground it up and made Grand Funk records out of it," he replied with a big smile. "But it sold six copies in a PX in Thailand."

"After graduating from Villanova, why did you do construction work?"

"I get a kick out of physical work. It's important to me. And the guys I met out at Sweeney's Construction Company, during my 'character development period,' they're my heroes. When I have free time I just go outside and help somebody put a boiler in." He sat forward in his chair. "The best time I ever had in construction was when I painted an elevator shaft with a big burly friend of mine, Bill Reid. I got the job because I'm not afraid of falling . . . so I usually did: two stories into concrete, that was one of my more spectacular falls."

———

By the winter of 1972, Jim had crisscrossed the country nearly a dozen times. It was a grueling schedule, but when he came home, his newfound success inspired him to write new songs around the kitchen table. "Bad, Bad Leroy Brown," "Careful Man," "Roller Derby Queen," and "Speedball Tucker" were all completed by Thanksgiving. And he was ready to do his second album before the new year began.

For one memorable set of shows before his return, Jim had been booked to open for Woody Allen. Woody had started out in a string of miserable little clubs but was now one of the major comedy stars in the country. He had already written and starred in *Everything You Wanted to Know about Sex*, *Bananas*, and *Take the Money and Run*.

"I'm really excited about playing with him," Jim told me one night on the phone. "I wonder if his phobias are for real."

At the first concert when Jim was opening for Allen, before he went onstage, Jim found the comedian pacing in the dressing room and wringing his hands. He looked like a caricature of himself, perseverating nervously.

"Do, do, do you think this stuff is good enough?" he asked Jim. "I mean, do you think what I have to say is really funny?" He was so painfully self-absorbed with stage fright that Jim wondered why he was putting himself through this. "I mean, do you think what I say will make 'em laugh?" He turned his head with the look of a badly disturbed owl. Jim thought Woody was hysterical, even funnier offstage than on.

With Allen as the headliner, Jim and Maury played the Bitter End on Bleecker Street in Greenwich Village in October and at Valley Forge in November. The hometown press cheered them on. One local Philadelphia reporter wrote: "So, Woody, you were pretty fortunate to have Croce in front of you."

One night, when Jim called me for our nightly conversation, I told him, "Honey, you made *Rolling Stone* again. They said you look like a happy guerrilla fighter just in from the hills."

Jim laughed, thinking the description was ridiculous, but not too far off the mark. "Those writers will say anything!" he said.

I held up the article as if it could bring him closer to me. "You know, sweet thing, I think you're becoming far more famous than you realize. Everywhere we go we see pictures of your wonderfully rugged face." When he didn't respond, I continued. "I just wish I could see it in person."

"I don't know, Ing," he said quickly. "It's not like this is really fun for me, either. It's fucking hard work."

"I know it is. It's just that I miss you so much."

"Me too," he replied, but I wasn't convinced. He was constantly invited out to parties, and I was saddened by the thought of what might really be going on. Groupies waited for him after every show, and I wasn't completely blind to how tempting that would be.

Confronting Jim with my doubts would only make him angry, so I asked, "Have you heard from Sal?"

"Yeah, I actually spoke to Sal tonight, and I called my mom too. She said to say hello. I bought her some Godiva chocolates. I know how much she loves them." There was a pause.

"Are you okay?"

"I'm doing good, Ing. I'll be home soon."

"Okay. sweetie. Love you."

"Me too," he said.

———

In October, the tour made a one-night stop in Bemidji, Minnesota. Jonathan opened with his routine; then Jim and Maury performed.

During an intermission, an attractive, well-dressed young woman worked her way backstage and introduced herself.

"I just talked to your dad," she said to Jim. "He told me he was really glad that you were doing so well."

Jim just stared at her. "Uh huh," he replied, caught between shock and disbelief.

"He was sitting right up there." She pointed to an empty seat near the top row. At first Jim thought the woman was playing a joke, but her manner and expression seemed serious. So he asked what the man looked like. She described Jim's father perfectly.

"He was tall; he wore glasses and had kind of salt and pepper hair. And he was wearing a plaid flannel shirt."

235

Jim was spooked. He looked at Jonathan, who shrugged.

"Well," the woman continued, "he said to tell you that he knew *You Don't Mess Around with Jim* was going to make it. Then he said he had to leave and asked me to pass his message on to you."

Jim shook his head as he watched her walk away. As soon as Jim got back to his room, he called me.

"Ing, you're not gonna believe this. Remember when you told me you thought you'd seen your dad about six months after he died? Well, when I just finished my concert tonight, this woman came up to me and told me she had spoken to my dad tonight. He told her to tell me that he knew *You Don't Mess Around with Jim* could make it. No one knew he said that but you and me."

I'LL HAVE TO SAY
I LOVE YOU IN A SONG

MAURY WAS ABLE TO REST while Jim did interviews, radio shows, meetings, and solo performances, but Jim was having more and more trouble getting to sleep and waking up on time. To maintain an impossible schedule, he was relying more and more on pharmaceuticals.

"I have no privacy. None! Whether I hang a 'Do Not Disturb' sign on the door or not, the maids just walk right in. I'm so fucking tired, and I keep getting sick," he told me in a call from his hotel room in Chicago.

"Please just finish this tour and come home," I told him.

"Don't lay a guilt trip on me."

"I'm not, Jim. I just want you to be okay," I insisted.

"I am okay, and I'm hanging up now. I don't want to deal with your shit."

"Please don't hang up angry. Let's just change the subject." He slammed down the receiver.

Five minutes later, he called back and said, "I'm sorry, Ing. I know I need time off, and I keep asking Tommy, but he's not listening. I don't know how or when I can get it. Are you and my little old man doing okay?"

"Yes, Jim," I said defensively. "We're fine."

"I don't mean to take this out on you, Ing, but it just happens. I just get pissed off."

"Good night, Jim. We'll talk tomorrow."

"Good night, Ing."

After he hung up the phone again, there was a knock at his door.

"Jim, we know you're in there," chorused two girls' voices. He didn't answer. They kept tapping and banging, then burst into laughter. Finally they left. Jim heard them knock on another door down the hall, and then the voices were gone.

Wired and weary, Jim picked up his guitar, turned on the tape recorder, and sang what he had so far of a new song, "One Less Set of Footsteps":

> *We been running away from*
> *Somethin' we both know,*
> *We've long run out of things to say*
> *And I think I better go.*
> *So don't be gettin' excited*
> *When you hear that slammin' door,*
> *'Cause there'll be one less set of footsteps*
> *On your floor in the morning.*

And we've been hidin' from somethin'
That should have never gone this far,
But after all it's what we've done
That makes us what we are.
And you've been talkin' in silence.
Well, if it's silence you adore,
Oh there'll be one less set of footsteps
On your floor in the mornin'.

Well there'll be one less set of footsteps
On your floor,
One less man to walk in.
One less pair of jeans upon your door,
One less voice a-talkin'.

Before completing the third verse, he turned the recorder off, grabbed his note pad, and put down some words for another new song, "These Dreams." He turned the recorder back on and sang:

Once we were lovers, but somehow things have changed;
Now we're just lonely people,
Trying to forget each other's names.
Now we're just lonely people,
Trying to forget each other's names.

Once we were lovers,
but that was long ago;
We lived together then
and now we do not even say hello.
We lived together then
and now we do not even say hello

What came between us,
Maybe we were just too young to know;
But now and then I feel the same.
And sometimes at night I think I hear you calling my name,

239

Mm mm mm, these dreams,
They keep me goin' these days

When he finished recording "These Dreams," he returned to "One Less Set of Footsteps" and completed the last verse. He also finished another verse and the chorus for "These Dreams." He fell asleep, satisfied that at least he had almost all the new songs ready for the second album.

The next morning, Maury looked at Jim shyly and said, "I don't know how you do it, man. You can keep those damn groupies to yourself! I feel awful this morning. I can't do this to Judy."

———

A week later, Jim came home unannounced.

"I want us to move away from Lyndell," he told me, marching into the kitchen the morning after he arrived.

"Why? You're never here."

"Yeah, but did you see those fans down there by Frank's Folly? They knew I was coming home before you did. I want to move where no one can find me."

What he couldn't tell me was that he was paranoid about his separate lives colliding. I didn't like the idea of moving even further into isolation, but I gave in by rationalizing that if Jim felt more insulated at home, he'd try to be there more often.

We found a large farmhouse near Coatesville that rented for only $125 a month in a tiny rural community more than half an hour's drive from Lyndell. I liked the house and the acres of rolling farmland that surrounded it, but I felt totally abandoned, and my concerns about Jim and our relationship grew steadily. No matter how hard I tried to say the right things, somehow our nightly conversations ended badly.

One night when Jim called from the road again, I apologized.

"Jim, I'm so sorry. I know you think I sound selfish when I ask when you're coming home. But honestly, I'm not good at this. And I don't know what I can do to make things right."

"I know, Ing." Then he was silent. "It's not you."

"Please can't I meet you somewhere?"

"I don't know if we can make that happen, Ing. It's tough. This is no life for a baby. What would he do all day? I'll be back home in a few weeks. I promise. We'll have time then."

240

He never had a good answer for why we couldn't occasionally join him, and I was suspicious that there were groupies or other women on the road. But I wanted to believe him, so I tried to ignore the signs.

———

In the beginning of November, between concerts, Jim and Maury took a couple of weeks off to record Jim's second album for ABC/Dunhill, called *Life and Times*. Even before they got into the studio, "Bad, Bad Leroy Brown" was selected as the first single off the new album. "Next Time, This Time," "A Good Time Man Like Me Ain't Got No Business (Singin' the Blues)," "Careful Man," "Alabama Rain," "Dreamin' Again," "Roller Derby Queen," "Speedball Tucker," "These Dreams," and "It Doesn't Have To Be That Way" were also included. "One Less Set of Footsteps," one of the final songs Jim had written before going into the studio, was a last-minute choice for the album. After producing the song, Tommy and Dennis felt it was such a strong cut they wanted to put it out as a single.

During Christmas break, a reporter from the *Philadelphia Inquirer* interviewed Jim at home in Coatesville. The starstruck reporter was pleasantly surprised that Jim allowed him to get so close. They sat down at the kitchen table to talk. I served them coffee and muffins. Jim had his message down pat.

"We've seen everything from Spanish moss to icebergs on this tour," he said. "It's been a steady grind of getting up at six in the morning to catch airplanes and piling into cars for hundred-mile drives to the next gig." The interviewer sipped his coffee and watched Jim's expressive gestures, smiling as he took notes. "We've been on everything," Jim continued. "Crop dusters, everything. I didn't even know biplanes still existed. Some places we played you had to drive to because the only other way would've been to parachute in."

The reporter took it all down and, when the interview was over, said, "This was great fun, Jim. Thanks for your time. I won't bother you any longer."

"It's not a bother," Jim said.

While he was home for the holidays, I tried to focus our activities around Adrian James and steered Jim away from talking about his obligations. Fortunately, we had lots of friends who would visit when he came home. And although I would have preferred to be alone with him, I did my best to give him space.

———

Shortly after Jim left on his next tour, he was flying in a small plane on his way to Dallas with Maury and Jonathan Moore when a heavy squall moved in from the Gulf of Mexico. Traveling with Jonathan made Jim feel safe because the comedian was also a first-rate pilot. Jonathan would often sit in the copilot's seat and make flight path decisions. The storm struck with sudden fury. The plane began to dance from side to side. The pilot ignored it and went on telling stories about the action he'd seen in Vietnam as a fighter pilot.

"I've crashed several times," he said over the sound of the pouring rain. "Once a general who was on board got killed!" He turned around to grin at Jim and Maury, and pulled up his trouser leg to reveal a plastic prosthesis. "Lost this in a crash, too," he told them.

Maury turned white. A moment later the plane hit a downdraft and dropped suddenly. The pilot lunged for the controls as the craft sank at a faster and ever-steeper angle. They plunged more than 2,000 feet before the plane could be stabilized. Everybody, including the pilot, was terrified. Finally Jonathan said, "Turn the plane around. Let's go back."

———

On December 23, Jim walked onstage at Madison Square Garden and received a standing ovation. "*You Don't Mess Around with Jim* has reached over the million mark in sales," the announcer said excitedly. "And now Jim has just completed his second album, *Life and Times*. Let's hear it for Jim Croce!" The crowd's roar was deafening. Jim had given in and finally invited me to join him for the New York concert. He arranged to meet me back at the hotel room after the show, which I suspected was a way to avoid any possible run-ins with groupies.

Judy and I had driven to New York together. I left Adrian James with my stepmom for the weekend. It was my first time away from the baby, and I knew he was in good hands. I was glad Jim wanted me to come to this concert and hoped if it went well, we could do this again.

The crowds were amazing. It had been months since I had attended one of Jim's shows, and though I knew his set by heart, I was always happy that audiences had such a good time listening to Jim's music and raps. After two encores, Jim escaped out the back door to leave and meet me in our room at the St. Moritz. He was intercepted by a demanding woman who wanted to go home with him. He hated to refuse anyone, but he talked his way out of it, explaining that his wife was expecting him back in the room.

242

I waited impatiently for him to arrive. It felt strange to be so nervous with my own husband, but I wanted our evening to go well. When he opened the door to the hotel room, I was primping in the bathroom.

"Hi sweetie," I called to him. "I loved the show tonight. Maury was great, too."

"Thanks," he said quietly, as I came into the living room to hug him. He was still holding his guitar case.

"Sorry I'm late. I'm exhausted." He sighed heavily. I hugged him tightly.

"Do you want to just sit and sing some songs together and unwind?" I asked.

"I just want to hold you, Ing. Just be here for me. Please don't leave me."

"Why would I leave you?"

Jim sat down and took his guitar out of the case. "I don't know. Things just get so crazy on the road."

"I know—it actually feels like we're on a date. Like old times."

He started playing "Four Strong Winds," and I harmonized on the chorus. No matter how far apart we were, music brought us home. He played "Child of Midnight" and "And I Remember Her" and asked me to sing Joni Mitchell's "Blue."

"Ing, I want to sing with you again, and we could be on the road together."

"Well, we can at least do this once in a while, until Adrian James is a little older."

"God, I've missed you, Ing," he said. "I don't mean to be such a bastard."

"Let's not talk about it now. I don't get a chance to be with you very often. Could you just come over here and hold me?"

––––––

The next morning, Jim suggested we stay in bed and order room service. I loved the opportunity to be alone with him, and with excitement I looked at the menu. I was stunned.

"I can't believe this, Jim: $7.99 for eggs and toast and $3.00 more for bacon. Who can afford these prices?"

There was a knock at the door. I jumped out of bed and threw on my robe and went to see who it was. A messenger handed me an Associated Press article with a note from Tommy that read, "Good going, Jim."

Jim was sitting at the desk with his guitar in hand. I began reading the review out loud.

Croce, 29, is bounding up the ladder of musical success after nearly a decade of passing the hat and hitting the road.

243

Then the reporter quoted Jim:

"I try to approach my songs so others can say they've had that kind of experience too. It's like those old radio shows when you used to hear the door creak open in the background and everybody saw something different coming through it."

I sat down on the bed and read further:

Somehow there's no way anyone could seriously question whether Croce has paid his so-called dues. It's all too obvious that he has. His songs let you know more than anything else, but so does his fist-like face.

"You're really doing it," I said and went over to hug him. "Everything you dreamed of is coming true! Come on, come to bed."

But he seemed to have a lot on his mind, and his response was muted. "New York makes me nervous."

"Oh please, let's stay for just a little while." I let my robe drop to the floor.

"I can't, Ing. I'm exhausted. Besides, I need to stop in New Jersey on the way home to see Phil Petillo. My guitar needs some work done before I have to get back on the road again." He bit his lip nervously.

I didn't want to ask why he was distancing himself from me. We showered, packed, and were soon off to visit Phil and Lucille Petillo.

Not only an expert guitar maker, Phil was also an inventor who had developed a line of guitar strings that Tommy and the Boys were promoting. The year before, Phil had made Jim a Petillo guitar and since then had repaired several others for him. He charged fairly for his work, but Jim knew the degree of devotion Phil extended couldn't be bought. Like Jim, Phil wasn't in it just for the money.

Lucille welcomed us warmly to the guitar studio and into their home.

"Please, stay for lunch," she insisted.

"Have you spoken to Tommy lately?" Jim asked Phil. Both the Petillos went silent. Phil and Tommy had been friends in New Jersey, and Tommy had introduced Jim to Phil when they began negotiations for Petillo Strings two years before.

"We're not exactly on speaking terms. We may end up in litigation over Petillo Strings. Haven't you heard anything about it?" Petillo asked.

"I've been on the road. What happened? I thought you and Tommy were close."

"So did we," answered Lucille. "We always thought he was like a brother."

Phil Petillo summarized the situation without going into too much detail.

"It was a bad mistake for us to get involved with those guys. I hope they're treating you okay," he said.

As we were leaving, Phil said, "You take care of yourself, Jimmy, and make sure you get some rest."

"Yeah, right," Jim said. And then he gave me a knowing glance.

———

When we arrived back in Pennsylvania, we picked up Adrian James from my stepmom's, and Jim called Flora.

"We have a little surprise we got for you in New York. Ing and I are gonna bring the baby over. We'll be there for dinner."

"God forbid," Flora scolded. "You took the baby to New York City with you? *Schifoso!* What kind of filthy place is that to bring a baby?"

"Mom, we didn't bring the baby to the city with us, but babies are born in New York every day. I got some cannoli for you from Ferrara's. I know how the Flower loves them."

When we arrived at Flora's, I hugged my mother-in-law with one arm and carried Adrian James into the kitchen on the other. Jim took off his cowboy boots and left them inside the front door. He brought Adrian's car seat into the kitchen and set the Ferrara's box on the plastic tablecloth. As he entered the kitchen, he leaned over to kiss his mother, but she turned toward the counter to get our lunch. She served Jim's favorite, a kohlrabi sandwich on Italian bread with olives and pepperoncini. She cleaned Adrian's pacifier at least fifteen times in between feeding him.

"Adrian is getting so big, Mom. I think he looks just like Jim. Don't you?" Flora kissed her grandson on the cheek.

"I love him so," she said.

"Does he look like Jim did when he was a baby?"

"Jimmy was the smartest little boy. People couldn't believe he was so smart. I don't know what happened to him."

I encouraged her to talk about good times, but Flora was upset with her son's career. She feared Jim was away from all of us too much, and though she couldn't express her anxiety to him, the tension between them had grown steadily. Their relationship had been strained since Jim's father's death, and the longer Jim was on the road, the worse it got.

"You're a grown man traveling around like a gypsy. Look at you, the way you dress. God forbid!"

Jim was hurt, but he controlled his feelings. "We do fine, Mom."

"What can I tell my friends when they ask me what you do?"

"You can tell them I work hard every day to make a living, and that my record is number one in the country. What more do I need to do to please you? Get a fucking job with a pension?"

"How dare you!"

Jim bit his lip and raced for his boots by the front door in the living room.

"Ing, get the baby. We're leaving!" He went back into the kitchen to get the baby's car seat.

"Why are you leaving like this? Are you crazy?" Flora yelled.

"I'll show you what crazy is, you fucking son of a bitch!" he shouted, cursing his mother out loud for the first time in his life. "Don't you ever talk to me like this again!"

"Is he crazy?" Flora looked at me with fear in her eyes. "What's the matter with him?"

"I'm so sorry, Mom," I said. "He's not himself. He's exhausted, but he'll be alright. We better go now." I headed quickly for the door.

"I should have spoken up to you a long time ago," he yelled. "I won't listen to you belittle me—never again. All I ever wanted was to make you happy. But I can't please you. Nobody can!" He slammed the door.

———

Jim's schedule continued nonstop. He was still opening for Woody Allen and Randy Newman. *You Don't Mess Around with Jim* was the number one record in the nation, and yet we could barely pay the bills. One night on the phone I asked:

"Has Tommy mentioned when we'll get a check for your royalties?"

"The accountants in LA take care of that now. But at least they're putting me up in nicer hotels," he said.

"Great, but we're still only getting $200 a week, and you've got a number one record. This doesn't make sense, Jim, with all the records you've sold and all the concerts you're doing."

"They say the money I make has to pay off the expenses before I can get paid."

I knew any further discussion was useless.

Jim and Maury left for Europe in February 1973 to promote *You Don't Mess Around with Jim*. They were warmly welcomed in London, Paris, and Amsterdam, and the reviews were very encouraging for their foreign sales. When they returned in February, the second album, *Life and Times*, was about to be released, and Elliott booked them with Loggins and Messina.

"I feel like I'm in overdrive," Maury complained after one show. He was stretched out on his hotel room bed. "When do we get a break?"

Jim looked up from the latest set of reviews that Joie, the secretary at BNB, had sent, which he'd brought to Maury's room to share.

"I'm worn out too, but we've got to keep going," he said. "It's because we are out here that we're getting press like this." He held up the most recent copy of *Cashbox* and read aloud:

> In a matter of months, Jim Croce has risen from the obscurity of a talented troubadour to the prominence of one of the brightest new performers on disc. Jim Croce is currently in the midst of his third single success, 'One Less Set Of Footsteps', bulleted at #37 this week from his second LP, 'Life and Times.' Jim has reinforced his recording prowess with extensive bookings around the United States, as evidenced by his tour now in progress with Loggins and Messina.

"Yeah," Maury said with a sniffle, "and what do they say about the stalwart Maury Muehleisen, always at your side?"

"You can't take reviews to the bank, Maury. But if you keep playing, I'll make you rich." They laughed.

"Yeah, just like you."

"Listen to this." Jim read more recent reviews, first one from *Billboard*:

> "Jim Croce—Life and Times"—Story songs of a very personal nature are the hallmark of Croce's works. His soaring voice carries him on his trips through life and we are privy to his experiences.

Then he read one from *Dealer's Magazine*:

> Croce is a hot poet—favorite of young people.

"And this is from the *Daily Trojan*," he said, reading on:

Jim Croce is the fastest rising newcomer on the pop music scene today. His newest album, 'Life and Times', will sky rocket him to even higher heights. One Less Set of Footsteps, the first cut on the first side will probably be his next big hit.

———

In March, Judy and I drove to the Philadelphia airport to pick up Jim and Maury, who had just completed another West Coast tour.

"I never know who to expect when Jim comes home," I told Judy as we stood at the gate holding Adrian's hands between us. "Every time he comes off the road, I don't know whether he's going to freak out or be himself."

"I'm sorry," she said.

"He's wound so tight it really frightens me." I picked up Adrian and took a deep breath, trying to feel positive in my anticipation. "I'm pregnant, Judy. And I just hope Jim is happy about it."

Jim got off the plane, still high from his well-received performances in California. He gave Adrian and me a quick hug, and then we rushed to the parking lot, trying to avoid the fans and stares on our way. During the hour-long drive home, Jim played the radio loudly and barely said a word, switching stations constantly.

"I can't wait 'till you hear this song I wrote on the road," he told me when we pulled into the driveway. He walked in the front door and headed straight to the tape deck. "Listen to this. It's about these groupies dedicated to making plaster molds of as many rock stars' dicks as they can. They're serious! They came to my dressing room a couple of nights ago, wanting to add me to their collection. I couldn't resist writing about them!" The tape began to play "Five Short Minutes of Love."

Well she was standin' by the dressing room after the show,
Askin' for my autograph and asked if she could go back to my
*   hotel room.*
But the rest is just a tragic tale:
Because five short minutes of lovin'
Done cost me twenty long years in jail.

Well, like a fool in a hurry, I took her to my room,
She casted me in plaster while I sang her a tune,
Then I said, oooh-oo-ee, sure is a tragic tale,

Because five short minutes of lovin'
Done brought me twenty long years in jail.

Well, then a judge and a jury sat me in a room,
They say that robbin' the cradle is worse than robbin the tomb.
Oooh-oo-ee, sure was a tragic tale, (wasn't worth it)
Because five short minutes of lovin'
Will cost me twenty long years in jail.

When I get out of this prison gonna be forty-five,
I'll know I used to like to do it, but I won't remember why.
And I'll say, Oooh-oo-ee, sure was a tragic tale
Because five short minutes of lovin'
Done cost me twenty long years in jail.

"And did you let them?" I asked when the song was done.

"Yeah, it was really something!"

"Yeah, I bet it was."

"It's all so crazy!" He shrugged. "But it's their thing, and if they dig it, they should do it."

"'That sounds just like you."

"What the hell are you so pissed off at? It's only a song!"

"It's not only a song. How stupid do you think I am?" Tears filled my eyes. "This crap has gone on for so long, you don't even know how blatant you are! Jim, I'm going to have another baby," I cried as I stormed out of the living room and ran upstairs to the bedroom with Adrian in my arms.

"Well, have it your goddamn self!" he yelled after me, then headed for the kitchen and grabbed his guitar.

An hour later, I walked into the kitchen to get Adrian James his lunch.

"Oh, I forgot to tell you," Jim said, as if nothing had happened. "A film crew is coming by this afternoon to shoot some footage for a promotional film. They want me to do more college concerts. I invited them to stay for dinner." Still seething, I didn't let the news get a rise out of me.

"So how many am I supposed to serve?"

"Fifteen or so," he replied flatly.

Holding back my tears, I started cutting tomatoes and vegetables to make a big batch of spaghetti sauce. I felt choked by the pressure we were under. He had promised that this time when he came home, we'd have time alone. But now, after another fight, and with a camera crew on its way, my hopes of our communicating seemed futile.

An hour later, Acorn Productions pulled their vehicles up the long driveway, and Jim went out to greet them. While the crew set up on the front porch of the house, Rick Trow, the head of the production company, walked around the property. Though we rented the large farmhouse for only $125 a month, it was surrounded by eighty acres of rolling hills. An Amish man named Amos leased the farmland and grazed his cattle there. And a pond filled with ducks was right out in front of the house.

"The ducks frighten Adrian," Jim said to Rick, "but he loves the cows. His first words after 'Mama' and 'Dada' were 'cow,' 'moo-cow.'"

"Kids are great, aren't they?" Rick said.

"Yeah, I nicknamed him Adrian Amos James after ol' Amos over there on the tractor. When we have our next son, I'll name him Andy."

Rick told me they were staying at an inn in Coatesville, and I was thankful they didn't all expect to sleep at the house. He explained that first he wanted to take some footage of the three of us doing what we did as a family. And that he'd be back the next day to work with Jim alone.

While I was cooking in the kitchen, Jim called to me to come out with Adrian so I could sing with him. The last thing I wanted to do was to be in an idealized PR piece on Jim Croce. I was disheveled. I had nothing to wear but jeans and a new T-shirt Jim had brought me with his face on it. I was totally unprepared to perform; I was livid, and I walked out grumpily and sang my part.

Rick and his crew were very nice. They seemed to really enjoy our music. After dinner, when they were getting ready to leave, I invited them all back for breakfast.

After putting Adrian to bed, I went into the living room where Jim was practicing.

"Jim," I said calmly, "I don't want to argue anymore. I know your coming home is painful for you, and it is for me too. If there's something I'm doing wrong, tell me." My lips trembled. "I don't mind taking the blame. But I need help now, because I can't go through this anymore." I sat down on the sofa, and tears fell from my eyes. Jim put down his guitar and held me. "It must be my fault, because no matter what I do, I make you angry."

"No, it's not your fault. I'm fucked up," Jim said. "I'm the one who needs help."

"Jim, maybe we both need help. Or maybe we should just end this, once and for all."

"No, Ing, please, I promise it'll get better. I'll get help, anything you want."

I wanted to believe him. But I didn't want to keep arguing every time we were together.

"I don't know what to say. I feel my life is falling apart, Ing. We're still driving a fucking broke-down car, and we barely have anything to wear!"

When we went to bed, he assured me he'd go for counseling. "And I promise I'll spend more time at home," he whispered. "I'll be different, you'll see. But, please, please don't leave."

———

In the beginning of March 1973, Jim performed as the opening act for the comedian George Carlin. Three days later, Barb Eraud, a reviewer for the University of Pittsburgh newspaper, wrote:

> Croce moved me more than any other artist I've ever seen—from Stones to Kinks to Yes to Poco to James Taylor to Carole King to anybody—nobody can put across a song the way he can. . . .
>
> Although Jim insists he isn't a comedian, his monologues were much more interesting, relevant and humorous than Carlin's. There was an intimacy established between him and his lead guitarist, Maury Muehleisen and the audience, until it was as if we were all sitting around a fireplace exchanging stories and fun.

In late March, Jim opened for Loggins and Messina at Carnegie Hall to two sell-out shows and rave reviews.

The following day, he was thankful for this review in the *New Musical Express*:

> Physically, he resembles a construction worker version of Hurricane Smith—long, lean, and denim clad with moustache and a curly mop of ink black hair. He introduces each song with anecdotes, biographical insights and an impeccable sense of timing. He is relaxed and urbane, and an absolutely marvelous put-down artist. He is a better stand-up or stool-perched comedian than many so called comics now working the circuit. His set really made the evening for me.

251

There was more praise from a variety of publications, and Jim was particularly excited that he made it into *Guitar Player* magazine, and that they mentioned Maury and Phil Petillo:

> *To set the record straight, Croce is hardly the bullish Cretan we're led to believe. To the contrary. His hands are not broad, like a baseball catcher's, he probably doesn't weigh 130 pounds, and he's not even six feet tall. . . . Jim's musical roots go back to his father's traditional jazz with Turk Murphy, Fats Waller, Bessie Smith, Eddie Lang and Joe Venuti. . . . Jim's favorite guitarists are Christopher Parkening, Merle Travis, and Jerry Reed. . . . When they play concerts as a duo, Jim generally stays with rhythm fingers, leaving the lead and fills to Maury, though they'll sometimes swap duties and mix them up. Croce uses a Martin D-35 but with a narrower neck that his friend and guitar maker, Phil Petillo, repaired for him. Petillo shaved down the Martin's struts to make the guitar resonate a little more. Jim prefers very low action. The strings are Petillo's own brand.*

Life and Times shot to the top of the charts. At a concert after the album's release, Jim told his audience how he came up with "Bad, Bad Leroy Brown":

"This song compresses the personalities of a number of people I've had the privilege to meet, including my sergeant at Fort Jackson and a fellow private I got to know down at Fort Dix. Leroy and I were stationed there and we were sittin' around talkin' one night. And he said he didn't like it anymore and that he was just gonna get up and go home. And he did. He went AWOL. He had the whole army out lookin' for him, but they couldn't find him.

"But then they didn't have to. He came back at the end of the month to pick up his paycheck . . . which was kind of a mistake." The crowd laughed. "But when he got out of the stockade it was a lot of fun to talk to him, because he said it had been an enlightening experience. He was serious, very serious. I mean, he's probably doing books or something now, delivering lectures on some corner about the benefits of being locked up by the military police. Good 'ol Leroy." He and Maury started to play "Bad, Bad Leroy Brown."

> *Well the south side of Chicago*
> *is the baddest part of town,*
> *And if you go down there*

You better just beware
Of a man name of Leroy Brown

Now Leroy more than trouble,
You see he stand 'bout six-foot-four,
All the downtown ladies call him "treetop lover"
All the men just call him, "Sir."

And he's bad, bad Leroy Brown,
the baddest man in the whole damned town;
Badder than old King Kong,
And meaner than a junkyard dog . . .

After high-spirited cheering, he and Maury began playing another cut from the new album, "These Dreams."

While the ballads on the second album didn't meet with the commercial success of "Operator" or "Time in a Bottle," *Rolling Stone* reporter Jon Landau appreciated them:

> *Croce sustains my interest through his depiction of the alternate sides of his romantic vision—one that encompasses the fantasy world of bizarre but human characters and the romantic world populated by lonely people who always manage to miss making their connection. "One Less Set of Footsteps" and "Next Time, This Time," are marked by an undercurrent of resentment against women but neither is vengeful in the style of early Dylan. Rather, they are the product of a disillusioned man.*

Jim continued to build his monologues with the audiences. Some of them were rehearsed and refined, but he often ad-libbed, depending on the crowd. He and Jonathan had a standing challenge to see who could be the raunchiest onstage. Jonathan would feel out an audience early with a few off-color jokes, which let Jim decide just how far he could go. Listeners who responded well were treated to bawdy ballads. Nearly half of his time onstage, though, was devoted to spinning out anecdotes from his past to help explain a song he was about to sing. Before "Roller Derby Queen" he talked about the woman who inspired the song, clearly competing with Jonathan to be outrageous and politically incorrect.

253

"You know up until last year most of my musical experience was centered around barrooms, country and western bars, kinds of places you see in movies like *Easy Rider*, with three or four chrome-plated pickup trucks sittin' out front and a rifle rack in the back window. And when you get up on the stage to play, they have you surrounded by chicken wire, so you don't get injured by beer bottles, flying pitchers, and all that stuff that's goin' on.

"Well, I met a lot of characters in these places, and a lot of them I ended up putting into songs.

"So I was playing one afternoon in one of these local bars where we live. And sittin' down about ten feet away from me was this cute little woman, chubby, about this high, and about as big as a fireplug. She had this blonde hair that stood up real tall. And I found out she drove the school bus in the township where we lived and she was a Spray Net freak.

"Ya know, did you ever see the old movies where Pancho Villa's men had bullets across their chests? Well that's the way she brings Spray Net cans back from the supermarket. So anyway, I have this rule of thumb that if you're 350 pounds, you're a person. And at 400 you become a place . . . and she was hanging in right in there. And every time I watched her clap, I could see the fat on her arm jiggling back and forth. It was a beautiful sight. And I got excited.

"So I started talking to her, and it turned out she came from Texas. She used to be a roller derby queen. And that afternoon I just knew I just had to write a song about her. Now we don't usually do it at home because her husband is a state trooper, and he can really, really mess up a nice day. But we're gonna do it for ya here. It's called 'I Fell in Love with a Roller Derby Queen.'"

With all the flying he and Maury were doing, Jim also developed stories to encapsulate their experiences.

"Of all the airlines we've been on, my favorite is Allegheny," he would tell an audience. "They give you an apple and a glass of water served inside an air sickness bag. It's more an omen than a meal. They are the originators of what we call the white-knuckle flights, the ones that make you feel like you're strapped in a dentist's chair with duct tape. They fly one hundred feet above the Pennsylvania Turnpike at two hundred miles an hour so they don't get lost."

At one concert, Jonathan came out like a reporter interviewing Jim about his favorite flight on Indian Airlines.

"Why did you choose this flight?" Jonathan asked with formal politeness.

"Oh, deary me," Jim would answer in a high, thin Indian voice he tried to make sound like Maharishi Mahesh Yogi's. "The answer to your question lies here." He'd put his fingertips together in meditation. "Fly Indian Airlines, the people who know how to get there, 'cause there's where they're from." After another few minutes of banter as reporter and Indian traveler, with a curt nod, Jim dismissed Jonathan and signaled to Maury to start the next song. Backstage after the show, the comedian praised his cohort.

"That was funny, Croce," he said. "We're a good team."

"Yeah, well, when they sign me up to replace Carson, I promise I'll have you on the show," Jim teased.

"I'm serious, Jim," Jonathan stated. "You'd be a great actor or a host. Maybe you really should consider television."

"I've thought about it," Jim replied. "It certainly would help cut back on traveling and solve problems at home. Hey, did I tell you, Ing's with child?"

"No, but congratulations!"

"Yeah, it might be good to get home for a while when she has the baby. But I'm afraid I'm not real good at home. My little man hardly knows me. And, for that matter, neither does my wife anymore."

"I'd like to meet Ingrid sometime," Jonathan suggested. "She must be something to keep up with you."

"You'd like her, Jonathan. She's really something, a great cook and very funny. We'll have to have you over sometime when we get off the road."

In May, Charlie Fox asked Jim to record the theme song for *The Last American Hero*, a Joe Wizan movie starring Jeff Bridges. The song "I Got a Name," by Charles Fox and Norman Gimbel, sounded as if it had been written for Jim. "We really want you to concentrate on the vocal, Jim. So you won't need to play guitar on this one."

When he stepped up to the studio microphone for the first time without his guitar, he felt a bit nervous. His guitar was his shield, and he felt exposed without it. He sang the song all the way through, as they requested. They then asked him to do some shorter versions for commercials.

Jim asked, "Am I doing okay?"

"You're doing great, Jim. Just keep singing," the engineer said from the sound booth.

When Jim and the Boys listened to the playback, they were all pleased and liked the song enough to decide to include "I Got a Name" on his next album.

By late spring of 1973, Jim had sold millions of records, sold out hundreds of concerts, and made guest appearances on the Johnny Carson and Dick Cavett shows.

"I've gotta rest," he said in a phone call to Tommy. "The road is really getting to me. I need time off."

255

"Not now, Jimmy," was the curt reply. "You know the schedule. And Jimmy"—Tommy paused—"cut out the drugs."

To keep Jim's spirits up, Jonathan made sure that no two performances were alike. One night, when Jim and Maury were performing for a college in LA, Jonathan hired two attractive women to ride their bikes onto the back of the stage in plain view of the audience but where Jim and Maury couldn't see them. The women were naked except for their socks. Jim and Maury were in the middle of "Operator" when the crowd gasped audibly and started to cheer.

The naked girls kept riding in a figure eight, and the audience began to howl. Jim and Maury stared at each other in amazement. Finally the women ran out across the stage and down the ramp in front of Jim and Maury. The musicians doubled over in laughter. Jonathan yelled out "Triumph!" from backstage.

After the show, the women waited for Jim.

"I can't let them suffer," he told Jonathan as he got ready to leave his dressing room.

"I agree," the comedian said. "Wives are for home. But the road is for the lads. It's not marriage problems we have—it's road problems!"

"Yeah, that kind of thinking is fine when I'm on the road, but fuck, the guilt eats me up when I'm with Ingrid." He grew serious. "I can barely relax and recuperate from all this wild-ass stuff. I don't know what's more stressful—being on the road or going home!"

The next morning he woke up and couldn't talk.

"Shit," he thought to himself. "What am I gonna do?" He had never missed a concert in his entire career, but now he would be forced to cancel the college tour that included Oklahoma, Mississippi, Texas, and Louisiana. Randy Newman's father was an ear, nose, and throat physician and agreed to examine Jim that day.

"If you don't stop singing for a while, you might never sing again," he said sternly. "Your prescription is silence and sunshine. I don't want you to speak one word—not even a whisper."

Jim boarded the next available flight to Florida. He had Maury call Rich to let him know he'd be coming down for a visit and had BNB's secretary call me at home.

"Jim is on doctor's orders to rest," Joie told me. "He's not allowed to talk to anyone—not even whisper. So he went to stay with Rich in Florida."

After a week at Rich and Diane's, he headed down to Key West. One night at dinner in the Chart Room at the Pierhouse Hotel, he ran into Jimmy Buffett, his label mate on ABC/Dunhill. They had met months earlier in Los Angeles.

256

"Jim, what are you doing here? Good to see you!" Jim couldn't speak but offered his hand, shook his head, and pulled out his pen and paper. "Remember, Jay Lasker introduced us in California, Jim? He thought you'd be a good role model for me," Buffett joked, "being older and all."

Jim smiled. He opened his spiral tablet and wrote: "Doing good! Have throat problems! Can't talk. How 'bout you?"

"Shit, I'm so broke I have to charm hotel guests into doing my dirty laundry while they do theirs. I'm sure you're beyond that." He looked hopefully at Jim. "Hey, I've got a Fender Telecaster and a hand-tooled leather guitar strap that says 'Jimmy.' Are you interested?"

"Maybe," Jim wrote. "How much?"

"I'll sell it for $100, but it's worth a lot more than that," Buffett bargained. The deal was struck.

"Next time I'm on radio, I'll play 'Great Filling Station Holdup.' Love that song. I'll mention your album. What's it called?" he wrote, and handed the notebook to Buffett.

"*White Sport Coat and a Pink Crustacean*,'" he replied. "I appreciate it. Tell everyone to buy it!"

From that meeting on, Jim and Buffett reconnected whenever their schedules allowed, and became good friends.

Within a couple weeks, Jim had regained his voice and was back playing at Doug Weston's Troubadour in Los Angeles and the Santa Monica Civic Center. The *Hollywood Reporter* called his delivery "sophisticated, intelligent and full of piercing imagery," while *Variety* said he "had them rolling in the aisles." *Billboard* also interviewed him in Los Angeles and mentioned his "throat attack." "This was an extreme deprivation for Croce," the reporter said, "who loves conversation. 'I wore out a couple of those little blackboards,' Jim told me."

The Troubadour and the Santa Monica Civic Center were close enough together for Jim to stay at the Sunset Marquis Motel for almost a month. California had become his home away from home, and he settled into the easy lifestyle.

One night after a Troubadour engagement, he met Cheech Marin, of the outlaw comedy team Cheech and Chong.

"I'm a real fan of you guys," Cheech said. "We should get together. Why don't you come over to my house?"

Jim and Maury took him up on it and arrived at Cheech's door after one of the Troubador shows, with their guitars and a six-pack of beer.

"You guys were very impressive tonight, man," Cheech said.

"Thanks," said Maury.

"Yeah, we appreciate it," Jim added. He looked around the house and felt comfortable from the start. With paintings and pottery all around, and the aroma of food cooking on the stove, he felt right at home.

"This pottery is beautiful, man. Where did you get it?" Jim asked, pointing to a tall, slender raku vase.

"I made it, man. I'm a mud head."

"So's my wife," Jim told him. "She'd love your work."

"I'm a good cook, too, so if you guys are hungry, I can make something."

"Thanks for the offer. Home cookin'—that's really nice," Jim said. "I'm not too hungry yet, but I've got some great stuff to share. Let me show you how to make a Lyndell hash pipe out of a beer can." He crushed the middle of the can, slit holes in the top with his pocketknife, worked an air channel inside, and filled the back with hash. Then he lit it and sucked the smoke out the pop-top hole.

"Far fuckin' out," said Cheech. He smiled and tried the Lyndell pipe. "It works great!"

Jim and Maury soon became regular visitors to Cheech's house in the Hollywood Hills, along with other musicians like Leon Russell, Harry Nilsson, and Dave Mason, who dropped over for jam sessions after concerts and often stayed until dawn.

"I like this lifestyle," Jim told Maury one night at Cheech's house when they were jamming with Hoyt Axton and banjo player Doug Dillard. "Maybe Ing and I could get a new start in California. I think she'd really like Cheech and his wife. And I think change would be good for us."

Before they left, he spent some time talking to Cheech on the balcony. Jim really felt good with Cheech. He was streetwise, well-educated, and knew a lot more than Jim did about the business. He respected him.

"You know," Jim confessed, "I'd like to try acting or hosting a talk show or something. Do you think I could do it?"

"Yeah, movies are fun," Cheech said. He gave him a scrutinizing stare. "You'd be good at it, man. Maybe we could do a movie together sometime."

Weeks later, Jim returned to Coatesville for a few days' rest between tours. Judy picked up Maury and Jim from the airport and dropped Jim off at home. Having been separated from us for many weeks, he stepped awkwardly toward the front door.

"Shit," he mumbled, "I feel like I should knock on my own goddamn door."

"You look exhausted," I said, hugging him.

"And you look very pregnant." He hugged me back. Adrian James ran into his father's arms. I had spent the morning preparing Jim's favorite meal. I was certain that after an hour he would grow restless and want to visit one of his buddies. I hoped dinner would keep him home for a while at least.

In the living room, Adrian proudly sang "Bab-a-loo," from the *I Love Lucy* show, strumming his ukulele in earnest with his slender little fingers. After dinner, Jim made some phone calls while I put away the dishes. I hesitantly went upstairs to put Adrian to bed, afraid Jim would leave the house while I was out of sight. But minutes later he joined me in the baby's room and followed me to the bedroom.

He built a fire in the old fireplace and lit a candle near the bed. While I was turning back the comforter, Jim walked back into Adrian's room.

"I want to check on my little man again," he said. "I love to watch him sleep."

When he returned, he lay down next to me, and soon we were touching. Just as we began to relax and enjoy the intimacy, he jumped up without any explanation.

"What's the matter, Jim? Do you want to talk about something? Are you worried about the rent or the bills?"

"No, I just need to leave."

While he played his guitar downstairs in the kitchen, I turned over and cried myself to sleep.

Around 4:30, he came back upstairs to wake me up. Sitting on the edge of the bed with his guitar in one hand, he gently shook me.

"Ing. Wake up, sweet thing. Wake up. I just wrote a song I want you to hear. I wrote it for you."

"Do you have to play it right now, Jim?"

"Please, Ing. I want you to hear it now. I need you to."

I sat up in bed. He adjusted a pillow for my back and kissed me on the cheek. Then he sang me his new song, "I'll Have to Say I Love You in a Song":

> *Well, I know it's kind of late*
> *I hope I didn't wake you,*
> *But what I've got to say can't wait*
> *I know you'd understand.*
>
> *Ev'ry time I tried to tell you*
> *The words just came out wrong,*
> *So I'll have to say I love you in a song.*

I know it's kind of strange
But ev'ry time I'm near you,
I just run out of things to say
I know you'd understand.

But ev'ry time the time was right
The words just came out wrong,
So I'll have to say I love you in a song

LOVER'S CROSS

THE WIND SWIRLED AROUND the single-engine Beechcraft as it took off from Chicago's O'Hare Field. A storm was moving eastward, toward their destination in Washington, DC, where they were scheduled to play the Cellar Door that evening. Jonathan sat silently in the front seat, looking intently out the cockpit window.

"Stop being so quiet," Jim yelled to Jonathan over the roar of the engine. "You're making me nervous."

While Jonathan sat still, looking down at the white-capped waves on the southern tip of Lake Michigan, the pilot radioed the tower.

"What's the wind pattern and velocity reading?" he asked. He started to gain cruising altitude, but the wind took hold of the plane and jerked them suddenly off their seats.

"Jesus!" Maury cried out. "This feels fucking dangerous." He clutched the sides of his seat so hard, his knuckles literally turned white. Then he shut his eyes and began humming to calm himself. Jonathan was transfixed on the instrument panel, making sure that the pilot had everything under control, double-checking his decisions.

For more than two hours the roller-coaster ride continued. The pilot began his descent toward the airport, and everyone breathed a deep sigh of relief.

Maury, his eyes still tightly closed, called out, "Are we there yet?"

As the plane flew lower, the turbulence worsened. The wings and body swung back and forth, bucking violently.

The cockpit of the plane went dark.

"Christ!" the pilot yelled. His words were drowned by the huge roaring engines of an ascending DC-9 that was so close Jonathan could see the rivets on the nose of the plane. The jet's wheels suddenly appeared fifteen feet in front of the windshield. Jim dove for the floor, but his seat belt jerked him back. Maury opened his eyes and mouth wide to scream, but no sound came out. The belly and the tail of the DC-9 rolled over the top of them with a deafening thunder that suddenly ceased.

"Bloody hell!" Jonathan cried. "The bastard barely missed us!"

The pilot's face went ashen as he fought to bring the Beechcraft under control. The tiny plane slid through the backwash of the jet, shuddered, then straightened out, and descended at a steep angle. Jonathan forcefully grabbed the yoke in front of him and took over. The plane was almost on the runway when a violent gust of wind tossed it sideways, beyond the taxi lane and toward a thick grove of oak trees. Jonathan struggled to bring it back on line, but it was too late to gain altitude. He pulled hard to the right, away from the trees, as the left wing mowed through a thick hedge like a giant clipper. The plane screeched as the branches scraped along the aluminum wing, but it held together and came to a stop with the left wing plunged into the hedge.

For a moment, nobody spoke. Jonathan turned and stared at Jim. Maury had shut his eyes again. They got out, stunned and silent, and headed toward the terminal.

"Shit!" Jonathan said softly. "Something's after us, Jim." He took out a Saint Christopher medal from his jacket pocket and handed it to him. "Here, take this. It's for good luck, man. In case next time I'm not there to save you."

———

By early June 1973, "Bad, Bad Leroy Brown" had sold more than a half million copies, and *You Don't Mess Around with Jim* had gone gold. Although Jim's concert price had risen to $10,000 per night, and he was playing constantly to packed houses, he was told that the money he was earning was still being used to pay for his expenses. Jim lived with the promise that royalties would be coming soon. He had appeared on *American Bandstand*, *Midnight Special*, *Rock Concert*, *The Helen Reddy Show*, and various television specials. "Time in a Bottle" had been chosen as the theme song for *She Lives*, a television movie starring Desi Arnaz Jr., about a woman stricken by cancer. Soon after a second appearance on *The Tonight Show*, Elliott, Jim's manager, called him on the road.

"Just wanted to let you know there's a change in your schedule. We've booked you to host *Midnight Special* on June 8, when you're back in LA next week, to be aired on ABC on June 15. And Cavett wants you in two weeks."

"That's great, Elliott. Keep booking me on TV as much as you can. I reach a lot more people with one television show than with a shitload of concerts. Besides, I can stay in California. I'm actually thinking about moving here."

"Well," Elliott continued, "as a matter of fact, in September I've got the twenty-fifth booked for the *Midnight Special* again and the twenty-sixth for *Rock Concert*."

"Good. Maybe I could get my own show someday."

"Well, at least you can cover for a week for Carson while he's on vacation. Would that work for you?"

"Wow, cover for Johnny Carson. That'd be great."

Jim interacted easily with Carson and had made an impression on the popular host. On his most recent *Tonight Show* appearance, when Johnny had asked him what he'd been doing lately, Jim had told him about his recent bouts with flying:

"The meaning of faith is giving your guitars to the airlines. They have this new thing now called 'special handling.' Usually you have to leave your guitar with them where you leave your suitcase, but now you can take it right to the door of the plane. So you get to actually watch them drop it."

"I hear you've been flying all over lately. How do you like it here in Los Angeles?" Johnny asked.

Jim squinted his left eye and answered, "The health craze is big now in California. Everyone is into this guru-commune routine of bein' real still and eating brown rice. You know, rice makes you nice. Well, shoot, rice never made me nice—it made me thin. And another thing: everyone is into bein' pure, but I don't buy it. I walked into a health food kitchen in Westwood yesterday, and they have the wheat germ and kelp flower. They have the soybean meal and ginseng root. And then way down at the end of the shelf, so no one can see it, is this carton of Camel cigarettes and a jar of instant coffee. I don't think it's all that it's cracked up to be."

After the commercial break, Jim sang "Bad, Bad, Leroy Brown" and then returned to his seat next to Johnny.

"Didn't I hear that you had bad luck with cars?" Carson asked.

"Yeah, I just wanted one car I could depend on," Jim smiled, holding up his index finger. "I was always stopping by used car lots and junkyards trying to find one that worked. Last year I owned thirteen cars. And that's the truth—a little bit more than one a month. The truck I own now has fifteen-inch wheels on one side and sixteen-inch on the other. It always feels like I'm going around a corner." He leaned into a pretend turn.

———

In late June, Jim and Maury finally got a week off between road trips, and they both came back to Pennsylvania. It was the first time in a year and half that we were going to have a whole week together. On the second day of their break, Elliott called Jim at the farm.

"I hate to tell you this, man, but we've had to add some concerts to your upcoming tour. I'm sorry, but you guys have to cut your break short."

"What the hell!" Jim started to yell at Elliott. "I knew this would happen. Can't they reschedule them for after our break?"

"It's just the way it worked out," Elliott told Jim, nonchalantly.

"Well, it's good-bye again," he told me. "They've added more concerts to the tour."

"Jim, this is crazy."

"Yeah, I know," he said, running his fingers through his hair in frustration. "But we have to do the dates they've scheduled." With the receiver still in his hand he grew pensive. "Elliott knows how much I need this break. Maybe he can figure something out to make this work." Then he dialed a number.

"Maury," he said. My heart dropped. I had been sure he was going to call Elliott back and have him rearrange his schedule. "We've got to head out tomorrow. Elliott just called, and they've booked more concerts."

"I don't think I can make it," Maury groaned. He was lying on Judy's bed. "I feel like I'm gonna die."

"What's the matter?" Jim asked.

"Allergies. I think it's the cat."

Jim exploded. "I'm not going alone!"

Then his voice became calm.

"Okay, Maury. I'll take care of it," he said.

"What do you mean?" Maury asked anxiously.

Jim slammed down the phone.

Maury turned paler than usual and slowly replaced the receiver.

"What'd he say?" asked Judy.

"He said he'd take care of it—whatever that means."

"I don't like the sound of that," Judy said.

"Yeah, he's wound up really tight."

After Jim hung up, I watched him go to the gun rack on the kitchen wall and take down the shotgun.

"What are you doing?" I asked nervously. He slapped his black-and-gold CAT cap on his head.

"Get Adrian's jacket," he ordered, walking toward the front door. "We're going for a ride to see Maury and Judy." The gun and his strange, dark mood scared me. But I was afraid to ask questions. I got the coats and carried Adrian to the pickup. Jim swung in behind the wheel without speaking. Impatiently he revved the engine, tucked some shells into the vest pocket of his denim jacket, and set the shotgun behind the seat. He turned up the country station on the radio. Thirty minutes later, after barely speaking, he turned the truck into Judy's driveway. He stopped in front of the house, left the engine running, grabbed the shotgun, and got out of the truck.

One of the neighbor's cats crouched at the end of the driveway. Adrian and I watched horrified from the pickup as he raised the shotgun. He took aim and squeezed the trigger. The gun bucked and let out a huge roar. He picked up the dead cat by the tail and strode sharply onto the porch. Maury and Judy stared at each other inside, mouths gaping. Jim rapped on the front window with the barrel of his shotgun. Judy jumped halfway across the room.

"I took care of it!" Jim yelled. "See you in the morning!" On his way back down the driveway, he tossed the cat into the brush and got in the truck. Adrian was crying. I sat in stunned silence.

———

Later that afternoon, when Jim went out to visit Bill Reid, and while Adrian was taking his nap, I called Judy and Maury. Maury answered.

"Maury, I'm scared to death about what happened today."

"He's crazy, Ingrid," Maury told me. "He's a madman. He can't go on like this much longer. And I can't be a part of this anymore."

"I know," I whispered. "But what can I do? I don't know him anymore. Please, Maury, don't abandon him. Please help us."

That evening, after Adrian was in his bed, I sat Jim down in the living room.

"I've made a decision today. I'm going to leave you if you don't get some help. I know there are other women. I know about all the crap that's going on, and I don't want to discuss it. I just want you to get some help."

Jim just sat there cornered, staring at me.

"You know about what other women?" he asked.

I ignored him and continued. "What you did today is the last straw, Jim. Either you get help, or Adrian and I are gone." I stormed out of the room and then stopped in the hallway when I heard him on the phone.

"How ya doin'?" he said. I listened to him pace back and forth as far as the phone cord would let him.

"I need a break badly. Can't you move these concerts to a later date?" He stopped pacing and stood still and listened for a moment. "No way! I can't stop taking them," he said. "I need them. I'd like to see you stay up on the natch for three days straight. If you care so damn much about me, get us off the fucking road!"

After he hung up, I walked back into the room and said, "You're still going aren't you?"

He nodded and headed upstairs to bed.

———

266

I called Elliott while Jim was on tour. I knew Jim would disapprove, but I didn't care. Things had gotten so bad I was desperately worried about his health and life.

"Please get him off the road, Elliott," I begged. "He's so messed up, I never know what he's going to do next."

"I know he's under a lot of pressure," Elliott admitted. "We'll get him off the road soon."

"Well if you don't, you'll have one less artist to promote."

"I understand."

"No, you don't," I insisted. "He's doing crazy things. Did he tell you about what he did at Maury and Judy's? He needs a break right now, not next week. Right now!"

"Okay, okay. He just has to finish this one final tour, and we'll give him time off. I promise."

"I hope you really mean it, Elliott." My voice was calmer. "Do you have any idea how serious this is?"

———

That summer, Jim played most of his gigs in Southern California. His agent had double-scheduled him on the West Coast so that in addition to concerts he could be readily available for television. In Los Angeles, Jim had been working with Corb Donahue, an artist relations representative for ABC/Dunhill who was also representing Jimmy Buffett. For over a year, Jim and Corb had developed a close friendship. Jim liked and trusted Corb. They could talk in depth about music and the music industry. Their conversations encompassed everything from world politics to Corb's passion, surfing. Corb thought Jim was brilliant and found his humor refreshing. "You know," Corb said one afternoon in Jim's hotel room, "when I first met you, I expected some big six-foot-six burly truck driver to walk through the door."

"Like Merle Haggard or Johnny Cash, right?" Jim laughed.

"Yeah, I thought you'd be a real bad-ass kind of guy. But shit, you're a pussycat. Of all the artists I've worked with, you're the only one who never says no. You make yourself available for anything the company asks, and you never complain."

"Yeah, and look where that's gotten me." Jim smiled and sat down at the desk to finish writing a note he had started.

"Writing thank-you notes?"

"Well, that's the least I can do for the people who buy my records." He folded down the top of the white note card. On the front was a pen and ink caricature of

Jim's face with a huge cigar and puffs of smoke. A printed message inside read, "Thanks for Messin' Around with Jim."

"Who do you send them to, anyway?"

"People who write me, disc jockeys, concert promoters, record distributors. Just nice folks. I even sent one to your boss."

"No wonder everyone loves you," he smiled.

"You know," he said, "I spend time with everyone except my own family. Shit, I haven't been home—I mean really home—for months. Don't get me wrong. I mean, I really love being on the road performing and meeting people. But it's hard with a family. And when I do get home, I'm so spun out I'm hardly there."

"You really do look tired, Jim," Corb said empathetically. "You're burnin' the candle at both ends."

"Yeah, well, I've been going nonstop for almost two years now," he added. "Ever wish you could just disappear?"

"Sure, and I do," said Corb. "You know, last month I took some vacation time and went down to Costa Rica. Maybe you and Ingrid could join my wife, Lee, and me in Central America when you get some time off. We'll take the babies and caravan down to Quepos. There are a couple of houses for sale there. Costa Rica would be a great place to hide away for a while. And I've been thinking land down there would be a great investment someday."

"Time off . . . that'd be nice," Jim muttered, putting away the note cards. "I just put a down payment on our first new truck, a Travelall. Maybe we could drive down with you sometime. Thanks for the invitation."

———

One June night, Jim called me.

"I want us to move to California," he said excitedly.

"Really?" I asked, surprised.

"Yeah, I've been thinking. San Diego is a great town. It would be easier on all of us to live on the West Coast. Just think, Ing . . . no winter."

"Sounds perfect to me." Jim still hadn't gone to get help, and I hadn't left him. I desperately wanted to keep our family together, and once Jim was off the road, I hoped he would see a doctor and stop taking drugs.

The idea of moving appealed to me. Coatesville was a lonely place, and I wanted Adrian to get to know his dad. So in late June we flew to California for the first time and met Jim in San Diego. We checked into the Hilton Hotel on Mission Bay and began looking for houses to buy. I found a really nice real estate agent who showed us around San Diego with the understanding that we only had a couple of days to find a house. On the first day, we found a two-bedroom ranch-style home in the wooded section of Point Loma that listed for $48,000. We made an offer of $45,000, and the house was ours.

Jim called Tommy.

"Ing and I have decided to move to San Diego and buy our first home, but I need to borrow some money for a down payment. I figure it shouldn't be a problem to get an advance."

"Well, I don't know Jim. This is kind of sudden," Tommy told him.

"Come on, Picardo. I still haven't received any royalties."

There was a long silence. To his surprise Tommy finally said, "Okay, Jim. I'll have the down payment wired tomorrow."

"I did it, Ing. We're actually buying our first home. If you can go to the bank tomorrow, you can deposit the check Tommy's sending."

"Don't you want to open the account with me, Jim?" I asked.

"I've gotta meet with some people in LA tomorrow, and besides, you're better at takin' care of business than I am."

The following day Jim returned to the hotel, having cut his trip short. I was writing letters. Adrian James, almost two, was sitting on the floor unscrewing the knobs from the dresser. Jim paced around the crowded hotel room, reading lyrics out loud for a new song. Not paying attention, he stepped on one of the dismantled knobs and twisted his ankle.

"Adrian," he yelled, "you can't play in the middle of the room!" He scooped him up and put him on the bed.

"Jesus Christ, I almost fell on my ass! Now don't move, little man." He pointed at his son.

"You sure are in a bad mood," I said, getting a tissue to wipe Adrian's nose. "What happened in LA?" I suspected he'd met with either his manager or some woman, and things had not gone well, or he was overcome with guilt. I didn't want to confront him, so I focused on Adrian James. I sat on the bed, took him in my arms, and stroked his soft, sweet hair. Without confrontation, Jim fell back into an armchair and tried to explain.

"Shit, I'm under a lot of pressure." He breathed deeply and added with his brow furrowed, "I've got two days to write a song for the new album and another for a movie soundtrack." He got up and flopped down on the bed, next to us. I took a deep breath. I wanted to hug him and just let all my feelings out, but it was time for Adrian's nap. So I got up and put Adrian in bed and sang him to sleep, as I often did, with "Rock-a-bye, Adrian James" to the tune of James Taylor's "Sweet Baby James."

Jim sat at the desk playing his guitar, recording the song he was writing. I started unpacking his suitcase and in the side pocket I found a small gift-wrapped box.

"What's this?" I picked it up to show him. He pushed pause on the cassette recorder and turned around to look at me holding the tiny box.

"Um, well . . ." he stammered, sitting up. "It's an S, a surprise I got for you." I opened it and took out a gold-link necklace, looked at it, and tucked it back in the box. My heart was heavy. I knew it wasn't really for me. Jim had always been great at selecting gifts, and this one was definitely not my style.

"Thanks," I said suspiciously. Then I spotted a similarly wrapped gift in the opposite side of the suitcase. "And what's this?"

"Another S. That's for you too." This necklace was made of earthy ceramic disks that had Egyptian designs.

"This one looks more like me," I said offhandedly and put it on, looking at Jim suspiciously.

"Goddamn it, Ingrid," he said heatedly, "I don't need your sarcasm. A simple thank you will do." I walked into the bathroom and started to cry. I ran a bath and got in. I was six months pregnant, and felt fat and ugly.

Through the door, I heard Jim working on his new song, "Lover's Cross."

> Well I guess that it was bound to happen,
> Was just a matter of time;
> But now I've come to my decision,
> And it's one of the painful kind.
> 'Cause now it seems that you wanted a martyr,
> Just a regular guy wouldn't do,
> And baby I can't hang upon no lover's cross for you.
>
> Yeah, I really got to hand it to you,
> 'Cause girl, you really tried.
> But for every time that we spent laughin',
> There were two times that I cried.
> 'Cause you were trying to make me a martyr,
> And that's the one thing I just couldn't do.
> And baby, I can't hang upon no lover's cross for you.

'Cause tables are meant for turnin',
And people are bound to change.
And bridges are meant for burnin',
When the people and memories they join aren't the same.

Still, I hope that you can find another,
Who can take what I could not.
He'll have to be a super guy,
Or maybe a super god.
'Cause I never was much of a martyr before,
And I ain't 'bout to start nothin' new,
And baby, I can't hang upon no lover's cross for you.

———

At the beginning of July, after a short visit to Coatesville, where I was packing for the move to California, Jim flew back to San Diego. He closed escrow and signed the final papers to move into the house on August 1. Then, while he was at the Los Angeles airport, before he and Maury left on their second European tour, he called to tell me he wanted to say good-bye to his little man. I could tell he was feeling bad and needed to just touch base, but it was so strained between us. Words were hard for both of us now.

Before I put Adrian on the phone, I told Jim that our friends George and Carole Spillane had agreed to drive our new Travelall and a moving van to California for us while Jim was in Europe, and that I planned to fly to San Diego with Adrian and meet them there.

A few days before the scheduled move, while Jim was still in Europe, George called to say Carole had been in a bad car accident. "It was pretty serious, Ing. She's in the hospital," George told me. "I'm sorry, but we won't be able to move you."

"Oh, George, I'm sorry for Carol. Don't worry about us. We'll figure something out when Jim gets back." Feeling anxious about the news, I took Adrian for a ride to Judy's. Shortly after we arrived, I started to feel dizzy and nauseous. I asked Judy to watch Adrian while I lay down on her bed. Suddenly, I felt strong contractions and stabbing pain. There was a rush of fluid.

"Jude!" I cried. "My water broke. Oh, my God, it's too soon to have the baby!"

Judy rushed me to the hospital in Bryn Mawr, a half hour from her home. George Spillane met us there and took Adrian home with him.

271

From the hospital bed, I called Jim in Amsterdam.

"I'm afraid we might lose the baby," I said as tears rolled down my cheeks. "Will you please come home? I really need you here, Jim."

"I can't leave the tour, Ing," was all he said. I hung up, feeling it was really over between us.

Eight hours later, alone in bed, I began giving birth. I pressed the nurse's call button again and again, and yelled out in pain, but the baby was coming, and there wasn't a nurse around. I struggled to deliver our baby alone. When I saw him move, I reached down to touch my son, who would be named Max. He looked just like Adrian James, but a little smaller. Several minutes later, a nurse appeared.

"What is it, Mrs. Croce?" she asked, studying her clipboard. When she looked up, she saw me crying. Maxwell James Croce had died in my arms within minutes of being born.

———

The next day, I checked myself out of the hospital and went home to finish packing. Judy came to help me, while George took care of Adrian James in Lyndell. He was sleeping on the couch with our little boy lying on his chest when the phone rang.

"George!" Judy said in a panicked voice. "Ingrid is very, very sick. I'm sure it's problems from the delivery. I'm taking her back to the hospital right away. I'll take her to Coatesville—it's closer—and call you from there."

I was delirious with pain when we reached the emergency room.

"Help me! Help me," I begged. The intern on duty quickly examined me. I was wearing ragged jeans and no makeup, and all the color had drained from my face.

"Are you on drugs?" he asked.

"No, I just lost my baby yesterday," I cried indignantly. "I'm not on drugs. I'm just in terrible pain! Please help me." A young Vietnamese doctor came to my rescue. She examined me and immediately ordered the intern to take me to intensive care. There she discovered I had septicemia, poisoning of the bloodstream from the placenta, which had not been totally removed. Since I was allergic to a number of antibiotics, controlling the infection was dangerous.

"She's not responding well to the medications we've used," the gynecologist told Judy the following day. "There's a good chance she may not make it." George placed an emergency call to Amsterdam, and Jim took the next flight back.

When he arrived at the airport, George was there with Adrian James to meet him with good news.

"The doctor reported that the new antibiotics they're giving Ingrid have started to work. She's not completely out of danger, but she's doing much better," George told Jim.

"Thank God. Come here, my little man," Jim said, picking up his son and hugging him tenderly. "I have an S for you from London. It's an English taxi."

"Boy, this has been a tough few weeks," George said. "I'm sure glad you're home." George put his husky arm around Jim's back and hugged him. "Carole ended up in the hospital ya know, from a car accident. And taking care of the women and children around here hasn't been easy!"

"George, stop at the grocery store on the way home. I'm going to buy you the biggest steak in town," Jim announced, smiling appreciatively as they drove away from the airport.

George pulled into the supermarket parking lot. Jim rushed in but couldn't find any steak. A clerk informed Jim of the nationwide meat shortage, so he settled for imported Italian salami, some Provolone cheese, Italian rolls, a case of stout, and a bottle of Tanqueray Gin. Joining Jim at the checkout counter with Adrian, George noticed that Jim hardly had enough money in his wallet to cover the bill.

"Sorry they didn't have steak, but I hope this will do!" Jim said, back at the house, pulling the salami and cheese out of the brown bag and opening a couple stouts. "Let's have some lunch before we go to the hospital."

He picked up Adrian James, put him in his seat, and placed small chunks of bread and salami on his tray.

"You didn't need to spend all your money, Jimmy."

"I owe you. And I'll be getting another stipend soon." Handing George a beer, he said, "Let's toast. *Saluti Perdudi*!"

George shook his head.

"A big international star like you should have more than 40 bucks on him. Something's terribly wrong here, Jim."

After lunch, Jim picked up his guitar and played "Lover's Cross" for George.

When he finished the song, he said, "You know, George, the thought of Ingrid dying really scares me. I've been a bastard."

"I know it hasn't been easy for you two, but you and Ingrid are both my friends. And you're right, Jim. You can't treat her like this. It's just not like you. You're always so kind to everyone else," George reminded him.

Jim looked tenderly at his son and kissed his tiny hand.

"I've gotta make some changes around here." He reached into his pocket and pulled out an airline cocktail napkin on which he'd scribbled some lyrics. He started picking a melody on the guitar and began to sing, his voice full of melancholy:

> *You can run far*
> *You can run farther*
> *You can run farther than that*
> *But one of these days*
> *One of these days*
> *You're gonna run right into you.*

———

Though I was still very weak, I washed my face in the hospital room sink, put on some blush, and brushed my hair.

I don't know why I care so much or why I'm even bothering, I thought to myself. Jim's refusal to come home when I was losing Max made me realize I was ready to give up on our marriage. But before Jim arrived at the hospital, I didn't want him to worry, so I did my best to look well. I couldn't deny that I still loved him.

Jim walked in holding a bouquet of wildflowers.

"You don't look bad for a dying woman," he said nervously. He handed me the flowers.

"Thanks." I took them and asked, "Is Adrian here? I really miss him."

"Yeah, he's downstairs, outside in the courtyard with George. They wouldn't let him come up."

"Please take care of him, Jim," I said wearily. I was still very ill and terribly depressed. I started to cry, overwhelmed by my feelings of loss for Max and for the Jim I used to know. "I think I better get some rest now," I managed. Jim looked remorsefully at me.

"I'm so sorry about the baby, Ing. I'm so sorry about . . . Just get better real soon, please. Adrian and I need you."

———

For the next few days I was in the hospital, Jim called and came to visit often, but I had little to say to him. He made plans for our belongings to be shipped to California. A married couple that owned a moving service offered to help us out for a reasonable fee. His wife would drive the Travelall, while the husband motored the moving van.

A month after losing Max, Adrian and I flew out to the new home with strict orders from the doctor not to overdo it. Our real estate agent, Louise Phillips, and her husband, Bill, picked us up at the airport and drove us to Point Loma. The Phillipses had stocked the refrigerator with groceries and put tropical plants all around the house.

"We just wanted to make you feel at home," Louise said. I had never had such a welcome.

"I can't believe your kindness," I said, overwhelmed. Right away, it felt like home. The next day Jim got a lift down to San Diego from LA with his road manager, Morgan Tell. He had bought me a potter's wheel and set it up in the garage.

"I want you to do your art again, Ing," he said gently, as he prepared dinner for us in the kitchen. "I'll be home for a while, working on the songs for the new album. I've told Elliott to keep my schedule light. The most I'll be gone is a few days a week. Losing the baby seems to be an acceptable excuse for some time off." Adrian sat coloring at a small table. "Just think, he'll be two years old in a couple weeks," Jim said. "Little man, go get your guitar." The toddler came back with his black-and-white plastic ukulele. He began strumming in earnest, and Jim picked up his guitar and started playing with him. "Wow, I can't believe he's so smart, Ing. He's harmonizing with me. I can't believe you made such a beautiful little boy."

"He looks like you did, Jim, with his knobby little knees."

"Oh no, he's much handsomer than me. I don't deserve you two."

A couple days later, when Jim returned from a gig in San Francisco, he brought me a kimono.

"Here, sweet thing, I thought you'd look pretty in this. Japanese women are petite like you. Come on, Ing, try it on." He held up the robe as I slipped into it. "I want you to have time for yourself today," Jim continued, as he tied the sash around my waist. "You look beautiful. Sit down and relax. It's my turn to do some work around here."

"Great," I told him. "I have the perfect project for you. I just bought some red-and-white striped wallpaper to decorate Adrian's room. You and your little man can hang it up together." I relaxed and started to read. Occasionally, I went into Adrian's bedroom to check on how my men were faring. The monumental project took most of the day, as Jim dipped the wallpaper sheets into the tub and carried them to the bedroom, while Adrian giggled, trying to wrap himself in the loose paper. By 6 PM, when I went to see their handiwork, Adrian was fast asleep in his newly papered room, which looked like a giant circus tent.

"Pretty good, huh, Ing?" Jim asked, kissing me on the forehead.

"Not bad at all," I said, surprised by his effort. For the first time in a long time I was starting to believe he really wanted to make our marriage work.

After the following weekend in LA, Jim walked into the house with his arms full.

"I've got S's for my favorite people," he said. I opened a large box and found a ceramic vase and a beautiful book on Japanese pottery. "The vase is raku," he said. "And the book is one that Cheech suggested. He said it was the best!"

"It's gorgeous, Jim. Thank you so much." I nuzzled my head at his neck and kissed him.

"Adrian 'Amos' James has an S too. Come with me, little man." Jim took his hand. "It's this way." We followed him to the garage, where a puppy tied with a red ribbon was asleep in a wicker basket. "It's an early birthday present," he said, bending down to pet the shiny, short brown coat. "He's three months old, and his name is Spooner. I figured my little ol' man needed a best friend." Adrian's big brown eyes gleamed, and he petted the sleeping puppy as carefully as Jim had.

During the next couple of days, Spooner took every opportunity to run out of the house and into the street.

"He's going to get run over!" I called out one afternoon as I flew after him. Jim and Adrian broke out in laughter as I ran back and forth into the neighbors' yards, trying to catch the puppy.

The following morning Jim wanted to go shopping for an antique desk. At a store on Adams Avenue in Normal Heights we found a rolltop over a century old. Inside the drawer were letters of the original owner, postmarked 1891.

"Can we afford $100 right now?" I asked.

"We deserve it," he said. "Besides, it's got a history." He bought it and arranged to have it delivered.

When we got home, I put Adrian down for his nap.

"You know, Ing, I'd still like to sing with you again," he said as I washed some dishes from lunch. "Maybe I can produce an album for you."

"I don't know, Jim. I think I'd rather make pots than go on the road. But maybe if I don't have to travel much," I told him as I considered it out loud. Although I enjoyed writing and singing with him more than anything, I wasn't interested in getting back into the business. But after two years of loneliness, and losing the baby, I was happy to see Jim's good nature return. "Sure," I agreed. "If you really want me to. But only if we do it together."

———

Jim flew to New York to record his third album for ABC/Dunhill, *I Got a Name*. In less than two weeks he recorded "Lover's Cross," "I'll Have to Say I Love You in a Song," "Five Short Minutes," "Workin' at the Car Wash Blues," "Top Hat Bar and Grille," "Recently," and "The Hard Way Every Time." In addition, he included a song Maury had written entitled "Salon and Saloon," one of Sal's called "Thursday," and a tune he and I had written, "Age," which we'd originally performed on our Capitol album.

"This is my last album for ABC/Dunhill. And I see no reason why I have to continue with Cashman & West anymore," he told me over the phone. Jim still didn't understand his legal obligations. But he did understand that after his hit singles and albums and two hard years on the road, he shouldn't be begging for money. "I feel great, Ing. Like I'm tying up loose ends. In a week I'm going to be done with touring for a while. And maybe I can start to focus on TV and be home more."

"I'd like that." I said.

"Yeah. You know, Maury's been doing a lot of writing lately. He even wrote a song for me," Jim said. "You'll have to hear it. And he wrote a song with Kenny Loggins that Kenny's putting on his new album."

"That's great; I'm really happy for him. He certainly deserves it."

"Yeah," Jim continued, "he's ready for a change. He and Judy saved some money, and they're buying a baby grand and some nice recording equipment. He's as eager to get off the road as I am."

———

Jim still had to do the makeup tour to play the concerts that had been canceled when he'd had problems with his voice. He called me from the recording studio in New York.

"Ing, sweet thing," he said enthusiastically, "get a babysitter for Friday night. I want to take you on a date. We need to talk." I knew Jim really would have preferred to have home cooking, but he knew that this would be a real treat for me. I rarely hired a sitter. Since Adrian was born, I had taken care of him on my own, except on a couple of occasions, when my stepmom or mother-in-law watched him.

I asked a new neighbor across the street with four young children of her own if she would mind babysitting Adrian for Friday night. Linda told me it would be her pleasure, and I thought that playing with the other children would be good for him.

277

Excited about our date, I looked in my closet and realized I had nothing to wear and, besides, Jim had told me my clothes looked too "back East." I drove down to an Ocean Beach thrift store to find something "California-looking." I wanted it to be a perfect night.

Adrian and I met Jim at the airport on Friday morning, September 14, and we spent the whole day together, bumming around San Diego like tourists. After a walk on the Ocean Beach Pier and a visit with a disc jockey friend, Larry Himmel, Jim took me to the Black, a local head shop, to get some incense. Then we went to another thrift store nearby, as Jim had told me he needed to replace his denim jacket, which had been stolen by a fan in Chicago. I also noticed he wasn't wearing his gold necklace with the Italian charm his parents had given him, but I said nothing. It kind of hit me that he might have given it away to the woman he'd bought that gold chain for, the S I'd found in his suitcase.

He tried on a jacket and a clerk with long black hair and a mustache came from behind him and stared.

"Far out, man—you look just like Jim Croce! I bet you could make a fortune imitating him."

"Do you think so?" Jim asked.

"I'm serious, man! You should do it."

"Are you going to get the jacket?" the clerk asked.

"No, not right now, but thanks," Jim said, eyeing the price tag. Jim and I left laughing about the hippy's comments.

"I wonder what he'd think if he knew you were really Jim Croce and too broke to buy a used jacket."

"I'm glad he didn't recognize me. I'd probably still be back there signing autographs, when I'd rather be with you." He kissed me on my cheek, and we all got into the Travelall and headed downtown.

Jim parked near Tiger Jimmy's tattoo parlor, and we walked up Broadway. We looked into the window of the tattoo studio. Jim now had several more tattoos, his most recent two butterflies, one on each shoulder, still healing, besides the rose on his chest, the spider on his arm, and the snake up his leg. I had softened to his appetite for body art. I had even thought about possibly getting a tattoo myself, or at least teasing him about it.

I told him, "I'm going to have 'Jim' tattooed right here on my hip, with a big X through it, crossing you out," my tone abrupt. He looked hurt, so I softened it. "Then I'm going to have another 'Jim' put right above it, because I could never cross you out, not for long anyway, though I probably should!" He laughed. I could always make him laugh, especially when I didn't intend to.

He put his arms around me, drawing me close, and kissed me deeply. Then he whispered in my ear: "I promise Ing, these crazy times are behind us. Forget tattoos. Let's go to the house so you can get ready for our date." He watched Adrian while I got ready. I knew he would rather have eaten at home, after all the restaurants on the road, but he knew going out to dinner was good for us. I could tell he was really trying hard to make things work.

When we were ready, we dropped Adrian with Linda and her four children. We drove back downtown to San Diego's Gaslamp Quarter. Walking around the desolate city, its streets full of beggars and ladies of the night, we found no restaurants or live music. When we finally stopped on the corner of Fifth and F, Jim joked that we should open a local restaurant and bar in the old Keating Building and call it Croce's.

"We could bring our friends in to play, Ing. It sure looks like San Diego could use some good food and music."

We got back into the car, drove up Fifth Avenue and finally found a Japanese restaurant offering sushi.

I'd never had sushi before, and when the food arrived, I asked Jim about the raw fish.

"You know what it is, Ing. I've taken you for sushi before. Remember, in LA?"

"That wasn't me, Jim," I replied, looking straight into his eyes. "I've never had sushi."

"Shit, yes, you have!" he insisted. Then he bit his lip to control his anger. After some silence, he apologized. "Listen," he said, "I need to talk to you. I've done some terrible things. I don't have any excuses. But the important thing is I want to be honest with you from now on. I just want to go back to the way we used to be, Ing."

I took his hand. "Look who's being serious now." I laughed.

"I am serious, Ing," Jim said.

"But I don't want to know about it, Jim," I told him. "I'm at a place right now where it doesn't even matter."

He was leaving for just one more week, and I wanted our last night together to be a good one.

———

The next morning I woke up in Jim's arms, and he was kissing me good morning.

"You feel so warm, Jim," I said, reaching up to kiss him gently. Embracing with the familiarity of years past, we began to make love, and he moved above me. I placed my hands on his back, just over his shoulders, and he winced.

"Don't touch me there. Remember, sweet thing. Those tattoos I got last week are still healing."

"Oh, I forgot." I leaned up on my elbows to see them in the light.

"Your butterflies are like the wings of an angel," I sighed, lying back on the pillow.

"Not exactly, Ing, I've been anything but an angel. We really do need to talk."

"I know all about it, Jim. We don't need to talk now." Jim had always been the silent one, but now he insisted on talking.

"I've got to do something about my life. I just don't know what to do." His voice filled with emotion. "I feel so lost. . . . I can't go on like this anymore. You have no idea how crazy it's gotten."

"You know, Jim, the truth is, I'm kinda numb."

"But I've manipulated you. I've failed you in every way."

His eyes filled with tears, and he hugged me to him. "No more, Ing. I promise you. No more. I want to cancel this trip, Ing."

He got up and left the room. Putting on my kimono, I followed him out to the kitchen. On the wall above the phone hung my favorite photo of Jim, taken by Paul Wilson at his last photo shoot. He stared at it. "My God, I've gotten so old. Look at me! I'm only thirty." He traced the dark lines beneath his eyes with his index finger.

"You look fine, Jim. You just need some rest," I added, trying to reassure myself as much as him.

"Yeah, I guess if it's only for one more week . . . But, if I do one more . . . then it'll be another . . . and then another. I just really want out!"

That last night together in the darkness, holding me closely, he told me, "Listen, Ing, if something happens to me . . . I mean if you don't hear from me or something, or I just disappear, don't worry. You'll hear from me in six months or so, I promise. I've been talking to Corb Donahue. He has a place in Costa Rica."

I held him closely for the last time.

I GOT A NAME

September 20, 1973

THE AUDIENCE HAD BEEN applauding nonstop for another encore. A few students were filing quietly toward the exits when Jim strode abruptly back into the bright spotlights at center stage. A cheer rolled through the crowd. Quickly, the fans scrambled back to their seats.

Jim greeted them with a broad smile.

"Natchitoches, where were you going?" he joked. He strummed his guitar slowly, giving everyone a moment to get back to their seats and quiet down.

"We'd like to finish tonight with a song called 'I Got a Name.' It was written by Norman Gimble and Charlie Fox, and it's going to be the theme song for a new movie called *The Last American Hero* starring Jeff Bridges. It's the title song from my new album too. You should be able to find it in the stores in about two weeks. It sounds something like this."

With a smile he nodded to Maury and took a deep breath. The weight of this concert was almost behind him. In unison, he and Maury played the introduction, and then, in the hushed blue light, Jim sang:

> *Like the pine trees lining the winding road,*
> *I've got a name; I've got a name.*
> *Like the singing bird and the croaking toad,*
> *I've got a name; I've got a name.*
> *And I carry it with me like my daddy did,*
> *But I'm living the dream that he kept hid.*
>
> *Movin' me down the highway,*
> *Rollin' me down the highway,*
> *Movin' ahead so life won't pass me by.*
>
> *Like the north wind whistlin' down the sky,*
> *I've got a song; I've got a song.*
> *Like the whippoorwill and the baby's cry,*
> *I've got a song, I've got a song.*
> *And I carry it with me and I sing it loud;*
> *If it gets me nowhere, I'll go there proud.*

Movin' me down the highway,
Rollin' me down the highway,
Movin' ahead so life won't pass me by.

And I'm gonna go there free . . .
Like the fool I am and I'll always be,
I've got a dream, I've got a dream.
They can change their minds, but they can't change me,
I've got a dream, I've got a dream.
Oh, I know I could share it if you'd want me to;
If you're going my way, I'll go with you.

Movin' me down the highway,
Rollin' me down the highway,
Movin' ahead so life won't pass me by.
Movin' me down the highway,
Rollin' me down the highway
Movin' ahead so life won't pass me by.

The crowd once again erupted in applause. Jim took off his guitar and bowed. He thanked them and quickly left the stage to call home.

I was in the kitchen guiding the deliveryman from AAA Furniture toward the den when the phone rang.

"Oh Jim, I'm so glad you called! No, you didn't wake me. It's still light here. I was just talking about you!"

"Really?"

"Yeah. The deliveryman is here with the rolltop desk. I told him that was my husband singing "Bad, Bad Leroy Brown" on the radio, and he said he loves that song. Anyway, where are you?"

"I'm backstage in Louisiana. I just finished the show."

"Are you okay? I'm worried about you, Jim."

"I'm exhausted, Ing. But just three more shows to go, and I'm home. I miss you and Adrian James so much."

"I miss you, too, Jim. How's Maury?"

"I'll tell you later. We've decided to leave tonight instead of tomorrow. We're flying out in about an hour."

283

"Oh! By the way, Jim, that birthday gift you got Adrian James must have been something you dreamed up to drive me crazy. That puppy is peeing on everything. But Adrian James loves him to death."

"How's my little old man?"

"He misses you, Jim. He points to your picture all the time."

"God, I can't wait to see him again! Hey, let's have a big birthday party for him in our new house." He paused. "Listen, Ing . . . I just called to tell you . . ."

Adrian James ran stark naked out the screen door and into the yard in hot pursuit of Spooner, the new puppy.

"Adrian!" I yelled, as the screen door slammed.

"Jim, Adrian's running across the yard after the puppy. I've got to hang up and run after him! He's not safe out there."

"Ingrid, please! Wait!"

"What is it, Jim? I've got to get Adrian! The gate is open."

Pausing, he said, "I love you, Ing."

I hesitated. It had been a long time since Jim had called just to say those words. "I love you too, Jim. Please, please call me later tonight, sweet thing. I've got to go right now. Good-bye."

Jim kept the phone to his ear for a few seconds longer. He placed the receiver back in its cradle. Morgan approached with Jim's guitar in its case. "I packed it up for you, man. Ready to go?"

"Thanks. Yeah, sure, Morgan."

He took the guitar from Morgan and walked toward the exit.

As his small entourage stepped through the rear door of the coliseum, a few dozen fans surrounded them. Jim graciously stopped and signed autographs.

"If anybody wants to tag along, you can follow us out to the airport," he said. The sudden exodus was comical as the fans hurried to their cars. "It looks like the start of the Grand Prix," he joked with his driver.

"Yeah, everyone's running, all right," Doug, the driver, drawled, "but damn, we've got to put this top up first. I should have done it earlier."

"Leave it down, Doug," Jim said. "It's a beautiful night."

"Yeah, but the seats are all damp now."

"Puttin' up the top won't change that. Leave it down."

The long procession of cars headed out toward the airport. Jim and Maury rode in the lead with Doug at the wheel. Morgan followed in a rental car accompanied by George Stevens and Ken Cortese. A parade of students trailed them.

"Doug, I want to apologize for not drawing a bigger crowd tonight," Jim said. "I'm really sorry. I know these makeup concerts are kinda tough sometimes."

"I should be apologizing to you," he answered. "Wasn't anybody's fault. I'm just blaming it on that tennis tournament, on ol' Bobby Riggs. He's an easy target!"

As the train of cars snaked its way through the dark streets, Maury turned to Jim and asked, "How was Ing? Is everything going good in California?"

"She's fine. The new puppy ran out the door with Adrian James in tow, and we had to cut the conversation short. Man, I can't wait to see my little man. Hey Maury, Ing and I are making plans for Adrian's second birthday. Can you and Judy come out to San Diego and help us celebrate? We certainly want his godmother there."

"Yeah, that sounds great!" Maury agreed.

Doug made a right turn, and in the reflection of the headlights Jim saw a small sign that read, "Airport." Below it, an arrow pointed the way.

"Sure aren't many lights around here," he said, as they drew closer to the airfield.

"Yeah, it's an uncontrolled field, you know, without a tower," Doug responded. "When the airport operator closes down at 6 PM, everyone goes home. Unless you know exactly where it is, this place can be tough to find." He maneuvered the convertible toward the waiting Beechcraft. Morgan parked the rental car next to the plane so he could easily load the luggage. Car doors slammed in the dark, as students got out of their cars and grabbed a last chance to talk with Jim Croce before takeoff.

Doug walked over in his friendly way to supervise the small crowd.

"Give him some room now," he directed. "Don't crowd him."

"Jim, where do you suppose the pilot is?" Morgan asked.

"I don't know." Jim looked around from the midst of fans encircling him. "He said he'd catch a cab."

"Well, that's the problem," Doug told him. "We don't have any cabs in our town, Jim. He'd have to walk or get a ride."

"I told him to be here by 10 o'clock, gassed up and ready to go," Morgan said, checking his watch. "Damn, it's almost 10:20 now! I might as well get the luggage on board."

The old Beechcraft twin-engine D-18 was in the tie-down area, alone and unattended. Morgan and Ken climbed onto the right wing and opened the door. Checking the instrument panel Morgan said aloud to himself, "I wonder if Bob has gassed her up yet."

Jim and Maury said their final good-byes to the students and then strolled around to the other side of the airplane to pass a joint in the warm night air.

As if out of nowhere, a car suddenly pulled up, and a man shouted out the window, "Hey! What are you boys doing over there?"

Jim's and Maury's eyes landed on the official insignia on the side of the car.

Morgan, while standing on the wing of the plane, replied, "We're waiting for our pilot!"

The man in the official-looking car immediately sped off.

"Oh shit," Jim said. They had a suitcase full of medicine, and the last thing they needed was some small-town cop snooping around. "Let's get the hell out of here as soon as Bob shows up."

The man of authority in the car, the coroner's photographer, was just back from an official assignment and had landed his own plane about ten minutes earlier. While driving by the main hangar, he had noticed a group of college students standing around some cars in the parking area and some unfamiliar men standing on and around the Beechcraft. In a small town all strangers arouse suspicion, especially late at night.

The photographer drove straight home and placed a call to the sheriff's deputy, Robert Self.

"The deputy is unavailable," the dispatcher said, "but I'll see that he receives the message as soon as he calls in."

Bob Elliott had taken a nap in his room at the Revere Inn Motel and woken up about 9:50 PM, just ten minutes before he was supposed to be at the airport. He rushed down to the lobby and tried to catch a cab but learned too late that there were no taxis in Natchitoches. At 10:00 PM he hurried south on foot down Washington Street in the general direction of the airport. Two weeks shy of fifty-eight, Bob had suffered a heart attack five months earlier. At 10:05 PM he made his way up the steps into the police station to make sure he was headed in the right direction. He was met at the door by Lieutenant Winbarg, who was on his way to meet Chief of Police Harry Hyams at a narcotics stakeout.

A few days earlier someone had discovered a satchel of drugs at the Natchitoches Parish Fairgrounds. The fair was scheduled to begin in a few days, and the local police believed someone associated with the circus was the most likely recipient of the drugs.

"Can I help you?" Winbarg asked, eyeing the disheveled and disoriented Elliott.

"Hi, my name's Bob Elliott. I'm a pilot, and I need directions to the airport."

Winbarg was suspicious, but pointing south, he said, "It's three miles thataway."

Bob headed out again, trying as best he could to run and make up time. Lieutenant Winbarg got into his car and drove to meet Chief Harry Hyams on the road out to the fairgrounds.

"Chief, I just gave a guy directions to the airport. He claims to be a pilot, but he looked like a circus man to me. He was wearing a wrinkled white shirt and dark blue pants."

Five minutes later, while Lieutenant Winbarg was still briefing the chief, Bob Elliott went jogging past their squad cars.

"There he goes, Harry," Winbarg said, pointing to the silhouette. "That's the guy." Chief Hyams radioed the two unmarked stakeout cars parked at the fairgrounds near the airport: "Be on the lookout for a white, middle-aged male approaching your position on foot," he ordered. In the dark, Bob passed the airport sign without seeing it and instead turned right on the next street, Fairgrounds Road.

Within a few minutes, the first stakeout officers heard him running down the road, within ten feet of their car. The officers observed Bob Elliott disappear in a southerly direction into the moonless night. He then came running into view of the second stakeout car.

The officer slowly got out of his car and said, "Hey, buddy! Hold it up! I'm a police officer! Come on over here!"

"Oh, thank God," said Bob. "Officer, I think I'm lost. I'm a pilot, and I'm trying to get to the airport. Can you give me a lift?"

Without answering, the officer radioed the chief.

"Bring the guy over here," Hyams replied. "I'll handle it." The officers drove over with Elliott and left him in the back seat while they conferred with the chief.

"He says he's a pilot and needs to get to the airport, Chief. But I'd bet my left nut he ain't." Hyams motioned toward the backseat of his own car with a jerk of his head.

"Stick him in the cage, Joe. I'll run him out and see what develops."

As Bob got out to switch cars, Hyams demanded, "Let me see your identification."

"I left it in the plane," he explained.

Hyams chuckled. "Well, let's just drive over there so you can show it to me."

At the airfield, the officer was surprised to see the group of students and the men standing by the plane. As he drove up, he shined his spotlight on Morgan, Maury, and Jim. All three men shielded their eyes, their hearts pounding.

"Good evening, boys," Hyams said in an exaggerated drawl. "Anybody recognize this guy?"

Morgan walked over to the car, "Yeah, officer. That's our pilot, Bob Elliott. Is there anything wrong?"

"No, I guess not," Hyams groaned, and got out and gave Jim and the others an examining stare. "That is, if you want to claim him. He managed to get himself lost out here in our big metropolis. I sure hope he has better luck navigating your plane."

"Thanks for your help, officer," Jim yelled out as the chief eased himself back into his patrol car.

"At your service," Hyams replied matter-of-factly, touching the brim of his cap. "Have a good trip."

Maury climbed into the Beechcraft and sat in the backseat opposite Ken. George paired up in the aisle with Morgan. Bob Elliott sat at the controls, busily going through a preflight checklist and studying the maps. Jim climbed up on the wing and sat down in the copilot's seat.

"Flyin' copilot, are ya?" Doug called up to him.

"Yeah. Maury and I've been takin' lessons." Before he shut the door, he extended his hand. Doug reached up, and they firmly clasped hands.

"Thanks for everything, Doug."

"Take care of yourself, and keep turning out those hits."

Jim shut the door and tightened his seatbelt.

Out the left window Bob yelled, "Clear!" and cranked over the engines. When they began to taxi, Jim looked back and gave one last wave to the fans in the parking area.

Doug got into his GTO and headed back to the university.

Bob Elliott pushed the throttle, and the plane roared down the runway. Once it was airborne, he kept the plane at a slow rate of climb. They were less than thirty feet off the ground and, unknowingly in the dark, aimed directly at a small stand of uncharted trees. Suddenly the plane skimmed the top of the first tree. They rammed into the second tree, and the left wing ripped away. The plane struck the ground and broke apart.

———

At 4:35 AM Pacific Time, the phone rang. I had been dreaming about my potter's wheel. It was spinning out of control, and I was trying to keep it balanced, but I couldn't make it happen. I needed Jim.

Even though I was sound asleep I grabbed it on the first ring, hoping it was him calling.

"Jim?" I asked.

"No, Ing. It's Mom. Are you all right?"

"Oh, hi, Mom. What's the matter?"

"Oh, Ingrid . . . I was just watching the *Today Show*. There was a terrible plane crash last night."

She paused.

"And Jim's dead, right?"

"Yes, Ing." She paused. "His plane crashed."

"And Maury too?"

"Everyone."

———

I buried Jim the following Monday at the Hayem Solomon Memorial Park, a small Jewish cemetery in Frazier, Pennsylvania, in the rural countryside near Valley Forge. It rained hard during the funeral. I chose this cemetery for Jim because he had loved the history of the area and because it was near his mother's home.

Rabbi Louis Kaplan, who had presided over Jim's conversion and our wedding, officiated.

"When I supervised Jim's conversion to Judaism," he said, "I was never sure whether he came to study or if he came to listen to my Bessie Smith records. But it didn't matter, because he always came with a heart full of love."

I sat in numbed grief. Sal, Rich Croce, and George Spillane read eulogies that told of their deep love for Jim.

Jay Lasker, president of ABC/Dunhill, recited the eulogy he'd written:

"Some people reach out and feel nothing. Jim reached out and in some way touched everyone. Some talk of love and goodness as if they alone remained its custodian. Jim gave his love and goodness as if it belonged to everyone. He told me last New Year's Day that he enjoyed taking care of his son's 2 AM bottle and even his diaper change because it gave him more time to spend with the boy, something he had precious little time for, in light of his heavy travel commitments. We are now all the losers for not being able to spend more time with Jim Croce."

Finally, the rabbi closed the service with a Jewish parable:

"A rabbi was walking through the marketplace when, lo, the prophet Elijah appeared to him. The rabbi asked Elijah, 'Is there anyone in this marketplace who has a share in the next world?' The prophet looked about and answered, 'No.' A moment later, two men passed. 'Wait,' said Elijah, 'those two men do have a share in heaven.' The rabbi approached the men and asked, "What is your occupation?' They replied, 'We are jesters; our job is to make men laugh.'"

———

Four days later, while I was still in Pennsylvania, Adrian celebrated his second birthday. Judy gave a party at her house, but the mood was somber. "Where's Daddy?" the two-year-old kept asking.

Before we flew back to San Diego, I took Adrian to visit the cemetery. Together we planted a sapling pine tree next to Jim's grave.

"A plane crash took Daddy away, and he won't be coming home anymore," I cried as I tried to explain. Adrian wiped away my tears.

"Don't cry, Mommy," he said. "Don't cry."

———

When I returned to San Diego, I found a letter Jim sent from Natchitoches waiting for me. I sang Adrian James to sleep and then went outside to sit on the front steps to read it.

> Dear Ing,
>
> I know I haven't been very nice to you for some time, but I thought it might be of some comfort, Sweet Thing, to understand that you haven't been the only recipient of JC's manipulations. But since you can't hear me and can't see me, I can't bullshit, using my sneaky logic and facial movements. I have to write it all down instead, which is lots more permanent. So it can be re-read instead of re-membered, so, it's really right on the line.
>
> I know that you see me for what I am, or should I say, as who I are. 'Cause I've been lots of people. If Medusa had personalities or attitudes instead of snakes for her features, her name would have been Jim Croce. But that's unfair to you and it's also unhealthy for me. And I now want to be the oldest man around, a man with a face full of wrinkles and lots of wisdom.

So this is a birth note, Baby. And when I get back everything will be different. We're gonna have a life together, Ing, I promise. I'm gonna concentrate on my health. I'm gonna become a public hermit. I'm gonna get my Masters Degree. I'm gonna write short stories and movie scripts. Who knows, I might even get a tan.

Give a kiss to my little man and tell him Daddy loves him.

Remember, it's the first sixty years that count and I've got thirty to go.

I Love you,

Jim

EPILOGUE

WHEN I HEARD THE TERRIBLE NEWS that my husband was gone, I felt broken. The thought that our son would grow up and never know his father devastated me.

For over a decade after losing Jim, I stayed busy raising Adrian James as a single mom and fighting for our rights in court. Finally, in 1984, when I was considering my next step after all the litigation was over—including a wrongful death suit in Texas, the closing of the estate in San Diego, and the lawsuit in New York over contracts and royalties—a friend called and told me she knew of an open storefront for rent in downtown San Diego's undeveloped Gaslamp Quarter.

I went to see the space in the historic Keating Building at the corner of Fifth and F Street, and immediately recognized it as the same place where Jim and I stopped on our last night together. We'd been looking for dinner and live music in our new hometown, and when we couldn't find it, we joked about opening a restaurant and bar together in that very spot Jim had suggested. I saw it as a sign. We'd invite fellow musicians to perform and friends to enjoy great food, as we'd done at our Pennsylvania farmhouse.

I signed my lease that week, and Croce's Restaurant was born as a tribute to Jim. I hoped to recreate the warmth and ambience from our early days of entertaining together in the '60s. After waiting a year and half to get our liquor license in the dilapidated downtown, I took a second lease and opened Croce's Jazz Bar, right next door to the restaurant.

Adrian James, already a fine piano player and singer-songwriter at the age of fifteen, honed his talent playing at Croce's. After releasing his first CD on Private Records at just nineteen, he was on his own as a solo artist. Today, Adrian James, known as A.J., is a successful singer-songwriter, guitarist, piano player extraordinaire, and self-taught musicologist. He runs a record company, Seedling Records; works with me managing Croce Music Group; and has a wonderful family of his own.

Every day I am grateful for all the wonderful people who join us at Croce's. I love to hear their stories about how Jim's music changed their lives, and in exchange I'm thankful for the opportunity to offer them a taste of the kind of hospitality Jim and I shared with our friends and family.

Over the years, I have often been asked when there would be a Jim Croce biography and movie. There were many opportunities, but the time was never right.

Now it is 2012, and I have completed the Jim Croce story. The book was cowritten with my husband, Jimmy Rock. I met him fourteen years after Jim Croce passed away. Jimmy Rock was thirty-seven, raised on a farm, never married, a pilot, drummer, singer-songwriter, and attorney. After everything I'd been through, including the years I spent in litigation, I never wanted to fall for another musician or even meet another attorney, but Jimmy and I were both surprised to find love at table 21 at Croce's.

When we were engaged in 1988, I asked Jimmy to leave his law practice to write this book with me. He tried to impress upon me that this would be a very daunting task, and unusual for a second husband to help write the biography of the first husband. Stubbornly, I persisted, and in 1991 we finished our first draft.

We spent years researching and writing the manuscript, but in the end I still wasn't ready to tell my story. So we put it away, hoping that someday the right time and circumstances would come to edit and publish it for Jim's fans.

When we'd started on this journey, Jimmy and I taped and filmed as many of Jim Croce's family members, friends, and fellow performers as possible. Jim's mother, Flora, kindly gave us everything she had of Jim's to help us with the project, as did Jim's brother, Rich. Fortunately we did our research when we did, as sadly, many people have since passed on.

During the years Jim Croce and I were together, we'd taped almost every one of our music sessions on a Wollensak reel-to-reel tape recorder, and later on cassette. Though almost all of his well-known songs were written at our kitchen table, when Jim wrote songs at construction sites or on tour, he taped them, too. So we were able to track the development of his lyrics and melodies.

On March 16, 1987, the night before a fire burned A.J.'s and my home to the ground, I had fortuitously taken all of Jim's photos and memorabilia to the restaurant to hang on the walls. I am admittedly a bit compulsive and have saved everything in a fairly organized fashion, from Jim's recordings, notebooks, letters, and diaries to press releases, travel schedules, books, medical records, family keepsakes, and even his brass baby shoes.

In 1989, while doing research for this biography, Jimmy Rock, A.J., and I chartered a private plane to fly to the small airport in Natchitoches, Louisiana, where Jim's life ended. We visited Prather Auditorium at Northwestern University and met with fans who attended Jim's final concert. After the visit, we drove back to the airfield and took off in the small plane, rising into the sky above the spot where Jim's plane crashed. After all those years, I finally found closure. And so, if nothing else, I knew that writing this book had given me that opportunity.

Then, one day in 2010, we ran into an old friend of ours, David Klowden, who had lived at our home when he and A.J. had a band together back in the late '80s. As close to a family member as he could be, David was, in addition to a musician, a writer, editor, and teacher, and one of the kindest and most down-to-earth people

I know. Because Jim Croce was a private man, we wanted a compassionate friend with whom to work. So we asked if he would consider editing our book with us, and this is the fruit of our labor.

The stories I told about my life in my cookbook, *Thyme in a Bottle*, were more delicious versions of what happened because they were written to provide a meaningful context for the recipes I'd collected over the years and perfected at Croce's Restaurant and Jazz Bar.

But this book is not an idealized version of that time. The gritty reality of the amphetamine-driven truckers' culture in "Speedball Tucker," the tale of a man's broken dreams in "Workin' at the Car Wash Blues," the theme of failure in "New York's Not My Home" and "Box #10," the rock 'n' roll madness of "Five Short Minutes of Lovin'," and the anger of losing a relationship in "One Less Set of Footsteps" are as truly a part of this story as the romantic sentiments of "Alabama Rain," "I'll Have to Say I Love You in a Song," "Photographs and Memories," and "Time in a Bottle." Jim put his life to music. His experiences and observations are memorable and resonate with us because they're real.

I hope in reading this book you came to understand that although Jim was far from perfect, his greatest flaws derived from the same source as his greatest gifts: he wanted to make everyone happy. I also hope that it has inspired you to help me keep his music and memory alive. I know he will be with me forever.

ACKNOWLEDGMENTS

RECALLING EVERYONE WHO has contributed to telling this story will be difficult, but I'm going to give it a try.

I must begin with Jim's mom and dad, Flora and Jim Croce, who taught him the lessons of generosity and graciousness and instilled the love of storytelling and song; Rich Croce, Jim's brother, for his dedication and guidance in the writing of this book; and the Babusci family in Rochester, New York—Linda and Mike Nicosia, Jeanette Fina and Lenny Fina—our relatives who shared their early memories of Jim.

I want to thank my father, Sidney Jacobson, for being like a second dad to Jim, and for always taking the time to listen. I want to thank my family—my twin sister Phyllis Blythe, stepmom Florence Jacobson, sister Janice Kohler, and brother Dr. Ken Jacobson—who welcomed Jim into their lives and loved him unconditionally.

Thanks to Jim's teachers, priests, rabbis, and the following list of special friends: Special thanks to Paul Wilson, who continues to befriend Jim's memory with his love and photographs, and to Judy Coffin, my closest friend, whose insights and memories of Maury were significant to this book. Joe Salviulo, Bill and Dee Reid, Rich "Reds" Bass, Emil Cianfrani, Frank Di Serfino, Melvin Goldfield, Chris Sigafoos (wherever you are), Carl and Sheila Feherenbach, Ronnie Miller, Mike DiBenedetto, Deborah Warner, Gene Pistilli, Pat Rosalia, Erin Dickens, Tim Hauser, George Spillane, Carole Spillane, Hy Mayerson, Bob and Ellen Knott, Gene Uphoff, Dolores Meehan, Paul Meehan, Harold and Berenice Jacobs, the Kaltenbach family, Lucille and Phil Petillo, and Larry Himmel. We also want to give special thanks to the Muehleisen family for keeping Maury's music and memory alive. To learn more about Maury, our dear, dear friend, please visit www.maurymuehleisen.com.

Thanks to musicians and friends from the road Joe Macho, Gary Chester, Ellie Greenwich, Tasha Thomas, Arlo and Jackie Guthrie, Nik Venet III, Cheech Marin, Tommy Chong, Jimmy Buffet, John Prine, James Taylor, Randy Newman, Kenny Loggins and Jim Messina, Wolfman Jack, Jonathan Moore, Corb Donahue, and Dick Clark.

We are thankful to Rick Trow for the film at the farm, Rita Bernstein for the photos at Moore College of Art, Al Parachini for the photos from June 1972, and Nik Venet for the 1969 Jim and Ingrid Croce album cover.

We want to thank Tracy Bedell for interviews, Will Mitchell for talking with us, and Doug Nichols for giving Jim and Maury a ride and for sharing his experiences of that last fateful day.

Thanks to Dick Boake for his friendship and for the Jim Croce Edition of the Martin Signature Guitar, which Jim Croce could never afford.

We appreciate the faith, friendship, and perseverance of our literary agent, Bill Gladstone.

Thank you to Roger Cooper of Vanguard for your encouragement and introducing us to Da Capo; the Da Capo team for all your help and support: John Radziewicz, vice president and publisher; Ben Schafer, executive editor; Annie Lenth, senior project editor; Jonathan Crowe, editor; Jonathan Sainesbury, art director; Kevin Hanover, vice president and director of marketing; Sean Maher, marketing manager; Kate Burke, associate director of publicity; Jeffrey Miller, attorney for your assistance in vetting this book; and Beth Wright of Trio Bookworks for editing our book. Above all, we want to thank Karstin Painter, who came to our rescue with a smile and her "can-do" attitude at the eleventh hour, and made our day!

David Klowden, thank you for helping us to edit, shape, and deliver this book to Da Capo.

Thank you, Anna King, for clearances and for helping us to promote all things Croce.

We are grateful to Diane Becker for being such a good friend and the only attorney from the old days that I can trust. I want to thank Karen Fairbank for her ongoing kindness, friendship, and legal counsel. I'm so glad she's on our side!

Thanks to our team who help Jimmy and me every day to keep Jim Croce's music and memory alive at Croce's Restaurant and Jazz Bar.

Special Thanks to my personal assistant and human resource manager Evelyn Caballero for being the kindest and most organized person I know. . . . You never let me down; and thanks to CFO Kim Melchoir, who assists me with all my "adventures" and keeps all the numbers perfectly straight! Finally, my deepest thanks to Tania Nelson, whose devotion to and care for us and our book has made her an official family member. Her careful insights and perspective have been immeasurable and greatly appreciated.

PHOTO CREDITS

Page ii: Jim practicing backstage, 1972. *Photo by Paul Wilson*

Page 1:   Jim in front of a Ford truck in Indianapolis, Indiana, 1972. *Photo by Al Parachini*

Page 15:   Teenage Jim with one of his first guitars.*

Page 39:   Jim and Paul Meehan, owner of Riddle Paddock, 1965.*

Page 57:   Jim and Ingrid on the steps with guitar, 1963.*

Page 77:   Jim at Moore College of Art, 1967. *Photo by Rita Bernstein*

Page 97:   Jim and Ingrid, 1966.*

Page 119:   Jim and Ingrid promo for Capital album, *Jim and Ingrid Croce*, in New York City, 1969. *Photo by Nik Venet*

Page 143:   Reds Mullen, Jim, and Emil Cianfrani at Sweeney's truck yard, 1971.*

Page 171:   Jim writing at their kitchen table in Lyndell, Pennsylvania.*

Page 193:   Jim at a diner, 1973. *Photo by Al Parachini*

Page 213:   Jim in Lyndell, Pennsylvania, 1971. *Photo by Paul Wilson*

Page 237:   Jim and Ingrid in Lyndell, Pennsylvania, 1971. *Photo by Paul Wilson*

Page 261:   Jim and Ingrid backstage at the Main Point. *Photo by Paul Wilson*

Page 281:   Jim and Maury backstage, 1973.

Page 293:   Jim. *Photo by Paul Wilson*

Photo courtesy of the Croce Family

SONG CREDITS

"Box Number 10"
Words and music by Jim Croce © 1971 (renewed 1999) Time in a Bottle Publishing and Croce Publishing. All Rights controlled and administered by EMI April Music Inc. All rights reserved. International copyright secured. Used by permission. *Reprinted by permission of Hal Leonard Corporation.*

"Careful Man"
Words and music by Jim Croce © 1972 (renewed 2000) Time in a Bottle Publishing and Croce Publishing. All Rights controlled and administered by EMI April Music Inc. All rights reserved. International copyright secured. Used by permission. *Reprinted by permission of Hal Leonard Corporation.*

"Cotton Eyed Joe"
Collected, adapted, and arranged by John A. Lomax and Alan Lomax. TRO © copyright 1934 (renewed) Ludlow Music, Inc., New York and Global Jukebox Publishing, Marshall, TX (As sung by Jim Croce). TRO-Ludlow Music, Inc., New York controls all publication rights for the World outside the U.S.A. International copyright secured. Made in U.S.A. All rights reserved, including public performance for profit. Used by permission.

"Dangerous Dan McGrew"
By Joan Whitney and Alex Kramer © copyright 1949 (renewed). All rights for the U.S. controlled by Bourne Co. All rights reserved. International copyright secured. ASCAP

"Don't Think Twice, It's All Right"
Copyright © 1963 by Warner Bros. Inc.; renewed 1991 by Special Rider Music. All rights reserved. International copyright secured. Reprinted by permission.

"Dreamin' Again"
Words and music by Jim Croce © 1972 (renewed 2000) Time in a Bottle Publishing and Croce Publishing. All Rights controlled and administered by EMI April Music Inc. All rights reserved. International copyright secured. Used by permission. *Reprinted by permission of Hal Leonard Corporation.*

"Five Short Minutes"
Words and music by Jim Croce © 1973 (renewed 2001) Time in a Bottle Publishing and Croce Publishing. All rights controlled and administered by EMI April Music Inc. All rights reserved. International copyright secured. Used by permission. *Reprinted by permission of Hal Leonard Corporation.*

"The Girl Who Invented Rock and Roll"
Words and Music by Joe Lubin. Copyright © 1957 (copyright renewed) by Daywin Music, Inc. All rights administered by Universal Music–Careers. International copyright secured. All rights reserved. *Reprinted by permission of Hal Leonard Corporation.*

"I Got a Name"
Words by Norman Gimbel. Music by Charles Fox. Copyright © 1973 (renewed) Warner-Tamerlane Publishing Corp. All rights reserved. Used by permission.

"Hey Tomorrow"
Words and music by Jim Croce and Ingrid Croce © 1969 (renewed 1997) Time in a Bottle Publishing and Croce Publishing. All Rights controlled and administered by EMI April Music Inc. All rights reserved. International copyright secured. Used by permission. *Reprinted by permission of Hal Leonard Corporation.*

"I Am Who I Am"
Words and music by Jim Croce and Ingrid Croce © 1969 (renewed 1997). Time in a Bottle Publishing, Croce Publishing and Denjac Music Co. All rights for Time in a Bottle Publishing and Croce Publishing controlled and administered by EMI April Music Inc. All rights reserved. International copyright secured. Used by permission. *Reprinted by permission of Hal Leonard Corporation.*

"I'll Have To Say I Love You In A Song"
Words and music by Jim Croce © 1973 (renewed 2001) Time in a Bottle Publishing and Croce Publishing. All Rights controlled and administered by EMI April Music Inc. All rights reserved. International copyright secured. Used by permission. *Reprinted by permission of Hal Leonard Corporation.*

"Lover's Cross"
Words and music by Jim Croce © 1973 (renewed 2001) Time in a Bottle Publishing and Croce Publishing. All Rights controlled and administered by EMI April Music Inc. All rights reserved. International copyright secured. Used by permission. *Reprinted by permission of Hal Leonard Corporation.*

"New York's Not My Home"
Words and music by Jim Croce © 1971 (renewed 1999) Time in a Bottle Publishing and Croce Publishing. All Rights controlled and administered by EMI April Music Inc. All rights reserved. International copyright secured. Used by permission. *Reprinted by permission of Hal Leonard Corporation.*

"Old Blue"
Words and Music by Roger McGuinn. © 1969 (renewed 1997) EMI Blackwood Music, Inc. and McHillby Music Publishing Co. All rights controlled and administered by EMI BLACKWOOD MUSIC INC. All rights reserved. International copyright secured. Used by permission. *Reprinted by permission of Hal Leonard Corporation.*

"One Less Set Of Footsteps"
Words and music by Jim Croce © 1972, 1973 (renewed 2000, 2001) Time in a Bottle Publishing and Croce Publishing. All Rights controlled and administered by EMI April Music Inc. All rights reserved. International copyright secured. Used by permission. *Reprinted by permission of Hal Leonard Corporation.*

"Photographs And Memories"
Words and music by Jim Croce © 1971 (renewed 1999) Time in a Bottle Publishing and Croce Publishing. All Rights controlled and administered by EMI April Music Inc. All rights reserved. International copyright secured. Used by permission. *Reprinted by permission of Hal Leonard Corporation.*

"Railroads And Riverboats"
Words and music by Jim Croce and Ingrid Croce © 1975 (renewed 2003) Time in a Bottle Publishing, Croce Publishing, and Denjac Music Co. All rights for Time in a Bottle Publishing and Croce Publishing controlled and administered by EMI April Music Inc. All rights reserved. International copyright secured. Used by permission. *Reprinted by permission of Hal Leonard Corporation.*

"Rapid Roy" (The Stoch; Car Boy)
Words and music by Jim Croce © 1971 (renewed1999) Time in a Bottle Publishing and Croce Publishing. All Rights controlled and administered by EMI April Music Inc. All rights reserved. International copyright secured. Used by permission. *Reprinted by permission of Hal Leonard Corporation.*

"Roller Derby Queen"
Words and music by Jim Croce © 1972 (renewed 2000) Time in a Bottle Publishing and Croce Publishing. All Rights controlled and administered by EMI April Music Inc. All rights reserved. International copyright secured. Used by permission. *Reprinted by permission of Hal Leonard Corporation.*

"Song for Canada"
Words and Music by Ian Tyson and Pete Gzowski. Copyright © 1965 (renewed) Four Strong Winds, Ltd. All rights administered by WB Music Corp. All rights reserved. Used by permission of Alfred Music Publishing.

"Speedball Tucker"
Words and music by Jim Croce © 1972 (renewed 2000) Time in a Bottle Publishing and Croce Publishing. All Rights controlled and administered by EMI April Music Inc. All rights reserved. International copyright secured. Used by permission. *Reprinted by permission of Hal Leonard Corporation.*

"These Dreams"
Words and music by Jim Croce © 1972 (renewed 2000) Time in a Bottle Publishing and Croce Publishing. All Rights controlled and administered by EMI April Music Inc. All rights reserved. International copyright secured. Used by permission. *Reprinted by permission of Hal Leonard Corporation.*

"Time in A Bottle"
Words and music by Jim Croce © 1971 (renewed 1999) Time in a Bottle Publishing and Croce Publishing. All Rights controlled and administered by EMI April Music Inc. All rights reserved. International copyright secured. Used by permission. *Reprinted by permission of Hal Leonard Corporation.*

"Tomorrow's Gonna Be A Brighter Day"
Words and music by Jim Croce © 1971 (renewed 1 999) Time in a Bottle Publishing and Croce Publishing. All Rights controlled and administered by EMI April Music Inc. All rights reserved. International copyright secured. Used by permission. *Reprinted by permission of Hal Leonard Corporation.*

"You Oughta See Pickles Now"
Words and Music by Dick Reynolds. © 1955 (renewed 1983) Central Songs, a division of Beechwood Music Corp. All rights reserved. International copyright secured. Used by permission. *Reprinted by permission of Hal Leonard Corporation.*

"Vespers"
Words and music by Jim Croce and Ingrid Croce © 1969 (renewed 1997) Time in a Bottle Publishing, Croce Publishing, and Denjac Music Co. All rights for Time in a Bottle Publishing and Croce Publishing controlled and administered by EMI April Music Inc. All rights reserved. International copyright secured. Used by permission. *Reprinted by permission of Hal Leonard Corporation.*

"What Do People Do"
Words and music by Jim Croce and Ingrid Croce ©1969 (renewed 1997). Time in a Bottle Publishing, Croce Publishing, and Denjac Music Co. All rights for Time in a Bottle and Croce Publishing controlled and administered by EMI April Music Inc. All rights reserved. International copyright secured. Used by permission. *Reprinted by permission of Hal Leonard Corporation.*

"You Don't Mess Around with Jim"
Words and music by Jim Croce © 1971 (renewed 1999) Time in a Bottle Publishing and Croce Publishing. All Rights controlled and administered by EMI April Music Inc. All rights reserved. International copyright secured. Used by permission. *Reprinted by permission of Hal Leonard Corporation.*